IVOR GURNEY'S

GLOUCESTERSHIRE

Exploring Poetry & Place

IVOR GURNEY'S
GLOUCESTERSHIRE

Exploring Poetry & Place

ELEANOR M. RAWLING

First published 2011

Reprinted 2012

The History Press
The Mill, Brimscombe Port
Stroud, Gloucestershire, GL5 2QG
www.thehistorypress.co.uk

British Library Cataloguing in Publication Data.
A catalogue record for this book is available from the British Library.

ISBN 978 0 7524 5353 8

Typesetting and origination by The History Press
Printed and bound in Great Britain by
Marston Book Services Limited, Didcot

CONTENTS

ACKNOWLEDGEMENTS

The book draws on a huge variety of resources and sources, ranging from geological texts to literary criticisms and the Gloucestershire Archives; from photographs and maps, old and new, to websites and blogs; from interviews and discussions to lone walking, running and photography in the Gloucestershire countryside.

Special thanks are due to the following for permission to use the items listed:

Carcanet Press Ltd, Manchester for a selection of Gurney's published poetry from *Collected Poems*, Kavanagh, 2004; *80 Poems or So*, Walter and Thornton, 1997; *Rewards of Wonder*, Walter, 2000, and *Best Poems and the Book of Five Makings*, Thornton and Walter, 1997.

The Ivor Gurney Trust for formerly unpublished poems and photographs, and extracts from letters, all from the Ivor Gurney Archives, housed in Gloucestershire Archives.

Gloucestershire Archives for four photographs: GL87.8 Westgate Street tram terminus 1897; SR38/29157 no. 7 Eastgate Street Fair, Mop Monday; SR38/29157 no.21 Gloucester Docks about 1882; GL57.30 Gloucester Cattle Market, Walwin Collection.

The Imperial War Museum for a print of a Paul Nash painting titled 'We Are Making a New World', 1918 (colour illustrations and Chapter 3).

The Ordnance Survey (Crown Copyright and database right 2010) for the locational map at 1:250,000 scale (colour illustrations).

Precision Terrain Surveys Ltd for the LIDAR image (Copyright Precision Terrain Surveys Ltd) of Cooper's Hill and High Brotheridge (colour illustrations).

The Trustees of the National Library of Scotland for a section of Ordnance Survey 1:2,500 Gloucestershire Sheet 25.1, published 1902, for the Gloucester map.(Figure 5.1 in Chapter 5)

Fineleaf Editions for the diagrams in Chapters 2, 6 and 7. These were drawn by William Dreghorn to illustrate his book *Geology Explained in the Severn Vale and Cotswolds* (1967). The book has been reprinted in 2005 by Fineleaf.

Alan Godfrey Maps for an extract from the Old Ordnance Survey Map, One Inch to One Mile Sheet 216, NW Gloucestershire 1896, for Figure 4.3 in Chapter 4.

Anthony Boden, author of *Stars in a Dark Night*, Sutton Publishing, 1986 (revised 2004), for the photographs of F. W. Harvey in Chapter 2 and the Chapmans with Gurney in Chapter 4.

Thanks are also due to:

The Ivor Gurney Society, particularly Philip Lancaster and Ian Venables, for their help and support.

Roger Ellis – artist and map maker who produced the illustrated map of Ivor Gurney's Gloucestershire (colour illustrations); the map for Chapter 2, Gurney's Cycle Ride; the map for Chapter 4, Gurney's Cottage and Dryhill Farm; Figure 5.5, The Twyver and the Abbey Stone; and Figure 6.4, Sailing the Severn in Chapter 6 (www.roger-ellis.com).

Simon Lee Dicker (Fire and Ice Creative Ltd) who produced the four Walk Maps for the Ivor Gurney walks: Above Ashleworth; A Blowy Severn Tided Place; High on Cooper's; On the Roman Hill (www.fireandicecreative.com).

Photographers: Philip Wade; Greig Simms. All other modern photographs were taken by the author.

My family – John, Helen and Richard – for help with drafting maps, editing photographs and reminding me that there is a life beyond writing a book.

FOREWORD

We are used to being reminded that Gloucester and Gloucestershire are fundamental to Ivor Gurney's work, so it is not surprising that someone who grew up in the county should find a passionate interest in what he wrote. But what is surprising is the way in which Eleanor Rawling has reinvented her topic. She comes to Gurney not as a literary critic, or a musician, but as a geographer and a theorist of geography who grew up walking and cycling the very lanes that Gurney knew. She knew Gurney's walks before she knew they were Gurney's walks. Now she probes beneath the landscape to find the geological basis of its characteristics; she looks, as Gurney loved to do, at its archaeology and its history and she tries to find out how and why the man and the place were so inextricably intertwined. She even suggests the landscape similarities of Severn and Somme.

She meticulously explores the paths that Gurney trod, recreating them and evoking them vividly so that they are available not only to those who can physically follow in his footsteps, but also to those who no longer can walk them. It becomes something like Gurney's experience when Helen Thomas took Edward's maps to Gurney in Dartford, and he followed the tracks turn by turn in his imagination.

So we don't have another literary criticism here. This is a new kind of book, new at least to me; an eclectic mix in which there is always some surprise lurking round the corner, a direction not anticipated, but one which illuminates some aspect of a poem. What it provides is a delightful ability to look afresh at Gurney, his county and his work.

'One comes across the strangest things in walks', wrote Gurney in 'Cotswold Ways', and Eleanor Rawling demonstrates emphatically just what he meant.

Professor R.K.R. Thornton, 2011

A note from the author:

For abbreviations of poetry collections and sources used in the text, see p. 152

Neither the author nor the publisher can be held responsible for any damage to individuals or property as a result of following walks described in this book.

1

BREATHING WAS LOVING: IVOR GURNEY'S GLOUCESTERSHIRE

OLD THOUGHT

Autumn, that name of creeper falling and tea-time loving,
Was once for me the thought of High Cotswold noon-air,
And the earth smell, turning brambles, and half-cirrus moving,
Mixed with the love of body and travel of good turf there.

O up in height, O snatch up, O swiftly going,
Common to beechwood, breathing was loving, the yet
Unknown Crickley cliffs trumpeted, set music on glowing
In my mind. White Cotswold, wine scarlet woods and leaf wreckage wet.

(Kavanagh, 2004, p.176)

A poem about walking in the Cotswold countryside but also a poem about much more than that, 'Old Thought' is a fitting way to introduce a book about Ivor Gurney and Gloucestershire. Ivor Gurney (1890–1937), the Gloucestershire composer and poet, is perhaps best known as a musician and First World War poet. Yet he also wrote vividly and prolifically about the places and landscapes of Gloucestershire. The eight lines of 'Old Thought' encompass many of the characteristics that make Ivor Gurney a fascinating poet of place, and one of the best writers to introduce the reader to Gloucestershire.

From the first word – 'autumn' – announcing the season and setting the scene in our minds ('creeper falling' and 'tea-time loving'), Gurney's poem ranges across a number of significant themes. He presents the sights, sense impressions and atmosphere of the Cotswold landscape as received by the walker, reminding us of the 'earth smell' so typical of autumn woodlands, of 'turning brambles' that are changing colour but also the possible cause of turning an ankle, and of the colour and dampness of beech-woods at this time of year ('wine scarlet woods and leaf wreckage wet'). The word 'wreckage' even sums up the likelihood of autumn gales. He revels in the act of walking, as a stimulant to the senses and thought ('the love of body and travel of good turf there' and 'O up in height, O snatch up, O swiftly going'). We can see glimpses of the sky as the walker strides along on the edge of the scarp slope ('half-cirrus moving') and hear

Ivor Gurney; the poet and composer in 1920, aged thirty.
(Photograph by Richard Hall, Gurney Archives)

Autumn on the Cotswold Edge: 'O up in height, O snatch up, O swiftly going'. Sheepscombe Common. (Greig Simms)

the joyful feeling of achievement at climbing a steep slope ('breathing was loving'). We learn of Gurney's belief in the close relationship between landscape, poetry and music ('Crickley cliffs trumpeted, set music on glowing in my mind'), the last two arising, as he believed, from the same 'springs of beauty'. And amidst all the wonder and enjoyment, there is a note of sadness and loss ('was once for me') as the poem hints that these experiences may not now be open to the writer.

Why Gurney? Why Place?

So Ivor Gurney is a unique guide, bringing sharp observational powers, the rhythms and cadences of music and poetry, a walker's closeness to the land, and, above all, a deep sense of belonging to these distinctive Gloucestershire landscapes. Gurney was born and brought up in Gloucestershire; his creativity was shaped by the Cotswolds and Severn Meadows of his home. When he was away from Gloucestershire, in London at the Royal College of Music (1911–15) and as a soldier (1915–17), he drew on his memories and imagination to recreate these places in his mind. Although he had started out as a musician, poetry became another important outlet for his creative energies and a source of comfort during the traumas of life as a First World War soldier. Eventually, Gloucestershire places became not only the subject of his poetry and music, but also an essential part of his being, so that his eventual confinement, from 1922 until his death in 1937, in a mental hospital far from his native Gloucestershire, may be seen as a particularly cruel blow. If Gurney's identity was shaped by Gloucestershire, equally the identity and character of Gloucestershire are forever shaped by Gurney's music and his poetry. This book will focus on the poetry, and aims to introduce Ivor Gurney, his poems and his Gloucestershire countryside to a wider audience.

It is only recently that the poetry of Ivor Gurney has become generally available and its quality and distinctiveness recognised. During his lifetime, Gurney only published two slim volumes of poetry (*Severn & Somme*, 1917 and *War's Embers*, 1919) although he was already making a name for himself as a musician. After his death in 1937, his music achieved continuing recognition but his poetry has taken longer to be noticed.

P.J. Kavanagh, who edited the latest edition of *Ivor Gurney: Collected Poems* (2004), suggests that there are two reasons for this – 'first, he was acknowledged to be a musician, a composer of songs, of genius – and we always doubt whether a man can be good at two things. Second, he was mentally unbalanced: from about 1912 when he was 22 he had been subject to mental breakdowns and in 1922, he was put in an asylum for the last fifteen years of his life. So Gurney was not only primarily a musician … he was a mad poet too, and the combination of all these things had caused him to be shunted off into a siding' (K, 2004, p.xx).

The efforts of Gurney's close friend, Marion Scott, in saving all his manuscripts during the war and asylum years, meant that a huge volume of unpublished material did survive after his death and the young composer, Gerald Finzi, who had been impressed with his music, took great pains to ensure that his poetry achieved recognition too (Boden, 2009). Despite these efforts, it was 1954 before another volume of his poetry appeared – *Poems by Ivor Gurney: principally selected from unpublished manuscripts, with a memoir by Edmund Blunden*. In 1973, *Poems of Ivor Gurney 1890–1937*, edited by Leonard Clark, was published, followed in 1978 by Michael Hurd's biography, *The Ordeal of Ivor Gurney* and P.J. Kavanagh's first volume of *Ivor Gurney: Selected Poems*, 1982. The late 1980s and 1990s saw a growing interest in Ivor Gurney, both as a musician and a poet.

Literary scholars have worked on the archives in Gloucester, new editions of *Severn & Somme* and *War's Embers* have appeared (Thornton ed., 1987) and reconstructed editions of Gurney's own selections of poetry have been published. These were prepared by him but never saw publication in his lifetime; *Best Poems and the Book of Five Makings* (Thornton and Walter ed., 1995), *80 Poems or So* (Walter and Thornton ed., 1997), *Rewards of Wonder* (Walter ed., 2000). In 1995, an Ivor Gurney Society was founded and, partly as a result, there has been a growing number of articles, books, broadcasts and recitals of his poetry and music. In 2008, a double biography of both Ivor Gurney and Marion Scott was published (Blevins, 2008). At the time of writing, the Gurney archives in Gloucester are being catalogued and reorganised to make them more accessible to researchers, and a full *Collected Poems* is on its way. As Kavanagh noted in the Foreword to the 2004 *Collected Poems*, 'Gurney's time does appear to have come.'

In all this, the twin foci of interest in analysing his poetry have often appeared to be his war experiences and his mental illness. Gurney, like many young men of his generation, joined up in the early stages of the 1914–18 war – in Gurney's case in 1915 on his second attempt – and he found his ability to write poetry a way of coping with the traumatic events he witnessed. Unlike many of the other 'war poets' such as Rupert Brooke, Siegfried Sassoon and Wilfred Owen, Gurney was not an officer but a common soldier and many of his poems reveal, with startling clarity, the details of everyday life for the ordinary soldier. In poems like 'The Silent One', 'First Time In' and 'Crucifix Corner', Gurney provides less rhetoric or protest than Brooke or Owen but perhaps a more accurate and poignant picture of what it was like to be there. In 'The Silent One', for example, the opening lines about a soldier hanging and dying on the barbed wire are made more traumatic because of the details of the man's chattering Bucks accent, and the almost offhand manner in which Gurney refuses to obey his officer and follow the man through a hole in the wire. Not surprisingly, poems like this are popular choices for anthologies of war poetry (e.g. Parsons, 1965; Hibberd and Onions, 1986; Stallworthy, 2002). What is most striking, to my mind, is how few poems refer only to experiences in France. Even in Gurney's poems about wartime happenings and soldier colleagues, the landscapes and places of Gloucestershire are ever present and a touchstone for his observations. A striking example is in 'Crucifix Corner', where despite the harsh detail of the regimental camp amid the mud and noise, he is drawn back to the Severn Meadows of his childhood – 'all things said 'Severn', the air was of those dusk meadows.' Or in the poem 'That Centre of Old', where 'in the still space at a strafe's end' he turns for escape to Cooper's Hill and autumn Cranham on the Cotswolds – 'Not anyway does ever Cotswold's fail – Her dear blue long dark slope fail.' He was not so much writing about the war, as using his Gloucestershire places to help him survive the war.

Similarly, Gurney's mental illness is something which fascinates commentators (Rattenbury, 1999; Hipp, 2005; Blevins, 2007). Although there is still disagreement about the precise nature of the illness, the diagnosis that he was bi-polar seems to be most widely accepted now, and it is also indisputable that Gurney had a continuing and debilitating stomach complaint, worsened by, or caused by, his erratic eating habits. Whatever the specifics of his condition, there is general agreement that some of Gurney's writing displays unusual rhythms and structures, occasionally odd turns of phrase, and erratic or missing punctuation. It would be tempting to put some of this down to mental disturbance. On the other hand, all commentators also agree that Gurney was capable of producing poetry of the highest quality, with deep meanings and clear succinct images at all periods, even in poems of the mid-1920s when his mental state was deteriorating (Rattenbury, 1999). Equally, some idiosyncrasies of expression are found in early poems as well as later ones and, increasingly, these are recognised as elements of his distinctive style and technique. Gurney's frequent habit of missing out linking words (such as 'and', 'is', 'were', 'in' and 'on') may result from the way he experiences places in a rush of emotion, embracing sensual encounters. Similarly, this book will explore the idea that his strange rhythms and unusual sentence structures may, perhaps, be linked with his need to move as he created – to walk, run or cycle through the countryside. Kavanagh has explained: 'He is a poet who should not be read line by line. His poems are more like jets of energy that hurry to their end' (2004, p.xxxi). His style and creative processes will be discussed later, but there does not seem to be any justification for making any direct links between so-called 'difficulties of style' and his mental condition. So, it seems that the label of mentally disturbed poet does not fit any more easily than that of war poet.

When I discovered Ivor Gurney's poetry, in my early twenties, I read the poems directly, without knowing any of this background. 'Cotswold Ways', 'The High Hills' and later 'Old Thought' and 'That Centre of Old', were some of the first poems I read in which my home area of the Cotswold Hills around Cooper's Hill was vividly pictured. Gurney's references to the 'soft winter morning of kind innocence', to the autumn woodlands with their 'boom of colour', and to Cooper's Hill as a place of escape and spiritual renewal, spoke directly to my experience. 'Yes I've been there. I've felt that!' What drew me to this poet with this startling leap of recognition, was the clarity and distinctiveness of his images of Gloucestershire places that I knew in a similar way, and his deep sense of belonging to this place. I felt that he was speaking to me directly. Years later, I nodded in agreement when I read Kavanagh's comment (K, 2004, p.xx) that 'because there are so many interesting distractions on the way to reading of Gurney's verse, my dearest wish would be for the reader to approach him first with no knowledge of his medical history ... So far as the sources of his poetry are concerned, he simply ignores his situation. This surely should be a hint to the reader to do the same.'

If Gurney's poetry is read and considered as it stands, it is not his war reminiscences or signs of insanity that strike the reader. The overwhelming feature that characterises it is his sense of knowing and belonging to one particular place – Ivor Gurney's Gloucestershire. This is why I have chosen the theme of 'place' as the broad idea on which this book is based – place in general and Gloucestershire in particular. I am not suggesting that existing commentators have ignored the importance of place; indeed, Michael Hurd (1978) spoke of Gurney's love of Gloucestershire and of his 'countryman's true clarity of vision'. Subsequent chapters (e.g. Hooker, 1982), articles (e.g. Scott, 1998; Lancaster, 2007) and introductions to his poetry (e.g. Walter and Thornton, 1997) have all referred to Gurney's identification with Gloucestershire and close attachment to particular places, as evident in his poetry and music. Geoffrey Grigson picked out six of Gurney's poems, as long ago as 1980, to appear in the *Faber Book of Poems and Places* and Kavanagh produced *People and Places*, a selection featuring Gurney's work in 1982. But place, as an overarching idea, has not been the major interpretative framework for Gurney's work, nor has Gloucestershire been the primary focus of any existing commentary about him.

As someone who has spent their professional career in geography and geography education, encountering the role of place in a different context, and one who has also been an avid student of literature and poetry, I feel that I have a different perspective to offer on Gurney's life and work. Place is a fundamental concept in geography and geographers have sought to illuminate the way in which people interact with and invest meaning in places (Rawling, 2011). One of the oldest traditions is that of regional geography, in which the characteristics of both physical and human features of a place are studied, with the aim of identifying a distinctive spirit or sense of place. Also relevant is the landscape history approach of W.G. Hoskins, whose best-known work is *The Making of the English Landscape* (1955, reprinted 1985). In this approach, the landscape is conceived as a series of vertical layers of underlying rock and soil, and centuries of human use and habitation. Understanding is achieved by 'digging deep' into these layers, drawing on geology, archaeology, history and a localist vision. As Hoskins explained (and no doubt Gurney would have approved), 'everything is older than we think' (Hoskins, 1985, p.12). Both place and landscape studies have taken many twists and turns since then, with geographers in the 1980s and 1990s (for example, David Harvey in 1996) being more concerned with revealing the social and economic forces that underlie place and landscape formation (we might think of Gurney's musings on the housing conditions for London's poor in 'North Woolwich' and 'A Wish') than with identifying regions or sense of place. Most recently, some cultural geographers are moving away from the idea of seeing the world as a detached spectator and are emphasising personal engagement with the world. A new kind of landscape study is foregrounding the ways in which individuals relate to the world, looking at photography, painting, walking, poetry and music, for example, as signs revealing how 'self and landscape are intertwined' (Wylie, 2007). For me, Gurney's poetry of Gloucestershire cries out to tell us how and why the man and the place were so inextricably intertwined.

So all these approaches are relevant to a new look at Ivor Gurney, throwing the spotlight directly on the place as well as on the poet and the poetry, and making as much use of geological diagrams and landscape descriptions as of critical observations about poetic language and rhythm. Although I am aware that this eclectic approach will lead to a strange mix that may not satisfy the literary or geographical purists, I am encouraged by Gurney's own observations in the essay 'On Earth' (recently published in 2009) that it was essential to dig deep down into the very soil of his own county in order to take the full measure of its beauty – 'It has always been strange to the writer … that our many textured, coloured, many grained earth stuff nor its larger aspect has had its adequate praise.' And later – 'Where are the praises of each county, each soil.' Gurney would have approved of Hoskins' efforts and I hope, of my own, in attempting to give this proper consideration. I believe that a wider and deeper view will result in an interesting read and some unusual perspectives. Equally significant perhaps, I am a walker and a native of Gloucestershire, and I grew up in the midst of the places that were dear to Ivor Gurney. I do not intend to compete with established literary critics; I merely wish to throw a new light on the place that lies at the heart of Ivor Gurney's life and poetry and so to illuminate the poet, the poetry and Gloucestershire.

The Sequence of Chapters

The book will be sequenced in a way that unfolds Gurney's life and poetry as if place really mattered. Chapters 2, 3 and 4 will introduce the poet and the place, examining Gurney's life in a way that interweaves biography with geography, and juxtaposes exploration of his creative development with investigation of the place and landscape. Chapters 5, 6 and 7 will take the opposite approach of starting with the places that were special to Gurney – the Old City (Gloucester), the Severn Meadows and the High Hills (Cotswolds) – using his names and ways of identifying them. The aim is to show how he spoke about – and through – these places, and how the places spoke through his poetry and music.

Chapter 2 addresses his life to 1911, including his introduction to the Gloucestershire countryside, the role of family, his friendship with Herbert Howells and Will Harvey, and the early development of his habit of walking and creating 'in-place'. Chapter 3 deals with Gurney's life 1911–17, when temporary absence in London or in France took him away from the Gloucestershire countryside and forced him to reassess what they meant to him. Perhaps not surprisingly, absence seemed to concentrate his mind and move him to express his feelings in poetry as a form of therapy for home-sickness and trauma, and as a means of keeping place memories alive. Chapter 4 details the gradual loss of Gurney's direct and creative contact with place, and with the spark of joy and creativity that this engendered. This loss was firstly a result of mental illness and depression and then, after 1922, because of his confinement in an asylum far from Gloucestershire, an action meant to address his condition but which may have exacerbated his discomfort and pain. Permanent exclusion from his Gloucestershire places led him to depend heavily on memory and imagination in order to maintain his identity and creative inspiration but, as Gurney himself knew, even this would (and did) fade. 'Memory is poor enough consolation / For the soul hopeless gone' he wrote in the immediate post-war period, as if predicting his eventual loss ('The High Hills', B, p.54 and K, 2004, p.81). Chapters 2, 3 and 4 all feature a special double-page spread focusing on some particular aspect or incident – Gurney's Cycle Ride (Chapter 2); The Dead Land Oppressed Me (Chapter 3); Gurney's Cottage and Dryhill Farm (Chapter 4).

Chapters 5, 6 and 7 each follow a common format: an introductory section will consider how Gurney came to know the place, and will examine any further details of the location and characteristics of these places, drawing on past histories and geographies. This is followed by an exploration of the way Gurney wrote about each place – can we discover some of the actual locations of his inspiration? How do the words of his poems illuminate or reshape Gloucestershire places? What else do they tell us about the way Gurney found meaning in these places? How did Gurney's self become so intertwined with the places of Gloucestershire? Features that were special to each location will be examined – for example, the importance of Gloucester Cathedral and its history, and how this related to Gurney's sense of place; his friendship with Will Harvey, and his enjoyment of sailing representing vital elements in his knowing the Severn Meadows; walking on Crickley Hill and discovering the Romans becoming crucial to his interest and involvement in the Cotswolds.

Included within Chapters 6 and 7 are suggested walking routes, with maps, illustrations and relevant poetry, providing an opportunity for the reader to undertake a more personalised entry into some of the Gloucestershire places so valued by Ivor Gurney. The walks are:

- Walk 1: Above Ashleworth (Severn Meadows above Gloucester)
- Walk 2: A Blowy Severn Tided Place (Severn Meadows below Gloucester at Framilode).
- Walk 3: High on Cooper's (The High Hills around Cooper's Hill and Cranham)
- Walk 4: On the Roman Hill (The High Hills centred on Crickley Hill)

In Chapter 8, I draw together some of the threads from previous chapters and highlight important general points about Ivor Gurney and Gloucestershire in particular, and poetry and place in general. The discussion ranges across the way Gurney's poetry captured in words the actual Gloucestershire, at a particular moment of historical and geographical time, and also created new interpretations of place, time and identity. More than this, the chapter aims to find the narrative – the story of Gurney and Gloucestershire – and to illuminate how Gurney's creative growth and development, and his physical and mental well-being, became inextricably linked with 'being in' this place. The relationship brought him joy; it also ended in pain when he was exiled 'out-of-place' in the asylum. At the end of the chapter, I return to my geographical background to propose a different way of mapping this relationship. Conventional maps, of which there are many throughout the book, are inadequate to express Gurney's Gloucestershire on their own, implying, as they do, that place is merely an objective feature separate from the poet as observer and creator. Figure 8.2, the last in the book, is designed to be laid (figuratively speaking) over the more conventional map of Ivor Gurney's Gloucestershire (colour illustration 12); it is concerned directly with this intimate person–place relationship and with what it tells us about the poetry and the man.

Gurney's Gloucestershire was a real place and, throughout the book, maps, diagrams, photographs and historic documentation have been used to identify the actual locations and typical landscapes he frequented, to reveal links and connections and to enable the interested observer to discover some of the sources of Gurney's inspiration. A locational map of this part of Gloucestershire (OS 1:250,000) is provided as the first colour illustration to aid identification of places and localities. Several block diagrams and landscape drawings (Figures 2.5, 6.1, 6.2, 6.3, 7.1, 7.2) have been reprinted directly from the classic 1967 book by William Dreghorn – *Geology Explained in the Severn Vale and Cotswolds* – by kind permission of Fineleaf Books (which reprinted the book in 2005). On two occasions, Gurney's movements through the landscape have been reconstructed from his poetry, essays and letters to create specially drawn maps – Gurney's Cycle Ride in Chapter 2; Sailing a Boat on the Severn in Chapter 6. The walking maps (Chapters 6 and 7) were drawn by Simon Lee Dicker, a specialist cartographer/designer (Fire and Ice Creative). A unique element of the book is a full colour illustrated map of Ivor Gurney's Gloucestershire occupying the middle colour pages of the book. It was constructed as a result of studying the places in Gurney's life and poetry, and was created with the help of expert cartographer and artist, Roger Ellis.

Exploration of Ivor Gurney's poetry and sense of place through these chapters will, I hope, not only enhance readers' understanding and enjoyment of Gloucestershire, and illuminate Gurney's life and poetry, but also alert us to our own relationship with the world around us at a time of increasing concern about our global places, environments and landscapes.

2

THE POET AND THE PLACE: LEARNING GLOUCESTERSHIRE

So, walking Gloucestershire, the child or boy learned his lessons,
But learned that high on Cooper's in June's scented silence,
Wild strawberries grew a host there, and by the rippling
Twyver, some fairy made scarlet unmatched cool bounties;
Who learned his music under the high sky dappling
the Gloucester ploughland with shadows – with colour dainties.

('Culpeper', GA, 1925)

The Boy of Gloucestershire

Ivor Bertie Gurney was born on 28 August 1890 at 3 Queen Street, a narrow thoroughfare adjoining Eastgate Street, close to the centre of Gloucester (Figure 2.1). He spent his formative years exploring his surroundings, finding adventure, happiness and mental stimulation, not only amongst the city's historic streets and buildings, but also in the diverse countryside of the Severn Meadows and the Cotswold Hills, that surround Gloucester on all sides. Although events later seemed to be pulling him away from these places, Gloucester and Gloucestershire were always his home, his refuge and his inspiration. As Gurney himself explained, 'the earth entered into my making and into my blood'. It is not possible to understand the poet or his poetry without exploring Gloucestershire at the same time.

In 1890, the year of Gurney's birth, Gloucester (with a population of almost 40,000) was the economic and political centre of the county, a busy, workmanlike place, still more important commercially than the slightly larger Cheltenham (almost 43,000), the rapidly growing spa town to the east. In form, at least, Gloucester was still a mediaeval city in the late nineteenth century, dominated by the cathedral, the riverside docks and the Cross – the place where the four main streets have met since Roman times. The central part of Gloucester was characterised by narrow streets and alleyways, many of them built over the remains of earlier streets and walkways and concealing reminders of earlier phases of Gloucester's history – Roman, Saxon, Norman, mediaeval and later. No. 3 Queen Street was built on the top of the old Roman wall, and the wall itself had been refashioned and used for shops in mediaeval times. So, appropriately for someone like Gurney who was fascinated by history and particularly by the Romans, his birthplace lay directly over layers of Gloucester's past. Since that time, the main Eastgate Street, and Queen Street itself, have been changed several times, including a major and rather brutal redevelopment of the old Eastgate Market in the 1960s, which reshaped the whole area behind the façades of Eastgate Street, Southgate Street and Brunswick Road. Queen Street disappeared completely, although a narrow walkway named Queen's Way follows the same line and maintains the memory

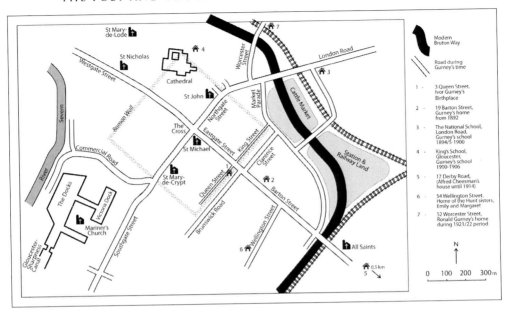

Fig. 2.1: Ivor Gurney's Gloucester.

of the Roman wall. A plaque commemorating Gurney's birthplace occupied a rather dark corner in this walkway until its relocation, in September 2009, to a more accessible site on the corner of Boots in Eastgate Street.

Present-day Eastgate Street is to most Gloucestrians a busy functional shopping street, in which shoppers bustle along the now pedestrianised street past Boots, the Eastgate Shopping Centre, a mobile phone outlet and Starbucks. The only obvious reminder of the past in this part of Gloucester is the striking tower of the former St Michael's Church at the Cross.

Nevertheless, the old Gloucester is never far away in this city, and despite the continuing economic and social changes in the twenty-first century, Gloucester retains a strong sense of historic place and past. As Gurney himself wrote, 'She is a city still and the centuries drape her yet; / Something in the air or light cannot or will not forget / The past ages of her and the toil which made her.' ('Time to Come', K, 2004)

David Gurney, Ivor's father, was a tailor who worked from his home premises so that the small house in Queen Street accommodated not only the tailor's shop but also the family – David, his wife Florence, Winifred (Ivor's older sister) and Ivor. Shortly after Ivor's birth, the family moved to a slightly bigger house and shop at 19 Barton Street, now the south-eastern extension of Eastgate Street.

Originally, Eastgate Street only went as far as the East Gate on the corner of what is now Brunswick Road, after which it became Bertonstret (Barton Street). In the 1980s the local council made the upper end, as far as the junction with the new inner ring road, an extension of Eastgate Street and most of the older housing, including 19 Barton Street, was knocked down. In Gurney's day, the original upper Barton Street would have been a lively area of urban residences and small shops, its fortunes improving since the opening of the railway station to the east of the town in the 1840s. The house at 19 Barton Street was of rather gloomy Victorian design, with double-fronted shop windows. Much of the lower floor, apart from a small living room and cramped kitchen/scullery, was given over to the tailoring business, while upstairs was one larger room and three very small bedrooms including the attic.

Ivor's brother, Ronald, was born at the house in 1894 and his sister, Dorothy, in 1900. It was from this Barton Street base that Gurney's childhood unfolded, and from which he visited the Gloucester shops and places of interest with his mother, attended the nearby National School

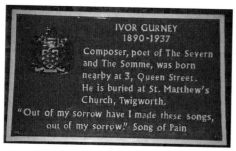

Above: The plaque commemorating Ivor Gurney's birthplace. Formally occupying the narrow alleyway directly over old Queen Street, it was moved in 2010 to a more accessible position near Boots on Eastgate Street. (Philip Wade)

Right: St Michael's Tower at the top of Eastgate Street. St Michael the Archangel's Church was originally built in the twelfth century and rebuilt twice, once in the fifteenth century and once in the nineteenth century. The church was demolished in 1956 leaving only the tower, which is Grade II listed.

in London Road (*see* Figure 2.1) and became a regular pupil at All Saints' Sunday School. The Church of All Saints played a crucial part in the life of Ivor Gurney. Not only did his parents, David and Florence, meet there but on the occasion of Ivor's christening (24 September 1890), the young curate of All Saints, Alfred Cheesman, became Gurney's godfather. The church can still be found, but it is now isolated on the outward edge of the inner ring road, and it is no longer a church but an Asian Community Centre.

Alfred Cheesman was then only twenty-five and this was his first appointment. He was by all accounts a quiet, conscientious man, devoted to helping his parishioners and, because of the chance that led him to be present at Gurney's christening, he was called on to be a second godfather and so became a lifelong friend and mentor to the young Ivor Gurney. Cheesman was Oxford educated; he loved books and music and during his twenty-four years at All Saints was able to support the intellectual growth and creative development of his young protégé, particularly after Ivor joined the church Sunday school (1896) and eventually the church choir (1899). Possibly influenced by Cheesman, the family purchased a piano in 1896 – apparently it had to be hauled up and in through the window of the large upstairs room at Barton Street – and Ivor began to extend his musical interest and skill.

In Gurney's early childhood, there were other features of the city environment that attracted him; for example, the busyness of Eastgate Street with its fairs and markets, the nearby cattle market, and the waterside. Gloucester Docks was a thriving commercial and trading centre positioned round the River Severn, which had been given a major boost by the completion of the Gloucester & Sharpness Canal (1827) and the coming of the railway in the 1840s.

The young Gurney was fascinated by the river, the ships and the seamen. An early poem, published in the 1919 *War's Embers* collection, recalled him as a child walking 'Down Commercial Road' to the docks with his mother, and being excited by the romance of the sailor's life. The rolling rhythm and jaunty rhyme scheme give this piece the feeling of a sea-shanty, well-suited to the theme, but not typical of his later Severn Meadows poetry.

DOWN COMMERCIAL ROAD

When I was small and packed with tales of desert islands far
My mother took me walking in a grey ugly street,
But there the sea-wind met us with a jolly smell of tar,

Clockwise from above:
19 Barton Street, the tailor's shop and
Gurney family home from soon after
Gurney's birth. (Gurney Archives)

All Saints' Church, where Gurney was
christened. At the time of writing, it is an
Asian Cultural Centre. (Photo 2010)

Eastgate Street Fair, Mop Monday in
the late nineteenth century. The tower
is that of St Michael the Archangel's,
where Eastgate Street meets The Cross.
(Gloucestershire Archives)

Gloucester Docks in 1882.
(Gloucestershire Archives)

Gurney's paternal grandmother at her house in
Maisemore. (Gurney Archives)

The riverside at Maisemore; low hills in the distance
(snow covered in this February 2010 photograph).

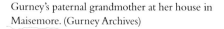

> A sailorman went past to town with slow rolling gait;
> And Gloucester she's famous in story.
>
> The trees and shining sky of June were good enough to see,
> Better than any books or tales the sailormen might tell –
> But tops'le spars against the blue made fairyland for me;
> The snorting tug made surges like the huge Atlantic swell.
> And Gloucester she's famous in story.

(War's Embers, 1919)

Another early poem – 'The Fisherman of Newnham' (WE) – has the dedication 'To my Father'
and describes how David Gurney 'set [Gurney] fishing by Frampton Hock', the river cliff at
Fretherne. David Gurney could trace his descent to the Severn Meadow villages of Maisemore,
Hartpury and Ashleworth. We know that he regularly led a family walk on a Sunday afternoon,
out of the city across Maisemore Ham (the flood meadows in the island between the two branches
of the River Severn) and so to Maisemore village where Gurney's paternal grandmother lived.
    Winifred Gurney remembered that:

> When Ivor was in the Cathedral Choir he was allowed to invite another choirboy, or more, to have tea
> with us before setting off. In these things, combined with trips down the Canal or the River, as well
> as country walks, Mother generally accompanied us, and they were the pleasantest days of our lives...

(Hurd, p.20)

Today one can still make the Maisemore walk if one is prepared for the landscape of concrete
pillars and viaducts, the deafening noise of traffic on the A40 and A417, and the sight of pylons
and electricity lines entangling the vision. Nevertheless, in the middle of Maisemore Ham, it is
still possible, even now, to feel the airy lightness of the floodplain landscape and to look beyond
the modern motor-car-inspired vista to see the pleasant low hills of the river terraces rising to the
north and west. It is easy to imagine the Gurney family making its way on a spring morning, with
the younger children running to jump muddy puddles or pick flowers along the path. A poem of
1925 recalls the bucolic pleasures of those early days:

THE SALT BOX

> There were three poplars there where my grandmother lived –
> She saw them at first waking – their foliage breathed
> Warning or content of all weathers. And on Sundays
> My father took us, and we picked up apples, or wandered

By ant hills or poppies; while the corncrake ground his strange cry in the wheat.
Till at half past six time
My father would rise; and say 'Well, mother I'm going
Up to the "Salt Box"' – past meadows of unmatched hay
Now ripening, it lay with thick hawthorn boundaried –
Company was there and perry of true farmers knowing
As worth knowing – Cool perry – And a faraway
Gloucestershire stretched like Heaven for blue and golden showing.

(Extract from longer poem,
Gurney Archives, 1925)

N.b. The Salt Box was the local 'beerhouse'. Perry is pear cider.

The walk alongside the River Severn and across the meadows introduced Ivor to the easiest way to escape from Gloucester into the countryside of riverside villages, low hills and woods, and to an enduring affection for these 'tiny knolls and orchards hidden beside the river / Muddy and strongly flowing', as he described them in the poem 'Strange Service' (S&S).

Gurney's mother, Florence, came from Bisley, a pretty village high up on the Cotswold plateau above Stroud; her Huguenot ancestors, the Luggs, had settled here in the seventeenth century. The Gurneys would undoubtedly have visited these relations but they do not appear to have made regular visits to this village, probably because of the greater distances involved. Some jottings on a piece of paper in the archives show Gurney considering the origin of the name Lugg – 'Huguenot I suppose' he has written. 'Flemish weaver – cloth in Stroud valley' – 'So with Maisemore, Upleadon, Ashleworth – Bisley I am proud.'

At the age of ten, and with Cheesman's encouragement, Gurney won a place in the Gloucester Cathedral Choir and an associated scholarship to the King's School, Gloucester. His horizons widened intellectually, socially and spatially. He proved to be only a reasonably attentive scholar but an active and successful sportsman, boasting that he had the second best batting average and the third best bowling record by the time he left school! (p.14, Hurd, 1978) He was certainly not shy or awkward at school, apparently showing an early skill in producing humorous rhymes and drawings in his school books, much to the amusement of friends, though perhaps not so appreciated by the teachers. The quality of education at the King's School was not high at

Left: Gurney's mother, Florence. *Right*: Gurney's father, David. Photographs taken in 1915 outside the family home at 19 Barton Street. (Gurney Archives)

Ivor Gurney playing the piano in 1905, aged fifteen years. (Gurney Archives)

Gurney's two sisters, Dorothy (the younger child) and Winifred. This photograph was taken about 1906/7. (Gurney Archives)

that time; the demands of the cathedral took precedence over academic learning, with music occupying the choristers for most of every morning. It was at King's School, however, that he improved his piano playing and learnt to play the organ, and we can surmise that his frequent choral activities in the cathedral helped to seal his affection and awe for this inspiring building, the place he often referred to as St Peter's Place. The spires of the cathedral, visible from the vale and the hills, became a backcloth to Gurney's life and a symbol of his county – 'Who says Gloucester sees a tall / Fair fashioned shape of stone arise, / That changes with the changing skies' he wrote in a later poem ('Old City', K, 2004).

Letters and reminiscences of Gurney's brother and sisters imply that Ivor was a precocious and rebellious child who rarely did what was expected of him and was frequently missing from home, wandering the streets and countryside on his own. The Gurney household was probably not an easy one for a talented but rather rebellious youngster to grow up in. The Barton Street quarters were somewhat cramped for the tailor's workshop and six inhabitants. Apparently Florence, Ivor's mother, was a rather unstable person with a tendency to dominate and push her husband and children. She often seemed complaining and cold, possibly as a result of her own frustrations and her desire for them to better themselves, although at other times she could be flamboyantly caring. David Gurney was a quieter, gentler person – 'Happiness revolved round Father,' wrote Winifred Gurney later. 'The pity of it was that Mother did not seem to enjoy her children, and so far as I could see she did not win their love' (W. Gurney reminiscences, Hurd, p.11). It would be unwise to accept this one viewpoint only. Winifred and Ronald were later jealous of Ivor's success and of their mother's support for him. Florence Gurney undoubtedly wanted her children to do well; it was she who was instrumental in purchasing the piano, it was she who pushed Ivor to practise his playing and she was tremendously proud of his various musical achievements.

Florence herself records that, in 1904, Ivor was asked at the last minute to stand in for one of the singers at the Three Choirs Festival in Gloucester and to perform on the stage alongside Madam Albani.

> Madam Albani would have him by her and he looked such a boy to her but they said he done it beautiful an unrehearsed piece and he was so frightened at his success when he got home, he hid in the kitchen everybody saying Ivor Gurney had been singing with Madam Albani.
>
> (Letter from Florence Gurney to Marion Scott, undated, GA)

It is not surprising that the other children felt that their mother was guilty of favouritism. Although Ivor was close to his mother as a child, later they often clashed and arguments would more often characterise their relationship.

An interesting insight into Ivor Gurney's relationship with his father is given in an unpublished poem (GA), written in 1925. In it, Gurney describes his father's love for, and knowledge of, the countryside, and explains that he sees himself following his father's desire that he should speak for Gloucestershire. He seems to hint that his father, who had a musical background, would like his son to create the images of Gloucestershire that he, himself, had 'never never, been able to say or sing'. The references to Petersburg and Count Tolstoy are because Gurney shared a birthday with the Russian poet and used the name as a link. In fact, Petersburg is also the name of an American Civil War battle site, and this poem is part of a group of 'American poems' in which Gurney makes many connections between his own life and American names (*see* p.71).

PETERSBURG

My father looked on ploughland and willed me.
His was the friendliness of every hill and tree
In all the west Gloucestershire, in all west Gloucestershire
Born of that earth, of like love brought to birth;
Knowing the flights of birds, and the song of the smallest
Bird – the names of flowers, and the likeliest place

Where first spring might bring Her lovely trifles in.
So on a night when Orion ruled with majestic light,
He remembered his past dreams, all broken, and hoped for grace
Whereby a son should say what he had never never,
Been able to say or sing of such beloved Earth.
Walked to Maisemore, and made his vows as his father
Had done before – So on the Day of one Master
Of me I was born – Leo Count Tolstoi – to be
War Poet, and lover, maker, server of earth, the born of Gloucestershire

(Gurney Archives, 1925)

As a result of David Gurney's success at tailoring, the family seemed to be moving into the ranks of the lower middle classes in the mid-1890s and the purchase of a piano in 1896 confirmed this. Nevertheless, it was a not a household with luxuries like books and quiet reading rooms so it was not surprising, perhaps, that as Ivor Gurney extended himself musically and intellectually, he liked to spend more time at his godfather's house nearby at 17 Derby Road, where these things were available. Gurney's godfather, Alfred Cheesman, took a great interest in the boy's development, encouraging him in music and introducing him to a wide range of literature and poetry. Gurney was definitely 'one of Cheesman's boys' according to his sister Winifred; indeed, between 1905 and 1911, Gurney spent such a lot of time with Cheesman that 'Ivor practically lived with him'. The photograph shows the dedication made to Alfred Cheesman in a book given by the young Ivor Gurney to his friend and mentor in 1907. The existence of this poem, only recently discovered, makes this the earliest known Gurney poem. Although it was known in Gloucester that the Revd Cheesman 'had a liking for lads', according to Hurd (1978) there was no hint that this was a homosexual attachment: 'No breath of scandal ever clung to his name. If indeed he loved, he kept his love to himself, content to be guide, philosopher and friend to such boys as had ears for his counsel' (Hurd, p. 10).

It was at this time too that the Hunt sisters (Emily and Margaret) became friends with the young Gurney, probably introduced to him by Cheesman. These two women, possibly half-sisters, lived close to the Gurney household at 54 Wellington Street, in a spacious house left to them by their mother after her death in 1907. Both sisters had been teachers in South Africa; they were well educated, musical and sympathetic to Ivor's talent and ambition. The sisters were comfortably off, owning a fine Bechstein piano and many books and newspapers. Gurney would spend long hours at the house, playing music and reading well into the evenings. Margaret, the

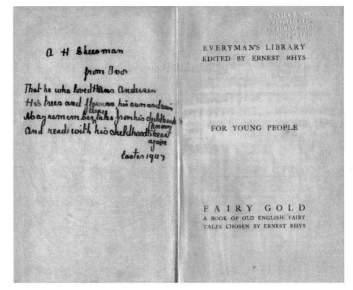

A 1907 dedication to Alfred Cheesman in a book which must have been presented to Cheesman as a present from the young Gurney. The book was found amongst Cheesman's papers by Graeme Middleton, and negotiations are under way to make sure that it is lodged in the archives. If the date is correct, then this is the earliest piece of Gurney's poetry we have.

The view up Barton Street today with the Cotswold scarp visible in the background.

younger sister, though fifteen years older than Ivor, was a special friend. Later, in a poem called 'The First Violets', Gurney recognised the way she had encouraged him to open his mind to the landscape around him.

> She had such love and after my music sent
> Me out to woodlands, and to wander by meadow or bent
> Lanes of Severn – I got them all into my music –
> I would wander my soul full of air, and return to her quick …
>
> (*Best Poems and the Book of Five Makings*, p.45)

Responding to all the encouragement and new experience, Gurney started writing music, apparently trying his hand on the first occasion when he should have been minding the tailor's shop for his father in 1904. But it was not just encouragement and a space to write that Gurney needed; he also needed inspiration, and even before Margaret Hunt's attentions, Gurney seems to have turned to walking the countryside for this. In this sense, Gurney's central Gloucester home was well-placed. Not only does the city sit astride the Severn Meadows but, as any Gloucestrian will affirm, it is not possible to live in Gloucester without being aware of the surrounding hills – the striking eminence of May Hill and the bulky outline of the Forest of Dean to the west, and the strong curve of the Cotswolds' scarp edge to the east (Figure 2.2). Gurney would have been aware of these different landscapes, beckoning alluringly. Even as a child, he would have found his way out of Gloucester, up the steep track known as Portway, which carries on from Barton Street and leads up the scarp slope of the Cotswolds to Cranham and 'dim wood lengths without end' ('Cotswold Ways'). Here he would have encountered his first experience of scarp-edge views and the rich odours of beech-woods, contrasting invitingly with the softer colours and more gentle landscapes of the Severn Vale. These early encounters were his 'springs of beauty'. As Gurney himself described it much later in 'Springs of Music', a 'beauty out of beauty suddenly thrust unasked upon a heart that dared not want more; had not dreamed of asking more, and was suddenly given completely eternal right in Cranham, Portway, Redmarley, Crickley – before the Paradise of Earth.' (Gurney, 1922)

The Golden Days

In 1906, when he was sixteen years old, a new period opened up in Gurney's life. He left the Cathedral Choir and the King's School and became an articled pupil of Dr Herbert Brewer, the organist in Gloucester Cathedral. Brewer was a respected musician in the Gloucestershire area, but according to Margaret Hunt and Marion Scott he was a competent, rather than an inspiring, tutor to Gurney. Nevertheless, Gurney was playing music, learning new skills and enjoying the experience of spending time in the cathedral. He was composing music with enthusiasm, setting

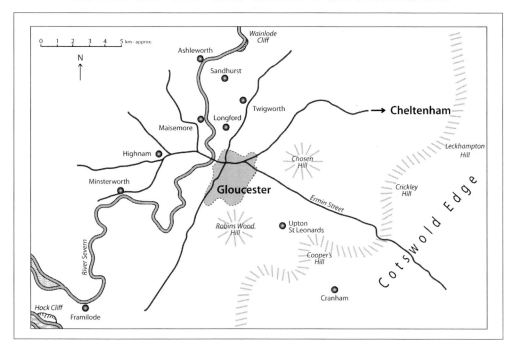

Fig. 2.2: Exploring the Local Area 1890–1911. This map is based on information provided on the Alan Godfrey Old Ordnance Survey Maps at 1 inch to 1 mile of Gloucester and District, 1896, and NW Gloucestershire, 1896. The dotted line shows the extent of Gloucester as it was in 1896.

songs to poetry – significantly, his choice of poetry included A.E. Housman, R.L. Stevenson and R. Bridges – but also producing pieces for piano and violin. Many of the latter are dedicated to the two Miss Hunts, whose encouragement, along with that of Alfred Cheesman, were crucial to his creative development, providing, at this time, a much needed and supportive audience. In 1905 he had passed some examinations of the professional organisation, the Royal College of Music of Organists, and so was able to take paid employment as an organist. For brief spells, he played for local churches, notably Whitminster, Hempsted and the distinctive Mariner's Church in the docks. He settled in most easily with the sailors and dockhands at the Mariner's Church; apparently his outspokenness did not endear him to the vicars' wives of Hempsted and Whitminster. The small income gave him some independence, which was bitterly resented by his brother, Ronald, who was then working unpaid in his father's shop.

More importantly, it was in the cathedral that Gurney met Herbert Howells, one of three pupils taken on by Brewer at that time. The third pupil was Ivor Davies, later known as Ivor Novello, but it was Howells who would become one of Gurney's closest friends and a great musician. A couple of years later, in 1908, a chance meeting on a tram resulted in Gurney also becoming friends with Will Harvey, a local boy who was studying law with a Gloucester solicitor, and who shared Gurney's and Howell's interests in music and the countryside. Although Harvey had briefly been at the King's School, he was two years older than Gurney and, since then, had been away at school in Lancashire, so they did not know each other well from school. Now however, these friendships ushered in what Blevins (2008) calls the 'golden days' for Gurney. He spent time with both Howells and Harvey, exploring Gloucester, going to concerts and walking along the riverside or on the nearby Chosen Hill. The boys shared ideas and opinions about music, books and local events.

It was with Howells that Gurney heard, and was excited by, Vaughan Williams' 'Fantasia on a Theme by Thomas Tallis' when it was first performed in 1910 at the Three Choirs Festival in Gloucester. On the other hand, it was probably Will Harvey who kindled Gurney's interest in writing poetry, since Harvey himself was developing his skills as a poet. It may have been Harvey

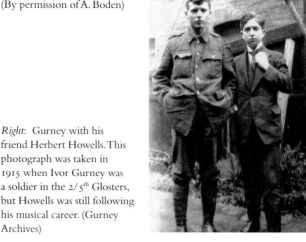

Left: Will Harvey, *c.* 1906.
(By permission of A. Boden)

Right: Gurney with his
friend Herbert Howells. This
photograph was taken in
1915 when Ivor Gurney was
a soldier in the 2/5th Glosters,
but Howells was still following
his musical career. (Gurney
Archives)

(or possibly Cheesman) who introduced Gurney to John Haines, a local solicitor and minor poet, who was already nurturing the talents of several other young poets and who became a good friend of Gurney.

Will Harvey was an intelligent and likeable young man. Winifred Gurney thought that the two boys were 'twin intellects … perfectly in harmony' (W. Gurney's reminiscences, GA). We know from Gurney's later poetry ('The Farm') that Will Harvey's family became very dear to him and that he spent a great deal of time in the family home, Redlands, 'a creeper-covered house' at Minsterworth near the River Severn. It was a large, comfortable and happy household where Gurney could mingle with the family; three brothers, a sister and the easy-going parents. 'Within the house were books, / A piano, dear to me / And round the house the rooks / Haunted each tall elm tree.' ('The Farm', WE, 1919) As Boden explains in his biography of Will Harvey, the home was always full of laughter, good food and, significantly, books and music. The two boys became virtually inseparable.

> Whenever possible, the pair would escape together to the welcoming farm at Minsterworth to help in the fields, to walk in the Severn Meadows, to pick fruit in the orchard, to play 'ping-pong' on the long dining room table or cricket with Will's brothers and friends, to set off with guns to bag rabbits for the pot, to make music, and always to talk.
>
> (Boden, p.22, 1988)

Both Hurd and Blevins make much of the fact that Gurney found the atmosphere in the Harvey home much more restful than in the sometimes tense and overcrowded conditions of Barton Street. It may partly have been a natural desire for independence, as well as his increasing sophistication, that led Gurney away from his own family at this time. 'He did not seem to belong to us … he simply called on us briefly, and left again without a word,' his sister Winifred remembered. While his family felt 'cut out', we do know that it was in this period that his passion for music and poetry, and the connection of both these with walking the Gloucestershire countryside, were greatly enhanced. The poem 'After-Glow', written in 1917 when Harvey was in a prisoner-of-war camp, is a poignant mix of wonder and inspiration roused by the natural beauty around him, the joys of the companionship found at Redlands with Will Harvey and his love of music.

AFTER-GLOW

Out of the smoke and dust of the little room
With tea-talk loud and laughter of happy boys,
I passed into the dusk. Suddenly the noise
Ceased with a shock, left me alone in the gloom,

To wonder at the miracle hanging high
Tangled in twigs, the silver crescent clear –
Time passed from mind. Time died; and then we were
Once more at home together, you and I.

The elms with arms of love wrapped us in shade
Who watched the ecstatic West with one desire,
One soul uprapt; and still another fire
Consumed us, and our joy yet greater made:
That Bach should sing for us, mix us in one
The joy of firelight and the sunken sun.

(S&S, p.47)

It was with Will Harvey too that Gurney followed up his love of sailing (*see* Chapter 6). Gurney was the proud owner of a small sailing boat, the *Dorothy*, named after his sister and purchased, it seems, from the lock-keeper. 'James the name of the man first sold me by payment / Of Five Pounds, this most treacherous and fine sailing / Vessel of mine, so leaking – but never failing.' ('Rappahannock', GA) It was kept at Framilode and was put to good use by the two boys in the wide channels of the Severn, downstream of Gloucester. Apparently, Gurney had a wild streak; he was contemptuous of risk and always pushing himself to greater physical efforts. He nearly capsized the boat on several occasions, but he also drew immense satisfaction from observing the changing moods of the river and the clouds moving over the hilly horizons of the Forest and Cotswolds. Will Harvey recalled the carefree pleasures of sailing 'upstream from Framilode to Bollopool' in his poem 'Ballade of River Sailing'. The boat also cemented Gurney's friendship with the lock-keeper, James Harris, (about whom a poem was later written) and, as Chapter 6 will show, the activity and inspiration of sailing feature strongly in Gurney's writing about the meadows.

So Gurney's young life was full of companionship and new interests but, at this time too, he developed some erratic personal habits. One concerned eating – he would go for long periods without food and then gorge himself on inappropriate items such as cakes and sugar buns. Another was his tendency to work through the night if the creative mood took him, and already he had taken to walking and cycling long distances on his own, in daylight or at night-time. One of the North American poems, written in Dartford in 1925, is entitled 'To Fort Yukon' and in it Gurney recalls how desperately he longed to be 'on Cotswolds' and the stealthy way he would creep out of the house at night whether or not he was given permission – Gurney bending the rules!

TO FORT YUKON (extract)

To walk at night on Cotswolds, on the high Camps old
Of Roman – March my first, three times given permission,
Often stealthily moving with soft feet below –
To where my boots and the door were; and to running far where
Painswick against High Heavens lifted Her brow.
(O Rome immortal, O Gloucester, O Cotswold spinnies,
How my love labours you repaid with love and promises)
So on – reading at return Shakespeare, Wordsworth in turn.

(GA, 1925)

GURNEY'S CYCLE RIDE

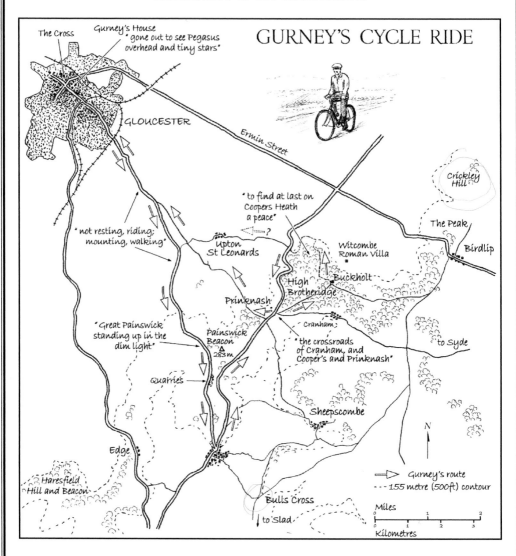

GURNEY'S CYCLE RIDE

The Cross

Gurney's House
'gone out to see Pegasus overhead and tiny stars'

GLOUCESTER

Ermin Street

Crickley Hill

'to find at last on Coopers Heath a peace'

The Peak

Birdlip

'not resting, riding; mounting, walking'

Upton St Leonards

Witcombe Roman Villa

High Brotheridge

Buckholt

Prinknash

Cranham

'Great Painswick standing up in the dim light'

Painswick Beacon
283 m

'the crossroads of Cranham, and Cooper's and Prinknash'

to Syde

Quarries

Sheepscombe

N

Edge

Haresfield Hill and Beacon

Bulls Cross

to Slad

Gurney's route
- - - 155 metre (500ft) contour

Miles
0   1   2

Kilometres
0   1   2   3

It is a cold clear night in late spring, with the stars showing brightly in the dark sky above Gloucester. At number 19 Barton Street, the household sleeps. But seventeen-year-old Ivor Gurney lies awake, imagining the dark outlines of the beech trees on High Brotheridge. He can almost hear the dry crackle of twigs and stirring of small creatures in the grass. He longs to watch the dawn wake on the scarp edge and to feel that surge of music and poetry in his soul. At last he can stand it no longer; he jumps out of bed and quietly dresses. Then, creeping past the open door of his sister's bedroom, he pauses to look at her sleeping form. Seven-year-old Dorothy stirs in her sleep – who knows what she is dreaming? Ivor tiptoes on down the stairs. Taking his bicycle from the narrow passageway, he manoeuvres it through the door and out into the cool night. Oh what wonderful stars – tiny sparkling worlds – and over there, is that Pegasus?

Cycling down Barton Street, he feels the thrill of secret joy at being the only person moving in the city. Soon he is cycling along Painswick Road and having to work harder as the road rises, first gradually, then steeply. The houses and streets are left behind; the only sounds are his own breathing and an occasional cry of a night creature. Now the hill is steeper and Ivor is sometimes forced to dismount and push the bike. But there is pleasure in this hard work and soon his efforts are rewarded by a glimpse of the dark bulk of Painswick Beacon rising above him…

DAWN

It is I have stirred restlessly in my bed,
At midnight, and dressed softly not to awaken
Others, and gone out to see Pegasus overhead
And tiny stars by no wind stirred or shaken.
With my bicycle taken
Carefully over rough stones not to make a sound
Nor waken my still sister, girl in her deep
Sleep, with hope of high beeches and Cranham instead
Of her dreams. (I did not dare at a girl's sleep)
Not resting, riding; mounting, walking till I had passed
Great Painswick standing up in the dim light for ever fast
And Roman calling to me, and challenging …
Free ever of beeches, save where the dead leaves cling
Of winter, that Spring left and Summer ever.
(That camp dipping nobly centrewards like a cup)
To pass that, and swift as running horse be driven
By quarry and sleeping house, and quiet townend –
Eastward, eastward, northward till I found my friend.

The cross-roads of Cranham, and Cooper's and Prinknash
(said Prinnadge)
To find my Roman nobleness, and to find music
At last, my dear thought flowing in my mind quick.
Looking up at the bright stars, beech twiggen, and to have knowledges
Of all the ages of life not told in pages.
My friends, the sentinels, and the corporal my courtesy.
To find at last on Coopers Heath a peace
Which enrapt me all in a cloak, my honourers
The dead Romans in whom ran (in me) blood the currents
And innumerous ages could not alter much, nor the
Truth of my imagining (proving) set down on pages.
They were there, Romans, quiet comrades and ponderers…
And Gloucester slept below them with her strange
Pattern of light, the old city, that was as them, as to me.

(GA, 1925)

The poem recounts the journey. Gurney was keenly aware of the Roman associations all around him ('Roman calling') – Roman Gloucester itself, farmhouses, villas (like Upton St Leonards) and roads such as Ermin Street. The summit of Painswick Beacon, then as now, was a grassy hilltop ('free ever of beeches') and the site of an Iron Age fort surrounded by ditch and rampart – Gurney refers to 'that camp dipping nobly centrewards like a cup'.

Soon he cycles downhill 'swift as a running horse' into Painswick. His route passes Catsbrain quarry and skirts the 'quiet townend' before he turns north-east along the main road (now the A46).

Gurney's 'friend' is presumably the road junction at Cranham Corner, where many roads gave him access to the Cotswold Edge – north-east to Cooper's Hill, Birdlip and Crickley; eastwards to Cranham, Syde ('Side') and Sheepscombe; south-west to Painswick, Edge, Slad and his mother's family village of Bisley.

He is inspired, as always, by the surroundings, finding music and his thoughts flowing quickly.

Rather than take the main road, I like to think he took the Birdlip road and turned through the dark woods at Buckholt to emerge on the Cooper's Hill summit and watch the lights of sleeping Gloucester until the dawn came up in the east. Gurney does not tell us about his return journey, perhaps through Upton St Leonards to join Portway. Or he might have cycled back to Cranham Corner to travel the complete length of Portway and so back to the sleeping household before it awoke.

Painswick Beacon and village, taken from Edge. (2010)

'Dawn', though written in 1925 in Dartford Asylum, provides a tantalising glimpse of his cycling activities. It shows us a young man, content in his own solitary explorations, who was already seeking peace and beauty in the natural world. There is more than a hint of Wordsworth's belief that 'one impulse from a vernal wood may teach you more of man' in Gurney's line suggesting that the 'bright stars' and 'beech twiggen' may provide 'knowledges of all the ages of life not told in pages'. Equally, we can note the rebellious and individualistic streak that led him to flout convention and take to wandering even in his teenage years.

There is no doubt that, at this point, music was his consuming interest or that his experiences of the countryside were the chief source of his compositions. He often roamed alone, creating the sounds in his mind, before rushing home to write them down. Wandering the countryside, exploring the sensations of the city, riverside and Cotswold Edge, creating music and discovering poetry – all these were a part of Gurney's 'golden days'. Whilst he could be a charming companion, he always displayed a restless energy and seemed to be more at home in the meadows, woods and hills than he ever was in any building or social gathering. This was a trait which was to follow him all his life. He treated his home in Barton Street and his various adopted homes with Cheesman, the Hunts or the Harveys, as merely temporary stopping places in which to compose or to read and discuss literature and music. Unconventional, wild, rebellious, erratic are all words that have been used to describe the young Gurney's behaviour and they may not be that unusual in a creative personality, but these attributes were also the symptoms of his intense and intimate identification with the Gloucestershire places. Before continuing his life story, we need to look in more depth at the character and geography of Gurney's Gloucestershire.

The Landscapes of Gloucestershire

(N.b. The locational map (in middle of book) may be useful to identify names and places.)

In one of the best known studies of the Gloucestershire landscape, Finberg (1975) set out a clear description of its characteristics: 'For of Gloucestershire, we may say, quite as truly as Caesar said of ancient Gaul, that it is divided into three parts' – the Forest of Dean, the Severn Vale and the Cotswold Hills. He went on to argue that 'were it not that recently improved communications have linked them much more closely together then ever before, there would be little or no justification for attempting to deal with all three in one narrative.' In fact, in the post-war period, and particularly since the 1970s, communications and personal mobility – particularly through use of the rail network, the motor car, the telephone and more recently electronic communications – have increased apace, so that the development of each part of Gloucestershire is closely bound to the rest of the county and to national and global trends. Equally, the growth of population, industry and tourism in the twentieth century has served, to some extent, to standardise settlement and services, and to minimise distinctive local differences. Nevertheless, whatever the underlying

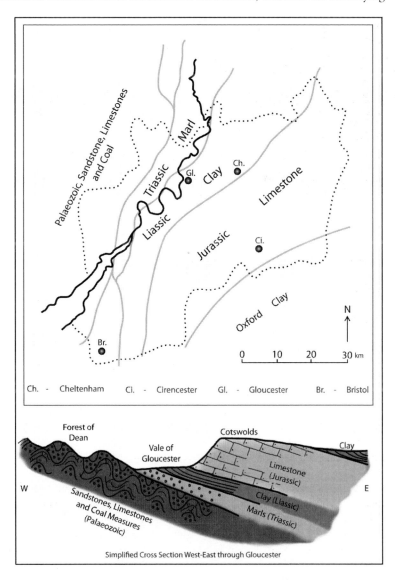

Fig. 2.3: Simplified Geology of Gloucestershire. The Gloucestershire boundary is that of the pre-1974 county.

processes of change, the landscape divisions of Gloucestershire remain strikingly distinctive to the observer. Natural England, the national advisory body on the environment, sub-divides Britain into 159 National Character Areas (NCAs) to provide an overview of the differences in landscape character at the national scale. The main part of Gloucestershire divides quite neatly into the same three areas (Figure 2.5) recognised by Finberg; the Forest of Dean and Lower Wye (NCA105), the Severn and Avon Vales (NCA106) and the Cotswolds (NCA107). In the north-west, there is also a small area around Dymock, Newent, and May Hill, well known to Gurney, which is described by Natural England as Over Severn (NCA104). The Bristol and Avon Valleys and Ridges (NCA 118) lies to the south and is less significant for this study (Natural England, 2010).

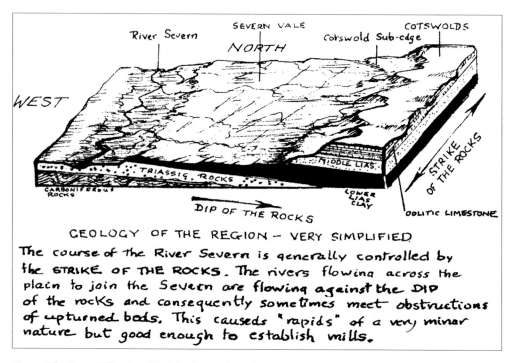

Fig. 2.4: The Severn Valley: Simplified Geology and Landscape. (W. Dreghorn, 1967)

The landscape distinctions are closely related to the geology (Figure 2.3). At its simplest level, the physical landscape is affected by the age and hardness of the underlying rocks. One of the best introductions to the Gloucestershire geology and landscape was provided by William Dreghorn in 1967 – *Geology Explained in the Severn Vale and Cotswolds* – and this classic text has now been reprinted (2005 by Fineleaf). Figure 2.4 shows Dreghorn's simplified block diagram of this area. The high ground of the Welsh borderlands and Forest of Dean are formed of older, harder rocks (the so-called Palaeozoic age rocks), which include the very resistant (Silurian) sandstones of May Hill, the redder (Devonian Old Red) sandstones of the Forest of Dean and its Carboniferous coal measures. To the north, the Malvern Hills, physically in Worcestershire but forming a dramatic

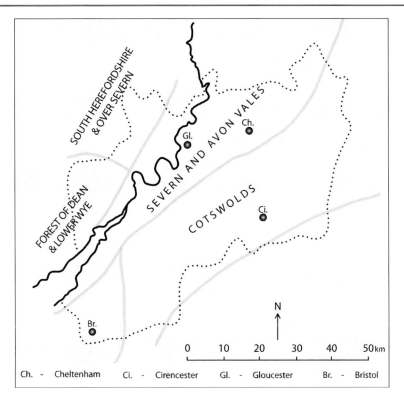

Fig. 2.5: The Landscape Character Areas of Gloucestershire. This map is based on information obtained from Natural England maps on the website www.naturalengland.org.uk. The Gloucestershire boundary is that of the pre-1974 county.

Over Severn (part of South Herefordshire and Over Severn) (NCA 104)
*   Fertile undulating farmland, with well-defined hedgerows and red sandstone farmsteads
*   Numerous churches and manor houses in small hamlets
*   Contrasting steep wooded slopes (e.g. May Hill) and more gentle vale and riverside slopes near the Severn and its tributaries

Forest of Dean and Lower Wye (NCA 105)
*   Well-wooded plateau with limestone and sandstone ridges between the valleys
*   Small-scale industry and remnants of earlier mining and industry
*   Strong sense of identity because of industrial history, landscape and past remoteness
*   Scattered settlements and small-holdings in the forest

Severn Vale (NCA 106)
*   Flat or gently undulating landscapes but with distinct vales, e.g. Gloucester, Leadon
*   Variety of land uses, from small pasture fields in the west to bigger fields and more intensive agriculture in the east
*   Ancient market towns and large villages along the river, with timber-framed and brick buildings
*   Prominent views of hills beyond the area, e.g. Cotswolds, Bredon, Malvern, May Hill

Cotswolds (NCA 107)
*   Defined by limestone geology; dramatic scarp rising from lowlands, with scarp foot springs and villages, steep combes and beech woodland
*   Rolling high 'wold' plateau, divided by narrow valleys, with some arable and some woodland
*   Prominent outlier hills in lowlands, e.g. Churchdown (Chosen) Hill, Robinswood Hill, Bredon Hill
*   Attractive villages, with grey or honey-coloured Cotswold limestone used in churches, houses and walls

visual backcloth to the Vale of Gloucester, are even more ancient. They are of Pre-Cambrian age, reminding us, as Fortey describes it, of a deeper hidden history when these hills were islands in a Cambrian sea (Fortey, 2010, p.83). The Malverns are frequently mentioned by Gurney, whose descriptions often refer to the striking outline of the hills seen from the Severn Vale – 'wavy Malvern under smoothy roof' as one poem intriguingly describes them ('The Square Thing', 80P). Further east are the younger rocks of Mesozoic age, consisting of the Triassic sandstones and marls of the Mercian Mudstones Group (formerly known as the Keuper Marls), the Lower Jurassic Lias clays of the Severn Vale and eventually the more permeable, and so more resistant, Middle Jurassic limestones of the Cotswold Hills. Because the layers of limestone are sloping or 'dipping' to the south-east, the Cotswold Hills present a steep cliff edge (or scarp) to the Vale, with the highest point being Cleeve Hill, rising 330m above Cheltenham. The River Severn follows a south-westerly course which is guided by the geology, picking out the softer clays and flowing between the two areas of higher land to west and east. The area best known to Gurney comprises the Vale and the Cotswold Edge, and so description will focus on these.

The Severn Vale is underlain by both the Triassic and the Liassic rocks. The Triassic deposits, occurring mainly to the west of the Severn, were formed under desert conditions, giving rise to the characteristic reddish Mercian sandstones and mudstones (formerly known as Keuper Red Marls) as seen, for instance, at Westbury on Severn's river cliff, the Garden Cliff south of Gloucester and also at Wainlode Cliff, north of Gloucester. The colour of the 'ruddy clay' was noticed by Gurney in his poem 'By Severn'. There are also occasional bands of a greeny-grey colour, now called Blue Anchor formation. They used to be known as Tea Green Marls because the environment at the time of the rock's formation was changing from hot, dry oxidising conditions to warm, humid reducing conditions, and so caused green ferrous oxide rather than red ferric oxide to dominate. The Lias clays formed under deep-water conditions and comprise the underlying rock, mainly to the east of the Severn. However, between the Triassic and Liassic layers, there are beds of shale, marls, and thin limestones with many fossils, a sequence representing the gradual flooding of the land by the sea. It was formerly known as the Rhaetic but is now generally considered to be part of the Lower Lias. It is significant for the landscape because it results in a low scarp that crosses the vale to the west of the river. This line of low hills, including the hills above Highnam and Ashleworth, was appreciated by Gurney, providing viewpoints and diverse walking options.

The river has been important in forming the landscape as we see it now. Floodplain alluvium covers the course of the Severn itself, as well as those of the tributaries such as the Leadon, Chelt, Frome and Cam. There are also remnants of ancient river terraces, marking the more elevated positions of the river and its predecessors throughout various glacial and interglacial periods. The Severn itself has its own moods; Finberg described it as temperamental:

> When Spring tides, particularly the famous Severn Bore, thunder up the estuary it is the most awe-inspiring of English rivers. A mature river, the geologist calls it, buts its conduct is wayward in the extreme. It frequently shifts channels, now favouring one bank, now another with deposits of rich alluvium.
>
> (1975, pp.25-6)

In the estuary the river is wide and powerful, producing huge waterscapes and pale, long horizons. In Gurney's day the senses were met by muted colours, watery reflections, marsh birds, reed beds, elver fishing (elvers are young eels) and boats of all kinds. According to the season, the walker would contend with river mists, flooded meadows, the roaring waters of the Severn Bore or soporific summer heat. Further upstream of Gloucester, the river narrows; there are meanders, more peaceful stretches of water lined with ash, willow and alder, occasional river cliffs as at Wainlode, and villages perched on the higher ground of river-formed terraces. The young Gurney found peace, adventure and inspiration in these environments, particularly in the company of his friend Will Harvey, and many of his poems feature the sights and sounds of the Severn. 'Near Midsummer', published in *War's Embers*, paints a picture of the river, contrasting the summer and winter conditions.

'Huge waterscapes and pale, long horizons' at Framilode.

NEAR MIDSUMMER (extract)
Severn's most fair today!
See what a tide of blue
She pours, and flecked alway
With gold, and what a crew
Of seagulls snowy white
Float round her to delight
Villagers, travellers.
A brown thick flood is hers
In winter when the rains
Wash down from Midland plains,
Halting wayfarers,
Low meadows flooding deep
With torrents from the steep
Mountains of Wales and small
Hillocks of no degree –
Streams jostling to the sea;
(Wrangling yet brotherly).
Blue June has altered all –
The river makes its fall
With murmurous still sound,
Past Pridings faery ground,
And steep-down Newnham cliff…

(WE, p.34)

In Gurney's day, the Vale was predominantly farmland, with dairy cattle on the heavier soils and floodplain areas, and arable or orchard on the better-drained terraces and more sandy soils. There were still remnants of the original oak woodlands but also ash, elm, diverse hedgerow shrubs and many orchards, bringing variety and interest to the landscape. The orchards of Gloucestershire were famous – apples, pears and plums – and of course the cider. Ivor Gurney's friend Will Harvey explained how he loved 'the tangled orchards blowing bright / With clouds of apple blossom' ('My Village', F. W. Harvey).

Many of the orchards disappeared after the Second World War, a situation regretted by Leonard Clarke (editor of a volume of Gurney's poetry). 'They are gone now, cider house and orchards / and billowing tides of blossom riding the slopes / with early bees raiding, and Severn a silver eel / twisting to the sea on far-away skyline.' (*Green Wood: A Gloucestershire Childhood,* 1962)

In the past, the prevalent building materials were timber and brick, and the characteristic half-timbered cruck cottages can still be seen in villages like Apperley, Ashleworth, Hasfield and Corse. Elsewhere the crumbly, Blue Lias stone that lies at the base of the Liassic sequence is often used in churches and country houses. A fine example of stone church, manor house and tithe barn can be seen at Ashleworth, a village which had connections with David Gurney's family and was much loved and written about by his son. One of Gurney's favourite walks was on Barrow Hill (*see* p.100), overlooking the village, and this features in one of his best-known poems, 'Above Ashleworth'.

Gurney turned again and again to the place he called the 'Severn Meadows' in his poetry and letters of longing – 'the best roads in England, the finest cider, the richest blossom in the most magical orchards, beauty in security…' he wrote in a letter to Marion Scott (22 March 1916) from the army training camp on Salisbury Plain, 'are not these only of my county, my home?'

Overall, the Severn Vale is a relatively narrow strip of land; the distance from the sandstone heights of the Forest of Dean to the limestone edge of the Cotswolds varies from 6-13 miles only. The Cotswolds present a steep, imposing edge or scarp when viewed from the Vale to the west, this scarp representing the transition west to east in Jurassic geology from the Liassic sands and clays of the Vale to the Inferior and Great Oolite limestones of the hills. At the bottom of the scarp are the Upper Lias clays, succeeded by a layer of sands before the limestone begins. This sequence makes for instability because the sands and blocks of limestone slip down over the clay and produce the bumpy, uneven lower slopes of the edge, as at Crickley Hill. The main scarp slope of the hill is made up of the Inferior Oolite limestones, of which there are different layers with different characteristics. First comes the Pea Grit, not a sandstone as the name might suggest but a limestone, which has distinctive pea-shaped grains (pisoliths) of calcium carbonate in it. The rock falls apart easily in frost and rainy conditions and it contains fossil remains, so it is not good building stone, but forms the cliff-like faces that line the path underneath Crickley Hill. When Gurney worked at Dryhill Farm in the 1919–21 period, he would have laboured on the fields under these cliffs and noted white dust from the crumbling Pea Grit rock on the tracks and lanes of Dryhill and Cold Slad. The Pea Grit cliffs extend all along to Leckhampton Hill to the north.

Note that there is a spring line where the waters percolating through the limestones meet the Upper Lias clays; Dryhill Farm, like many others, was sited on this spring line, as was the Roman villa nearby that fascinated Gurney. Above the Pea Grit are the upper and lower freestones (so-called because they form large free-standing blocks of limestone suitable for building) and the ragstones which split in thinner layers and so are best used for Cotswold walls. These limestones are oolitic, that is they are made up of egg-shaped grains (or ooliths) of calcium carbonate, and they form the main mass of the upper Crickley Hill slopes. The Great Oolite limestones appear further to the east and are the rock type of the high wolds, although a fault line has allowed fine quality Great Oolite limestones to outcrop on Cooper's Hill, which is one reason why the Cooper's Hill quarry stone was so prized by the early builders of Gloucester.

The steep line of the Cotswold Edge is most clear-cut in the northern and middle sections of the Cotswolds from Dover Hill, west of Chipping Campden, to Crickley Hill, east of Gloucester.

Left: Devil's Chimney, Leckhampton; a distinctive feature on the Cotswold Edge, above Leckhampton, so named because local legend assumed that it was the chimney of the devil's underground dwelling place. The nineteenth-century geologist, S. Buckman, suggested that the strange shape of the Devil's Chimney could be put down to differential erosion, involving the softer outer rock being worn away to leave only the inner harder rock remaining. However, it is more likely that the Devil's Chimney was left behind by eighteenth-century quarry workers, who quarried around it as a joke.

Right: May Hill on a snowy day in February 2010. The summit, despite its clump of trees, has the solitary bleakness of a mountain and can be seen from Gloucester and the Cotswolds.

Further south towards Stroud, Wotton under Edge, Dursley and Bath, the scarp slope is lower and more dissected into winding valleys and combes. As Gurney explained in his poem, observing the view from a small hill near Ashleworth – 'The Cotswolds stand out eastward as if never / A curve of them the hand of time might change; / Beauty sleeps most confidently forever.' ('Above Ashleworth', K, 2004) The northerly hills of the scarp edge are all high – Dover Hill (230m), Willersley Hill, Broadway Hill (313m), Shenbarrow Hill (about 303m) and Salter's Hill (about 290m) and, beyond the Winchcombe gap, the out-flung promontories of Langley Hill (274m) and Nottingham Hill (279m). But the scarp edge rises to its highest point in Cleeve Hill (330m), an impressive mountain-like shape with rounded moorland summit and wooded lower slopes. Running south-westwards again from Cleeve is the part of the edge best known to Ivor Gurney and mentioned most frequently in his poetry. The cliffed edge of Leckhampton Hill (293m) looks down on Cheltenham, followed closely by Shurdington Hill, then the heights of Crickley (267m), showing bare white limestone scars and dark wooded slopes before the edge curves round to Birdlip, High Brotheridge (282m) with its Cooper's Hill promontory (268m), with Witcombe tucked in the embayment beneath. In the early 1900s, there was still an air of remoteness about the edge, as recognised by Gurney:

CRICKLEY HILL (first verse only)
The orchis, trefoil, harebells nod all day,
High above Gloucester and the Severn Plain.
Few come there, where the curlew ever and again
Cries faintly, and no traveller makes stay,
Since steep the road is,
And the villages
Hidden by hedges wonderful in late May.

(K, 2004, p.39)

The Birdlip, Cooper's and Cranham stretches of the Edge are covered in the fine mature beech-woods of Witcombe, High Brotheridge, Buckholt, Kite's Wood and Pope's Wood, obscuring the scarp, although it reveals its prominence again with Painswick Beacon (283m), Scotsquar Hill (about 250m)and Haresfield Beacon (about 220m). These high summits were favoured places for the building of bronze-age and iron-age camps and burial mounds, whilst the Romans favoured sheltered embayments for their villa sites. All these features fascinated Gurney. Further south-west, the Stroudwater Valleys, feeding the River Frome, form a deep, winding and steep-sided bay in the Cotswold Edge, with many villages and outlying settlements clinging to the slopes to the east and south of Stroud. This area was the heart of the Cotswold weaving industry in the seventeenth and eighteenth centuries and the valley landscapes, with their former mills and weavers' terraced housing, still have a distinct identity based on their past. Gurney's walks and cycle rides often brought him as far as the high hills above the Stroud valleys, as he recounts in the poem 'Brimscombe' when, on a night-time walk, he found the village 'wrapped past life in sleep'.

The Edge is apparent again, although more fragmented with inlets and promontories, in Penn Hill (about 200m), Coaley Peak (about 250m), Cam Long Down (220m), Stinchcombe Hill (219m) and Nibley Knoll (203m) until it reaches Wotton under Edge. Although the south-west extremity of the Cotswold Edge is near Bath (and indeed that is where the modern walking route, the Cotswold Way, finishes), the southern portion was not as well known to Gurney and will not be dealt with here. South of Dursley, the scarp edge is lower and its prominence has been reduced by the many intruding valleys and promontories.

The edge is everywhere, cut deeply by westward-flowing springs and streams – Gurney described one of these (possibly Hatherley Brook which rises beneath Crickley) as 'Going placid westward, a small daughter between Crickley and Severn ('Small Chubby Dams', B, p.80). Sometimes the edge is broken by a deep embayment, offering a site for settlement, such as Winchcombe, Witcombe and Painswick.

A ridge of thin sandy limestone (the so-called Liassic Marlstone) runs across the vale at the foot of the scarp slope (see Figure 2.4). Since it is nearly horizontal, it forms a bench best seen looking north-west below Painswick Beacon, and it also forms distinct ledges on the tops of Chosen Hill and Robinswood Hill near Gloucester. These two hills are examples of outliers, or the remnants left behind when the edge has been eroded back. The marlstone capping has helped protect them from further erosion. Other outliers in the vale are Oxenton Hill, Dumbleton Hill and Bredon Hill. The tiny Chosen Hill was of special significance to Ivor Gurney and Herbert Howells, who used it as a favourite walking area, easily reached from Gloucester. It is difficult to recall the air of remote rurality that must have characterised Chosen Hill in the 1900s. Now it is surrounded on all sides by the suburbs of Gloucester, and the M5 passes noisily beneath its slopes. Nevertheless, an extract from Massingham's book *Cotswold Country* (1937) provides the appropriate flavour for Gurney's experiences:

High on a steep and isolated tor, so typical of the lias, I could see from the criss-cross of lanes the 'chosen church' of Churchdown. It was a mild December day, pensive in mist, and, as I climbed, I noticed the white fleeces of Traveller's Joy, festooned like Christmas decorations upon the trees crowning the conical hills that were grouped about the mount. Many of the trees bore mistletoe. To the west, the silver streak of Severn was paler than the mist; to the east, the scalloped, tossing line of the edge wound in and out in cunning variety of bluff and recess. All was novel among the half-shrouded distances, but where I stood was a patch of West Dorset. The church in its unique position…

(Massingham, 1937, p.68)

Views from Chosen Hill were almost certainly the inspiration for some of Gurney's best poems, including, possibly, 'When from the Curve', which refers to Gurney's process of creating music and poetry, and may have been inspired by the view of the woodland curving around Cooper's Hill. Later, Herbert Howells was to dedicate his 'Piano Quartet in A Minor' to 'the hill at Chosen and Ivor Gurney who knows it'. These outliers add variety and interest to the flat vale farmlands and today are still treasured as recreational 'lungs' for the towns of Gloucester and Cheltenham – Robinswood Hill, in particular, boasting a country park and a dry ski slope.

To the east of the edge lie the high Cotswold plateau regions, characterised by rolling uplands, large fields, mature beech-woods and villages hidden in combes or depressions. The whole area gradually slopes down eastwards and is cut into by the longer east-flowing streams of the Coln, the Leach and the Windrush. Eventually, the Cotswold region disappears in Oxfordshire somewhere beyond Witney and Chipping Norton, where the Great Oolite limestone is buried beneath the clays of the upper Thames valley and Vale of Oxford. These far eastern Cotswold places feature less frequently in Ivor Gurney's writing, although he did write poems about the small towns of Northleach and Burford and mentioned the Windrush Valley villages.

At the time Gurney was growing up, the Cotswolds was a rural and agricultural region, its economy no longer completely focused on sheep as it had been in earlier centuries when the Stroudwater Valley was the centre of a thriving cloth industry. By the early nineteenth century, farming for the bigger landowners had become a profitable mix of cereal growing and the keeping of sheep and cattle, with well-managed rotations maintaining productivity. Later in the century, agricultural decline set in, with competition from New World agriculture and the drift of people away from the land. Although the big landowners weathered the decline, life was very hard for the small farmers and the landless farm labourers as Gurney himself knew, spending several months working as a labourer at Dryhill Farm, beneath Crickley Hill, in the 1918–22 period.

A striking feature of the Cotswold landscape was, and still is, the visual coherence of the village landscapes. All the buildings are built of the characteristic Jurassic limestone, providing a harmony of colour, texture and design that is quite unique. Fortey (2010) describes the villages as 'the apotheosis of Jurassic stone' and fortunately many have been preserved in a visual sense, if not in function, now that 'The Cotswolds' is a protected landscape and a desirable place to live for the twenty-first century flexible worker or retiree. The villages, explains Fortey, 'were built on the backs of sheep, on the prosperity of the wool trade. Stone is pressed into service for everything; no wooden windows, rather there are mullioned windows divided by stone columns; walls of stone; market crosses of stone, bridges of stone.' Above all, the roof grows from the same geological source – the slate used is not real slate but simply thinly bedded limestones that are perfectly in keeping with the whole building. In 'Changes', Gurney laments the insensitivity of new building in the Cotswold villages: 'Villas are set up where the sheepfolds were, / And plate glass impudent stares at the sun, / For byres and stack-boards, threshing is for ever done, / New things are there, shining new-fangled gear.' Even in Gurney's day, it was no longer just farm workers who lived in the villages. There were experiments in communal living – as at Whiteway near Gurney's mother's village of Bisley – and there were increasing numbers of artists, designers and writers who were taking themselves off to rural hideaways, including William Morris at Kelmscott, Ernest Gimson and Sidney Barnsley at Sapperton and C.R. Ashbee at Chipping Campden.

The area described by Natural England as Over Severn includes the diverse countryside around Redmarley, Dymock, Newent and May Hill. The small hamlets and red sandstone farmsteads were known to Gurney because he sometimes cycled this way in his exploration of Gloucestershire; he wrote a poem about Redmarley 'clear shining after rain'. As for May Hill, the 'half-revealed tree-clad thing', as Gurney called it ('Twigworth'), it is conspicuous at 296m, even with the hilly Forest of Dean countryside behind it, but May Hill is not a limestone outlier related to the Cotswolds.

'Beauty sleeps most confidently forever.' Looking along the Cotswold Edge towards Cooper's Hill, from Crickley Hill. The outlier, Robinswood Hill, is far right.

Chosen Hill church – 'in its unique position'.

The harmony of Cotswold stone – the village of Painswick 'built on the backs of sheep'.

It is what geologists call an inlier because it is a mass of older rock (Silurian age) set within the younger rock (of Devonian and Carboniferous age) of the Forest of Dean. Because the May Hill rocks were originally bent upwards in a dome shape, erosion near the summit of the dome has revealed the older rocks inside. There are panoramic views from May Hill. It is, and was in Gurney's day, one of the most popular beauty spots for Gloucester residents to visit.

Finally, the Malvern Hills, though not in Gloucestershire, are a dominant landscape feature for those who live and work in the Severn Vale or on the Cotswold Edge. The Malverns are composed of very old (Pre-Cambrian) crystalline rocks which rise suddenly from the surrounding plains. The folding that brought this range into being was the same that caused the May Hill dome to be uplifted. The Malvern Hills stand sentinel over northern Gloucestershire countryside, running due north/south, ever-present and ever noticed by the inhabitants of Gloucestershire, whether the hills are lost in mist or standing gleaming in the sun. As Gurney wrote: 'What Malvern is the day is, and its touchstone / Gray velvet or moon-marked; rich or bare as bone; / One looks towards Malvern and is made one with the whole; / The world swings round him as the Bear to the Pole' ('The Touchstone', B, p.83).

This, then, is Gurney's Gloucestershire, the place that nurtured his growing talent and was to provide both a real refuge and a refuge of the mind – 'the central fires of secret memory' as he himself called it. We can see that the accident of his birthplace, surrounded as he was by the diverse environments of Vale and Cotswold, gave him access to an amazing wealth of landscapes and sensations, but it was his personal mix of restless physical energy, poetic sensitivity and open engagement with these environments that led him to move beyond being an interested observer and to see the place as an essential part of his being.

THAT COUNTY

Go up, Go up your ways of varying love,
Take each his darling path wherever lie
The central fires of secret memory;
Whether Helvellyn tower the lakes above;
Or black Plinlimmon time and tempest prove;
Or any English heights of bravery.
I will go climb my little hills to see
Severn, and Malverns, May Hill's tiny grove.

No Everest is here, no peaks of power
Astonish men. But on the winding ways
White in the frost-time, blinding in full June blaze,
A man may take all quiet heart's delight –
Village and quarry, taverns and many a tower
That saw Armada beacons set alight.

(*War's Embers*, 1919, p.89)

3

THE POET AND THE PLACE:
LEAVING GLOUCESTERSHIRE

You hills of home, woodlands, white roads and inns
That star and line our darling land, still keep
Memory of us; for when day first begins
We think of you and dream in the first sleep
Of you and yours –
Trees, bare rock, flowers
Daring the blast on Crickley's distant steep.

('Crickley Hill', extract, K, 2004, p.39)

Making Music in London

In 1911 Ivor Gurney left Gloucestershire to take up a place as a student at the Royal College of Music (RCM) in London. This was the culmination of his own efforts but it was Cheesman who had arranged for Gurney to sit the examinations and who also managed to raise funds locally to match the RCM scholarship of £40 a year. In autumn 1911, Gurney seemed to be buoyed up by pride and self confidence. He had so impressed the interview panel at the RCM, including the musicians Sir Hubert Parry and Sir Charles Stanford (who was to become Gurney's tutor), that he had been awarded a full open scholarship. Apparently, his musical talent was reminiscent of Schubert. 'By God! It is Schubert!', Parry was said to have exclaimed, as the rather wild unkempt figure of Gurney entered the interview room (Plunket Greene and Scott, 1938). Someone who also noticed the striking but untidy-looking Gurney was Marion Scott, a musician herself, registrar at the RCM and soon to become Gurney's most trusted friend. She remembers seeing the young Gurney for the first time: 'The boy was wearing a thick dark blue Severn pilot's coat more suggestive of an out-of-door life than the composition lesson with Sir Charles Stanford for which … he was clearly bound.' (Plunket Greene and Scott, 1938)

Despite, or perhaps because of, the high expectations about his musical development, Gurney was also apprehensive about leaving his home county and friends. In fact, Herbert Howells followed him to the Royal College in 1912 and another young Australian student beginning his course in the same year, Arthur Benjamin, soon became a new friend. Gurney, Howells and Benjamin were all pupils of Sir Charles Stanford and enjoyed talking, listening to music and exploring London together. They were very different, however. Blevins suggests that while Howells and Benjamin were conventional and tidy in dress and manner, Gurney often appeared shambling, dishevelled and sometimes rudely outspoken. 'At times his flamboyant, theatrical behaviour embarrassed those in his presence and left an impression of an immature high-strung young man.' (Blevins, 2008, p.22)

Significantly, the Gloucestershire countryside of Gurney's inspiration had also been left behind when he went to the RCM. Living in 'digs' at 15 Barclay Road, Fulham, he did not settle easily

Gurney in 1911 at RCM. (Permission of the Ivor Gurney Trust)

to college life and to London. It was no longer possible for him to rush out into the Severn Meadows, to sail his boat on the river, or cycle and walk up the Cotswold byways, although such escapes had become increasingly necessary to his mental well-being and creativity. In 'Chance to Work' (K, 2004, p.349) he regrets that he had to swap 'City's surroundings for Nature's sweetest teachings and pities' and that he found the first term 'a hard term, such that good memory asks not to look back upon'. When back in Gloucester for the holidays (August 1913), Gurney wrote to Harvey: 'My dear chap. You don't know what Portway was today – you don't know! I could only sing for joy and cry in my heart with pure happiness. Great black shadows, white violets, intensely blue sky, and a sun like wine to the soul. Damn London!' (Letter, 17 August, 1913)

We know that he did find interest in the city streets, the riverside and the fine buildings of central London, and was later to recall these in poetry about the city. He even continued his Gloucestershire habit of walking at night or as the dawn broke. 'Only the poet strolls about at ease, / Wondering what mortal thing his soul may please,' he wrote in the poem 'London Dawn', but he also confessed that 'clear lamps and dim stars' and 'worry of heart-ache' were poor consolation for the trees, meadows and skies of Gloucestershire ('London').

LONDON DAWN

Dawn comes up on London
And night's undone.
Stars are routed
And street lamps outed.
Sodden great clouds begin sail again
Like all-night anchored galleons to the main
From careful shallows to the far-withdrawn
Wide outer seas of sky.
Sleepers above river change their pain,
Lockhart's* shows lively up Blackfriars Lane.
Motors dash by
With 'Mirrors', 'Mails', 'Telegraphs', what not?
South shore of Thames on London shows a blot
And first careful coffee-stall is withdrawn.

Only the poet strolls about at ease,
Wondering what mortal thing his soul may please,
And spitting at the drains, while Paul's as ever
Is mighty and a king of sky and river,
And cares no more, Much-Father, for this one
Broke child, although a poet-born and clever,
Than any spit-kid of seven million
Must drudge all day until his earning's done.
A huffler** has her red sails just a-quiver;
Sun's very near now and the tide's a-run.

(K, 2004, p.62)

*Lockhart's was a London tea shop/café ** a huffler was a particular kind of Thames river craft

Left: Portway, the small road leading out of Gloucester and up the Cotswold Edge. 'Great black shadows, white violets, intensely blue sky, and a sun like wine to the soul.' This photograph was taken in summer 2010.

Right: The Millennium Bridge and St Paul's Cathedral in 2010. Gurney was fascinated by the shape of St Paul's on the London skyline.

He did not settle to organised tutorials and music practices either. Stanford declared him to be highly talented and potentially one of the best pupils he had received, but he also described him as 'one of the least teachable' (Howells, 1938, p.14). According to Howells, Gurney was outspoken, disorganised and careless, often arriving at classes late and with untidy manuscripts – not something which endeared him to the neat and authoritarian Stanford. On one occasion, Stanford threw Gurney out of the room for rudely criticising a correction that Stanford had made to one of Gurney's compositions. 'I see you've jiggered the whole thing,' Gurney had commented (Palmer, 1992, p.352). The relationship between the flamboyant Gurney and the inflexible and abrasive Stanford was always stormy.

From about 1912 or 1913, Gurney seems to have started writing poetry – perhaps not surprisingly, given Harvey's encouragement and the emotional stress of leaving Gloucestershire behind. A brief two-verse piece was included within a letter to Harvey from London, probably in 1913 and, after this, letters to Harvey often contained some lines of verse for comment. We know from letters and reminiscences of Gurney's friends that he was reading widely – including Yeats, Housman and Hardy. In 1913 he mentioned in a letter to Harvey (p.4, Letters, June 1913) that he had just seen *The Playboy of the Western World* at the Court Theatre and expressed the view that it 'contains some of the most beautiful love passages in Literature'.

It was an exciting time for the artistically inclined to be in London. The early years of the twentieth century witnessed the beginnings of deep change in social, economic and political conditions and, not surprisingly, it was artists, musicians and writers who were often at the forefront of such change. Traditional artistic themes of idealism, splendour and sentimentality were being replaced by the desire to challenge accepted viewpoints, confront everyday life and experiment with new ways of presenting reality. Innovations were taking place in form and technique in all the arts. It was in London that one could most easily hear the newer music of Ravel, Debussy, Stravinsky or see paintings by the Cubists or, in 1910, witness Roger Fry's exhibition of the newly-named Post-Impressionists. Gurney, Howells and Benjamin attended the première of Ralph Vaughan Williams' 'Sea Symphony' in February 1913, Gurney arising from his sickbed, desperate not to miss it. Afterwards, Howells and Benjamin were overcome with excitement and bursting with new ideas for their own work, and even Gurney, still feeling ill and retiring back to bed for three days, told Marion Scott that 'it was worth it' (Letter, February 1913). Writers like E.M. Forster, James Joyce, Virginia Woolf, D.H. Lawrence, Katherine Mansfield and eventually T.S. Eliot experimented with the multiplicity of viewpoints that came to characterise Modernism. New literary magazines were being established, such as the *New Age* and *Rhythm*, and literary London was bubbling with ideas about the possibility of breaking out from what were seen as the numbing effects of solid and respectable Victorian poetry. In 1912, the first volume of five in the Georgian Poetry series was published (Edward Marsh and Rupert Brooke ed., 1912), its editors hoping – as the preface suggested – that 'English poetry is now once again putting on a new strength and beauty'. In January 1913, Harold Monro's poetry bookshop was opened in Devonshire Street, London, to which Gurney became a regular visitor. Ironically, the Georgian poets themselves were later seen as lightweight and over-sentimental and the post-war poets were equally anxious to break away from the Georgian image.

One of Gurney's closest confidantes at this time was Marion Scott, and it was to her that he began sending drafts of his poetry as well as his musical creations. She seems to have recognised his creative genius but also his underlying insecurity and fragility. Throughout the first two years of his course, she kept in close contact, inviting him to concerts and musical events and, possibly, acting as a replacement for the Hunt sisters in his life. Significantly, it was Marion Scott who was most aware of Gurney's increasing ill-health and depression (what he called 'bloody indigestion' and 'beastly nervousness').

In February 1913, in the same letter in which he had described the Vaughan Williams première, he wrote to her explaining that he was 'oh so sick of everything, and by no means looking forward to work'. Finally, in May 1913, suffering from what seems to have been severe depression, he returned to Gloucestershire, to stay, not at home, but in the cottage of James Harris, the lock-keeper at Framilode. Here the peaceful riverside environment, the views of the hills and the opportunity to undertake some physical work and sailing seem to have aided his recovery. 'I have been here a week,' he wrote to Marion Scott in May 1913, 'and oh what a difference. And oh! Framilode on good behaviour!' He even tried to persuade Marion to visit Framilode herself – 'Come to Framilode, Fretherne, Elmore, Arlingham, Saul. Framilode on the map is just where the Severn does this sort of antic' (and here Gurney drew a quick sketch of the river bend). By early June, he was back in Fulham, London and 'on the mend' as he explained in another letter to Marion Scott (June 1913). This time, he described to her the view from the 'small hill not a mile from where I stayed (or stopped as they say there)'. The hill to which he referred can easily be identified as Barrow Hill (Figure 3.1), less than a mile from Lock House and about 205ft in height. There are many paths up this hill today from Framilode, Priding, Overton and Fretherne and, although it is only a short climb, one is greeted by an amazing panorama of hills, enhanced by the smooth silvery surface of the Severn on three sides. Gurney finished his letter to Marion Scott with the heartfelt observation that 'London is worse than ever to bear after that', and a tongue-in-cheek comment – 'Still let us hope that the militants [suffragettes] will blow it up soon.'

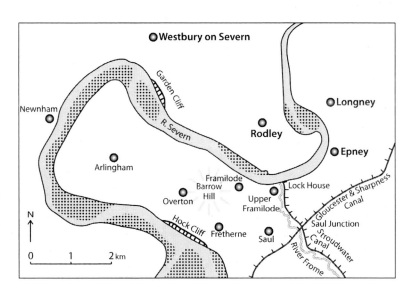

Fig. 3.1: A Small Hill; Barrow Hill near Framilode. This map has been based on current OS map information, but the scale is approximate only and the features are as in Gurney's day (about 1910–20). The Stroudwater Canal was then in operation alongside the River Frome.

Despite some continuing nervous illness and stomach trouble, Gurney seems to have managed to stay at his studies in London throughout the 1913/1914 academic year. What is more, there were signs of real originality and talent, notably Gurney's composition of what he called 'The Elizas', settings of five Elizabethan lyrics to music. He wrote to Harvey in early 1914: 'Willy, Willy, I have done five of the most delightful and beautiful songs you ever cast your beaming eyes upon', a judgement since confirmed by others. In addition, his interest in poetry was ever growing, as he commented in the same letter: 'Have you written much? Doesn't this sacred hunger for spring nourish that fire in you? If it does not yet, get, as I have just got, Davies' *Farewell to Poesy, Foliage* (his latest book) and *Songs of Joy* – the finest lyric poetry in English.' (Letter, early 1914)

W.H. Davies was the man who came to be known as the 'Supertramp' after the publication of his autobiography in 1908. Davies had spent many years tramping or hitching round North America and wrote forthright poems about common people, his experiences on the road and also about childhood, wild flowers and the natural world. The spring that Gurney mentions expectantly in his letter was followed by the glorious summer of 1914 and, although there is no hard evidence, it seems likely that Gurney spent it in his beloved Gloucestershire, walking the hills and the riverside, sailing his boat and enjoying the companionship of Howells and Harvey. It is probable that he became better acquainted with John Haines, maybe even hearing from him about the 'Dymock poets', including Wilfrid Gibson, Lascelles Abercrombie and the American poet Robert Frost. This group was living near Dymock on the Gloucestershire/Herefordshire border and they were all making names for themselves in literary circles.

But, of course, 4 August 1914 was the time when the First World War was declared, and the pleasures of a Gloucestershire summer were overshadowed for all its inhabitants by events elsewhere in Europe. Gurney apparently tried to join up immediately, as Will Harvey did, but Gurney was unsuccessful because of defective eyesight. He spent the autumn of 1914 back at the Royal College of Music but enjoying weekends with some new friends, the Chapman family in High Wycombe. Gurney had found a weekend job as organist at Christ Church, High Wycombe, where Edward Chapman was the churchwarden. His wife and four children made Gurney part of the family; indeed, Gurney became so attached to the eldest daughter, Kitty, that he proposed marriage. The proposal was refused as Kitty was still only seventeen, but Boden's book of letters from the 1915–17 period (*Stars in a Dark Night*, 2004) reveal that the happy times that Gurney enjoyed in High Wycombe undoubtedly helped him during the war.

In February 1915 Gurney applied again to join the army, and that same month wrote to Will Harvey to proclaim his success: 'Well, here I am a soldier – and in your own regiment's 2nd reserve.' He became a private in the 2/5 Battalion, Gloucestershire regiment, usually known as 2/5th Glosters. It was what he wanted at the time but it ensured that he would spend two more years away from his Gloucestershire places.

Becoming a Soldier

For all new soldiers, the first few months were taken up in training. Gurney spent the rest of 1915 in Northampton, Chelmsford and Epping. He described the training in a letter to Howells:

> The aim of training troops is to make them as tired as possible without teaching them anything. Take 'em on a route march, stand 'em on their heads, muck about with 'em in any fashion so long as they get sick and tired of soldiering.
>
> (Letter, June 1915)

From this point on, we have an interesting record of Gurney's life because he wrote many letters, mainly to Marion Scott and to his old friends Herbert Howells and Will Harvey, but also to new friends like the Chapman family at High Wycombe and Ethel Voynich, the novelist introduced to him by Marion Scott. He began writing poetry in earnest; presumably it was easier than trying to

Left: Ivor Gurney with Matilda Chapman ('La Comtesse', as Gurney called her) and Marjorie, nicknamed 'Mickey', the youngest of the four Chapman children. This photograph was taken in the Chapmans' garden in 1919. (By kind permission of A. Boden)

Right: Cranham trees 'transfigured to shapes of colour and form'. (2010)

compose music given the regimental accommodation, and it provided an outlet for his creativity. The letters show an amazing range of topics covered, from comments on the food and anecdotes about his companions to observations about writers and literary matters. Gurney was reading a great deal, including discovering the poet Walt Whitman, whose work he later claimed had been a key influence on his own writing: 'Walt Whitman is my latest rediscovery, and he has taken me like a flood. One of the greatest of teachers.' (Letter to Ethel Voynich, September 1915) But one topic that appears often is a sense of loss of the Gloucestershire countryside:

> But here's the spring. And Framilode, Minsterworth, Maisemore and the Severn villages must be full of flowers and peace.
>
> (To Mrs Voynich from Essex, February 1915)

> Sometimes my heart aches for Framilode, and my little leaky boat; my gun and the ever-changing Severn, now so full in Flood.
>
> (To Herbert Howells from Essex, April 1915)

> My leave starts on Thursday most likely – 5 whole days. O Cranham, Minsterworth, Framilode, Maisemore. All of you love me and I return the compliment. It is you that have poured into my as yet defective mould that fluid of beauty which shall one day take form in me and make others aware of your graces and sweet looks.
>
> (To Marion Scott from Essex, September 1915)

> Here in Essex, there are no sunsets, and no colour; no mystery in woods, no sense of other worldliness… When my mind can escape from its imprisoning body, it reaches out desperately to the memory of Malverns, purple and later black against afterglow, or Cranham trees transfigured to shapes of colour and form, seeming without substance, merely imagined, stuff of dreams.
>
> (To Marion Scott, October 1915)

Between February and May 1916, Gurney's battalion spent a cold, hard time at Tidworth on Salisbury Plain, making final preparations. In April 1916, Gurney was allowed a few days leave before the battalion went to France and he spent this back in Gloucestershire. A day's cycling took him 'through Maisemore, Hartpury, Corse, Staunton – near the Malverns now' and eventually to Redmarley:

> ... that little village set under the shadow of the Malverns and set with orchards thick and fair with blossom and flowers. Cowslips, daffodils, bluebells, ladysmocks; all Shakespearian like the country – a perfect setting for the old comedy'*.
>
> (Letter to Marion Scott, 25 April 1916) *presumably *A Midsummer Night's Dream*

It was on this occasion that Gurney found his way to the village of Ryton, hoping to meet Abercrombie, one of the Dymock poets. The poet was away but Gurney did spend a happy half day at Abercrombie's house – 'I wheeled the pram, did feats of daring to amuse the three children and talked of books and music with Mrs Abercrombie,' noting 'the genius of the place: all set in blue of the sky, green of the fields and leaves and that red, that red of the soil.' (Letter to Marion Scott, May 1916)

Finally in May 1916, the Glosters arrived in France and, for the next eighteen months, Gurney experienced the full range of terror, discomfort, companionship, boredom and occasional satisfaction that was the life of a soldier in this war. At the time that the 2/5th Glosters arrived, the war was setting into the pattern of slow trench warfare with both armies dug into long lines of mud and planking, stretching from Switzerland to the sea (Figure 3.2). The Glosters were first stationed at Riez Bailleul, west of Laventie, where they went through the usual instruction and introduction to their new conditions. Gurney's poem 'Riez Bailleul' reveals how he was already drawing on his Gloucestershire memories in an attempt to calm his fears about the forthcoming trials of trench warfare.

> RIEZ BAILLEUL (extract)
> Riez Bailleul in blue tea-time
> Called back the Severn lanes, and roads
> Where the small ash leaves lie, and floods
> Of hawthorn leaves turned with night's rime,
> No Severn though nor great valley clouds.
>
> Now in the thought comparisons
> Go with those here-and-theres and fancy
> Sees on the china firelight dancy
> The wall lit where the sofa runs.
> A dear light like Sirius or spring sun's.
>
> But the trench thoughts will not go, tomorrow
> Up to the line …
>
> (RW, p.57; K, 2004, p.146)

The expression 'go with those here-and-theres' sums up the poet's preference to let his mind indulge in thought comparisons, preferring to remember the 'firelight dancy / The wall lit where the sofa runs' (possibly at Redlands) rather than dwell on the events to come.

Soon (mid-June) the Glosters had their first experience of independent front-line fighting, in the Laventie sector, and after this they were thoroughly caught up in the life of an active battalion. The normal routine was for troops to spend three to seven days in a front-line trench facing the enemy; then similar time periods in both a support trench and a reserve trench at progressively greater distances from the enemy. Finally, they would be 'on rest' several miles from the line, after which the sequence would begin again. The Glosters were in the Laventie sector for several months; their rest location was normally La Gorgue, often mentioned by Gurney and seemingly one of the places he did his writing and musical composition. The logic of the 'fight and rest'

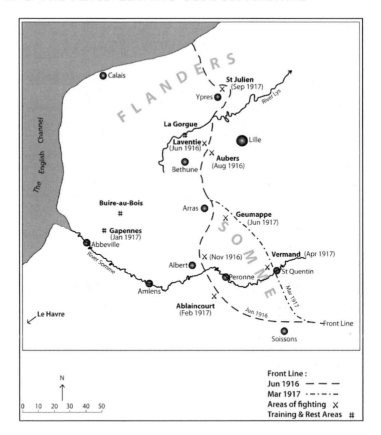

Fig. 3.2: Gurney's France. The information on this map has been gathered from *The Story of the 2/5th Battalion Gloucestershire Regiment 1914–1918* by A.F. Barnes (Gloucester, Crypt House Press, 1930)

system was one thing, but Hurd describes the reality of the conditions Gurney and his colleagues would have met, although the Glosters had not, so far, experienced a trench winter.

> In this unimaginable arena, vast armies of men fought each other and tried not to die. They also fought fear and despair, hunger and cold, disease, boredom, and all the absurdity of a situation whose cause no-one could remember or explain; they fought rats and lice and pestilential flies, the stink of rotting corpses and the fetid smell of human ordure; they fought loneliness and excessive inescapable company; they fought noise and sudden silence; and, above all, they fought the devouring excremental mud.
>
> (Hurd, p.66)

Gurney made a good soldier; he was fit and, perhaps surprisingly for one who liked solitude, he did enjoy the company of many of his fellow soldiers, being particularly pleased to meet those who shared his love of music, singing or poetry. On 7 June 1916, he told Marion Scott about a group of Welsh soldiers:

> They talk their native language and sing their own folksongs with sweet natural voices. I did not sleep at all the first day in my dugout – there was too much to be said, asked and experienced: and pleasure in watching their quick expressions, for oblivion. It was one of the most notable evenings of my life.
>
> (Letter, 7 June 1916)

This experience found expression in the poem 'First Time In' (K, 2004, p.128), in which Gurney welcomes the sense of companionship and the shared sadness of those missing their homelands, whether in the Black Mountains or the Cotswolds. Strangely enough, the discipline of army life, the physical exercise and the regular (if not high quality!) meals seemed to suit him, although he

Left: A Severn lane at Wick Street near Ashleworth. 'Riez Bailleul in blue tea-time / Called back Severn lanes.'

Right: Making hay near Painswick. 'Out of the window we can watch men making hay in a fashion reminding us distractingly of Home.' (Letter, 22 June 1916) This photograph was taken in 2010.

longed for more bread: 'the tales of my woe on this subject have ascended to the Lord Almighty with no result!' (Letters, 1916) For a while, too, he did not suffer from his debilitating nervous problems, despite or perhaps because of the intensity of the action. After the first really significant action in the Laventie-Fauquissart sector, Gurney wrote to Marion Scott describing:

> … a strafe which a machine gunner who had been through Loos said was worse than Loos while it lasted which was 1 ¼ hours … They began it and were reduced to showing white lights, which we shot away, and sending up a white rocket. Floreat Gloucestriensis! It was a great time; full of fear of course, but not as bad as neurasthenia.
>
> (Letter, 22 June 1916)

Laventie was a surprisingly pleasant place to be stationed:

> It was rather a unique little town, built in the form of a cross, with its red brick church in the centre. Though it was only a mile or so from the front line of the Fauquissart sector, the civilians lived on there and farmed a certain amount of the land around … the billets were fairly habitable and the plane trees still stood in the streets. There were some beautiful lawns and gardens behind some of the big houses.
>
> (Barnes, 1930)

Gurney seemed to agree with this judgement, and to find some calm and creativity; in his poem, 'Laventie' (B, p.69), he paints a sympathetic picture of this small town with its distinctive architecture (the red-brick church), the cafés and the beautiful gardens.

> But Laventie, most of all, I think is to soldiers
> The Town itself with plane trees, and small spa air;
> And vin, rouge-blanc, chocolats, citron, grenadine:
> One might buy in small delectable cafés there.
> The broken church, and vegetables fields bare;
> Neat French market town look so clean,
> And the clarity, amiability of North French air.
> Like water flowing beneath the dark plough and high Heaven,
> Music's delight to please the poet pack-marching there.
>
> (Blunden, p.69/70)

Making War and Making Poetry

In October 1916, the Glosters left the Laventie-Fauquissart sector and trekked south via Robecq to join the last days of Haig's Somme offensive in the Ablaincourt sector. Here they suffered some of the worst conditions they had yet experienced. The land had been reduced to huge crater holes and acres of mud:

> … men clinging to shell holes, mud deep enough to submerge a gun team and limber, masses of unburied dead strewn over the battle fields; no sign of organised trenches, but merely shell holes joined up to one another – and last, … No landmarks anywhere. The whole scene was one bleak wilderness of death.
>
> (Barnes, p.53)

The men were forced 'to live like rats' and were relieved when they were drawn well back to Gapennes for training in December 1916.

Despite all this, Gurney was now writing poetry at an urgent pace; it was as if he was stimulated by the high intensity of life at the front and needed to express his emotions. Every poem was sent to Marion Scott and, in October 1916, Gurney tentatively suggested that they might find a publisher. Marion Scott followed this up, with the result that Sidgwick & Jackson (Harvey's publishers) agreed to publish Gurney's first collection of poetry. Although Gurney was pleased to call himself a war poet, he explained in the Preface to *Severn & Somme*, that it was not about the 'Glosters' and the war directly:

> What I really want to do with this book is (1) to leave something definite behind if I am knocked out (2) to say out what Gloucester is, and is to me; and so to make Gloucester people think about their county (3) to have some good stuff in it whatever one might say about the whole (4) to make people realise a little what ordinary life is.
>
> (Letter to Marion Scott, 23 February 1917)

So his poetry never assumes a celebratory tone. After some initial patriotic sentiment in poems such as 'Maisemore' and 'To the Poet Before Battle' (which suggests some influence of Rupert Brooke), Gurney settled into a more down-to-earth style, recording the experiences of himself, as a common soldier ('Firelight', 'The Estaminet') or remembering Gloucestershire places ('Afterglow', 'The Fire Kindled'). 'Strange Service' (S&S, p.23) marks the beginning of his disillusionment with the war; for example, the first stanza runs: 'Little did I dream England, that you bore me / Under the Cotswold hills beside the water meadows, / To do you dreadful service, here, beyond your borders / And your enfolding seas.' It also reveals that Gurney knew he was relying on memory, as fragile as the reflections of waterside reeds on the surface of the Severn, to keep Gloucestershire places fresh in his mind: 'Now these are memories only, and your skies and rushy sky-pools / Fragile mirrors easily broken by moving airs…' Even stronger protest was registered in the sonnet 'Pain', one of five written in memory of Rupert Brooke.

> Seeing the pitiful eyes of men foredone,
> Or horses shot, too tired merely to stir,
> Dying in shell holes both, slain by the mud.
> Men broken, shrieking even to hear a gun –
> Till pain grinds down, or lethargy numbs her,
> The amazed heart cries angrily out on God.
>
> Extract from 'Pain' (S&S, p.66)

'Pain' batters the senses with horror; Gurney spoke for all his companions when he finished with the line: 'The amazed heart cries angrily out on God.' Such images recall the experience of the 2/5th Glosters in the Ablaincourt sector. Later, when recovering in hospital and starting to put together his second book, *War's Embers*, he reflected that 'What is happening is that my real groove lay in Nature and Music, whereas Pain and Protest forced the other book [i.e. *Severn & Somme*] into being.' (Letters, 1917)

It is important to remember, however, that many of the best poems about the war were written later – as Gurney himself commented (about Rupert Brooke), 'great poets, great creators are not much influenced by immediate events; those must sink in to the very foundations and be absorbed.' (Letters) And so it was with Gurney; the *Severn & Somme* collection is of interest as part of his development and immediate response to the war. There are some fine poems and signs of Gurney's potential, but some of it is immature and derivative compared to his later work.

Later poems, some subsequently published in *80 Poems or So*, *Rewards of Wonder*, and *Best Poems and the Book of Five Makings*, all draw on the full breadth of his experience, sharpened and clarified by post-war events, by the traumas of entering the asylum and by the increasing intensity of his identification with Gloucestershire. As far as the war is concerned, there are poems about the companionship experienced ('First Time In', K, 2004, p.128), the boring routines and those who rebelled against them (as in 'The Bohemians', K, 2004, p.243), the ubiquitous mud ('The Ford', RW, p.45) and the everyday horrors of war. The latter are sometimes dealt with at a level of deep personal suffering ('Half Dead', K, 2004, p.112) and at other times displaying a flat detachedness that serves to highlight the scene, as in 'The Silent One', where a fellow soldier is dying on the barbed wire in front of Gurney's eyes (K, 2004, p.250). However, what is also striking about Gurney's writings about wartime France, and distinguishes his work from other war poets, is how often he makes direct mention of his own Gloucestershire places.

Flanders, where the Glosters were first stationed, is essentially a flat plain of sands and clays, but it is not featureless. There are several low ridges and hills, almost imperceptible, perhaps, to the observer accustomed to the more striking relief of Gloucestershire. Nevertheless, even a few metres of height, as on the Passchendaele Ridge, allowed better visibility of the enemy trenches. As a soldier, Gurney would have appreciated the strategic significance of the hills; as a Gloucestershire poet it was inevitable that the landscape often brought to mind his own low hills of the Severn Vale ('not only hills but friends of mine and kindly' as he wrote in 'Strange Service'). Further south, the more rolling chalk plateau east of Amiens may have provided some landscape similarities with the Cotswold Hills, although without the dramatic scarp edge and cliff faces. At various stages in the war, Gurney was also stationed by rivers – the Lys in Flanders, the Somme running out to the sea near Abbeville – all large enough to remind him of the Severn. Anxious as he was to return to his creative homeland, it is not surprising that he kept seeing glimpses of Gloucestershire in the shape of a river bend, the edge of a hill shoulder, a copse outlined on the horizon, or a stream flowing through meadows.

In his letters, Gurney drew on memories of Gloucestershire, finding hints of the Stroud area in a river valley near Laventie (Letters, 7 June), noting the French villagers making hay despite the guns (22 June), and on one occasion being taken back to Gloucestershire by the call of a cuckoo: 'Once we were outside our dugout cleaning mess tins, when a cuckoo sounded its call from the shattered wood at the back. What could I think of but Framilode, Minsterworth, Cranham, and the old haunts of home.' (June 1916, to Catherine Abercrombie)

Not surprisingly, these experiences were to feature in poems written at the time, as well as in those written later when he was back in Gloucestershire or in Dartford Asylum. In 'Crucifix Corner', recalling the mud and chaos at the water dump where carts came every day to fill tanks with muddy chlorinated water, Gurney can look beyond the present moment to summon up images of the misty meadows of home: 'All things said Severn, the air was of those dusk meadows.' (K, 2004, p.135) In 'Laventie Ridge', he writes: 'The low ridge of Laventie / Looked like Wainlode's / Coming up from Sandhurst's / Orchard guarded roads.' (RW, p.68) In 'Crickley Hill', Gurney discovers that another soldier is also reminded of Crickley Hill by the look of a country lane near Buire au Bois, where the battalion was on rest:

When on a sudden, 'Crickley' he said. How I started
At that old darling name of home! And turned
Fell into a torrent of words warm-hearted
Till clear above the stars of summer burned
In velvety smooth skies.
We shared memories
And the old raptures from each other learned.

(K, 2004, p. 39)

In 'That Centre of Old', it is Cooper's Hill 'plain almost as experience' and 'autumn Cranham with its boom of colour' to which he turns 'after a strafe end' (K, 2004, p. 142). It is as if the Severn Meadows and the Cotswold Hills became the ideal places of memory, the touchstones of hidden happiness, or at least of an identity, that he could cling to whenever a sight or sound sparked off his imagination.

In the still space
At a strafe-end grateful for silence and body's grace
(Whole body – and after hell's hammering and clamouring).
Then memory purified made rewarding shapes
Of all that spirit runs towards in escapes,
And Cooper's Hill showed plain almost as experience.
Soft winter's mornings of kind innocence, high June's
Girl's air of untouched purity, and on Cooper's Hill
Or autumn Cranham with its boom of colour…
Not anyway does ever Cotswold's fail – Her dear blue long dark slope fail –
Of the imagining promise in full exile.

('That Centre of Old', K, 2004, p. 142)

Amazingly, despite the difficult conditions, he was also composing music; at least five songs were written in the trenches at this time and the first four, in particular, are considered to be of high quality. 'By a Bierside' set John Masefield's poem to music; 'In Flanders' is a musical setting of Will Harvey's poem; 'Severn Meadows' is a song set to Gurney's own words, and 'Even Such is Time' is based on Sir Walter Raleigh's farewell to life on the eve of his execution. 'Severn Meadows' is a particularly appropriate choice, both the words and music expressing the same longing for return.

SONG (Severn Meadows)
Only the wanderer
    Knows England's graces,
Or can anew see clear
    Familiar faces.

And who loves joy as he
    That dwells in shadows?
Do not forget me quite,
    O Severn meadows.

(S&S, p. 42)

The setting of Harvey's poem is poignant because in August 1916, Gurney had heard some bad news: 'Willy Harvey, my best friend, went out on patrol a week ago, and never came back.' (Letter to Marion Scott, 24 August 1916) He believed him to be dead. In his mind, Harvey and Gloucestershire were intricately linked: 'Ah his name is a part of autumn – and a Gloucester autumn – to me. And the falling of leaves has one more regret for me for ever.'

THE DEAD LAND OPPRESSED ME

Gurney at Rouen, after
being wounded in 1917.
(Gurney Archives)

Having always been sensitive to the natural world around him – the orchis, trefoil and harebells of the high Cotswold Commons, the beech-woods of the scarp edge, and the elm trees and hawthorns of the Severn Vale – Gurney was appalled by the devastation of the landscape caused by the war in France: 'You cannot think how ghastly these battlefields look under a grey sky. Torn trees are the most terrible things I have ever seen. Absolute blight and curse is on the face of everything.' (Letter to Marion Scott, 10 March 1917)

In 'Trees', he tries to recall, instead, the fine beech-woods on the Cotswold Edge at Cooper's Hill and Cranham.

TREES

The dead land oppressed me;
   I turned my thoughts away,
And went where hill and meadow
   Are shadowless and gay.

Where Coopers stands by Cranham,
   Where the hill-gashes white
Show golden in the sunshine,
   Our sunshine, God's delight.

Beauty my feet stayed at last
   Where green was most cool,
Trees worthy of all worship
   I worshipped … then, O fool,

Let my thoughts slide unwitting
   To other, dreadful trees, …
And found me standing, staring
   Sick of heart – at these.

(S&S, p.61)

'We are Making a New World', Paul Nash, painted 1918. Based on a drawing completed in 1917, this is one of the most memorable images of the First World War. The sun is rising on a scene of almost total devastation. (Printed by kind permission of the Imperial War Museum, London)

The artist Paul Nash seemed as moved as Gurney. In a letter to his wife on 7 March 1917, Nash describes a wood on the way to the frontline trenches:

> ... in a wood passed through on our way up, a place with an evil name, pitted and pocked with shells the trees torn to shreds, often reeking with poison gas – a most desolate ruinous place two months back, today it was a vivid green; the most broken trees even had sprouted somewhere in the midst, from the depth of the wood's bruised heart poured out the throbbing song of a nightingale. Ridiculous, mad incongruity!

Gurney also regretted the destruction of trees at home, caused by the need for timber during the war. 'Possessions' refers to the beeches cut down on the scarp slope above Witcombe.

POSSESSIONS
France has victory, England yet firm shall stay,
But what shall please the wind now the trees are away
War took on Witcombe steep?
It breathes there and wonders at old roarings
October time at all lights; and the new clearings
For memory are like to weep.
War need not cut down trees, three hundred miles over Sea
Children of those the Romans saw – lovely trunk and great sail trees!
Not on Cranham, not on Cooper's of camps;
Friend to the great October stars – and the July sky lamps.

(Rewards of Wonder, p.92)

Fortunately Harvey had not been killed but captured, and he spent the rest of the war in prisoner of war camps – relatively safe, as Gurney and the battalion discovered in October 1916. Gurney still worried that now it might be himself who didn't make it home so that they could meet again. His feelings for Harvey were expressed in several poems which appeared in *Severn & Somme* and *War's Embers*.

In February 1917, training finished; the Glosters marched via L'Etoile and Amiens to join the fighting in the Ablaincourt sector. By this time, the Germans were retreating rapidly to shorten the line, but it was decided that an Allied three-pronged attack centred on a line joining Arras, Cambrai and St Quentin should go ahead anyway, despite the difficulties of crossing the devastated landscape to find the enemy. The poem 'Near Vermand' (K, 2004, p.147), written after the war, describes the severely cold conditions suffered by the Glosters at this time. Gurney describes how even though 'lying flat on my belly shivering in clutch frost', he noticed as he looked eastward over the low ridge that …

> … low woods to the left (Cotswold her spinnies if ever)
> Showed through snow flurries and the clearer star weather,
> And nothing but chill and wonder lived in the mind; nothing
> But loathing and fine beauty, and wet loathed clothing.

The juxtaposition of 'loathing' and 'fine beauty' is startling – even at the height of discomfort and fear, Gurney's mind could hold a fine appreciation of Cotswold beauty. A few days later, on 6 April 1917, it was near Vermand that Gurney was wounded and sent back to hospital in Rouen. Edward Thomas was not so lucky; he was killed at Arras on Easter Sunday 1917. From hospital, Gurney told Marion Scott how he longed for Gloucestershire again: 'I cannot keep out of my mind what April has meant to me in past years – Minsterworth, Framilode, and his [F. W. Harvey's] companionship. And my sick mind holds desperately on to such memories for beauty's sake; and the hope of Joy.' (to Marion Scott, 14 April 1917)

He rejoined the battalion in May and was made a member of No. 1 Section, 184 Machine Gun Company, although these still served alongside the 2/5th Glosters. After some trench repairing work at Geumappe, and a rest period at Buire au Bois, the Glosters were sent to the Ypres sector to join the 3rd battle of Ypres (or Passchendaele as it became known). Events had already been going badly for the allied forces when the Glosters arrived to support the efforts near St Julien. In a later poem ('Moving up to Ypres'), Gurney describes the frightening conditions of heavy bombardment as they moved to a 'fearful place' to the north-east of Ypres.

By early September he was in line with the 184 Machine Gun Company (he refers to 'Londoners, Northerners, strange Gloucesters that I knew not') on a slight ridge above St Julien with the 2/5 Glosters infantry, his old battalion, spread out below him. Behind him he could see the scarred skyline of Ypres. The war diary of the 184 Machine Gunners tells how an unexpected gas attack on 12 September resulted in eight men being gassed, and Gurney was one of them. In a formerly unpublished poem, Gurney writes in a confusing stream of words, trying to deal with the traumas of that day by drawing out the terrors of losing grip on place and time.

> Having seen a Pachaendael★ lit with a flare of firs
> And Ypres a dawn light ruddy and golden of desire,
> The stuck tanks – and shook at our guns going in
> As my body would not stay still at such Hell of din:
> Worse than any of theirs – and seen Gloucesters going over;
> Many for the last time – by accident gone further.
> Dwelt in two pillboxes, had open station –
> And lost of geography any the least notion,
> Seeing Verey lights going up from all quarters,
> And all German, and yet to go onwards where the
> Tangle of time and space might be somehow dissolved,

Left: The spires of Ypres from Gallipoli Farm area in 2010. In 1917, Gurney saw the ruined skyline of Ypres.

Right: The Gurney Memorial at Gallipoli Farm, St Julien. This was established by the 'In Flanders Field' Museum of Ypres to commemorate the location in which Gurney was gassed in September 1917. This photograph was taken in 2010.

> Mixed with Londoners, Northerners and strange Gloucesters
> Whom I knew not – and seen shattered Ypres by canal waters.
>
> (GA, 1925)

★ Gurney's spelling of Passchendaele

A memorial now stands at Gallipoli Farm within a few metres of the place where this occurred. Although the effects of the gas appear to have been slow to appear, the authorities deemed Gurney's condition severe enough to warrant treatment, and by mid-September 1917 he was back in Britain in hospital, but not yet back in Gloucestershire. The previous six years had seen dramatic changes in his life. The young twenty-one-year-old who had hardly travelled beyond Gloucestershire in 1911, had first grown accustomed to living outside the county in London, and then been thrown directly into a distressing war in a foreign country. In both cases, his natural resilience meant that he survived, in both cases, probably better than he thought he would. Paradoxically too, absence from Gloucestershire had stimulated him to write poetry as well as music.

In the 1915–17 period, his output of poetry was very high, resulting in his first book of poems (*Severn & Somme*), material for the second book (*War's Embers*) and a range of intense experiences on which he could reflect and draw for the rest of his life. It is tempting to blame the traumas of war service for his subsequent mental breakdown; however, the seeds of his mental problems were already apparent before the war and, in fact, Gurney found that the discipline and hard physical activity of army life actually kept his nervous problems at bay (Hipp, 2005). More significant seem to have been the feelings of bitterness and betrayal he increasingly felt at the conduct of the war and the treatment of returning soldiers. He returned to Britain determined to reconnect with the beauty of the countryside and of music and poetry, all since long denied, as he explained in

'After Music', a poem he wrote in Edinburgh War Hospital on 8 October 1917 and sent in a letter to Marion Scott. His war experience had crystallised for him the supreme importance of Gloucestershire to his identity and creativity. Looking back now, we might wonder whether such place dependence was going to cause problems in the future, as indeed Gurney seems to have hinted in the final line. He has been drawn back from losing his identity in the hell of the war only to immerse himself in the creative passion of a particular place – 'if wisely' … only 'the Gods can tell'.

AFTER MUSIC

Why I am on fire now, and tremulous
With sense of beauty long denied; the first
Opening of floodgate to the glorious burst
Of Freedom from the Fate that limits us
To work in darkness pining for the light,
Thirsting for sweet untainted draughts of air,
Clouds sunset coloured, Music … O Music's bare
White heat of silver passion fiercely bright!
While sweating at the foul task, we can taste
No Joy that's clean, no Love but something lets
It from its power, the wisest soul forgets
What's beautiful, or delicate, or chaste.
Orpheus drew me, (as once his bride) from Hell.
If wisely, her or me, the Gods can tell.

(WE, p.49)

4

THE POET AND THE PLACE: LOSING GLOUCESTERSHIRE

WHAT EVIL COIL
What evil coil of Fate has fastened me
Who cannot move to sight, whose bread is sight,
And in nothing has more bare delight
Than dawn or the violet or the winter tree.
Stuck in the mud – Blinkered up, roped for the Fair.
What use to vessel breath that lengthens pain?
O but the empty joys of wasted air
That blow on Crickley and whimper wanting me!

(B, p.33)

Hope and Despair

Back in England, Gurney had high hopes for his recovery. Exclaiming with delight about the clean sheets and clean clothes of Bangour Hospital in a letter to Marion Scott, he also told her that he had even played the piano:

I played for two hours, mostly in accompaniment, and I found to my joy that what I had hoped is true – that the effort to concentrate is a pleasure to me; which means that, in so much, neurasthenia is a thing of the past. And that what I have would go if I lived in my old life once again, with an added incalculable Joy added thereto. Rejoice with me my friend, for that which was lost is found; or shall I say rather its hiding place is known.

(Letter, 26 September 1917)

Initially the publication of his book of poems *Severn & Somme* (November 1917) brought him great satisfaction and the reviews were good. He felt that he had been recognised as a 'war poet' though, as explained, many of the poems were not about the war *per se*, but about Gloucestershire and his own feelings. However, the next few years were full of disruption to any kind of normal life, and Gurney's nervous illness and periods of depression grew worse rather than better. He was moved between institutions – Newcastle General Hospital, Brancepeth Castle Convalescent Home, Lord Derby's War Hospital Warrington and, eventually, the Middlesex War Hospital in St Albans. The problem was that, although the physical effects of gassing appeared to have receded, Gurney now showed signs of mental illness, categorised by the authorities – who knew little about all the after effects of trauma that so many men were showing – as 'shell-shock'.

In March 1918, Gurney told Marion Scott that he had spoken to the friendly spirit of Beethoven and that Bach and Schumann were there also; on 19 June 1918 he sent a suicide note to her explaining that 'I know you would rather know me dead than mad.' (Letter) The hospital authorities found him wandering beside the canal in Warrington, having tried but been unable to kill himself. With a strange prescience, Gurney's poem, 'The Three Spectres', published in *Severn & Somme* in 1917, seemed to foretell such anguish. The first two spectres predict wounding or death in France, but the last one had seemed to hint at Gurney's fate to 'stay untouched until the war's last dawning' before his 'one hour of agony'.

It was not just the traumas of war service and gassing, and the frustrated desire to be normal again and walk in his Gloucestershire countryside; personal incidents in his life at the time added to his instability. Gurney had begun a relationship with a nurse, Annie Drummond, at the Bangour War Hospital, but despite his high hopes for a permanent relationship and marriage, she was not as serious about this and it all finished sometime in 1918. Indeed this may even have been the trigger for the suicide attempt. Gurney's father, David, was taken ill with cancer in early 1918 and eventually died in May 1919, and Margaret Hunt died in March 1919. There is evidence in Gurney's letters and his poems that he was also feeling sadness at losing his army comrades but tinged with a belief that he had let them down, and a gradually growing bitterness about the way returning war heroes were being treated.

Hurd (1978, p.126) wonders if some unpleasant bullying had happened to him at Seaton Delaval Command depot, to which he briefly returned in April 1918 and where he may have been considered a malingerer. The army discharged him in October 1918 but without a full pension (because his illness had not been wholly caused by the war), and for the next few years he was reduced to finding temporary employment while he tried to pick up the pieces of his creative life and find some kind of mental stability.

The period from October 1918 to September 1922 was a crucial one in Gurney's life. He no longer had a clear role; he was no longer a soldier but he had not fully established himself as a musician. He had gained success with his poetry but he wasn't yet an accepted poet. This point was confirmed for him in 1921, when he failed to have his poetry published in one of the Georgian Poetry series edited by George Marsh; and again in 1922 when a third planned volume of poetry (later called *80 Poems or So*) was turned down by Sidgwick & Jackson. He suffered from mental instability and depression but had been discharged from the army and hospital, so his friends and family were left trying to cope with his condition. During 1918–19, his family tried to settle him in Barton Street again. The extent of his illness is clear from the letters of friends and family at the time, mentioning, amongst other things, his erratic eating habits: 'His chief trouble is concerned with food – he would eat nothing all day. He asserts that if he gives way to the desire for food he is unable to stop, … if he has lunch he invariably goes out afterwards and buys large quantities of cakes and eats them and continues doing so as long as he has the money.' (John Haines, 1918, letter to Marion Scott)

John Haines tried hard to look after Gurney, taking him for walks, lending him books and keeping a watchful eye on him. This was not easy, as Gurney often responded to his own violently changing mood swings by disappearing to walk the hills or riverside. On one occasion, Dorothy Gurney explained in a letter to Marion Scott, October 1918, how Gurney had walked from Lydney to Newport (23 miles) and back the next day in order to find work on a boat sailing from Newport. She was worried, but noticed that this walk 'evidently did him good' (Hurd, p.129). In the light of later medical knowledge, we know that the body produces endorphins after vigorous exercise and this can raise mood appreciably. Gurney seems to have taken up his old habit of night walking again too, leaving the sleeping household at 19 Barton Street to climb Portway or to explore a silent Gloucester. Even some of the hard labouring jobs he took on at this time seem to have helped. 'I am glad to tell you,' Gurney wrote to Marion Scott on 2 November, 'that I am better myself after a fortnight's hauling of heavy things about the Munitions works: but that is a job that won't last long –fortunately.' (Letter)

Friends made every effort to settle Gurney down and keep him on a more even mental balance. Late in 1918 his mood seemed to swing upwards again. He spent Christmas 1918 with

Ethel Voynich in Cornwall near Gurnard's Head, managing to write a new song setting and to pen notes and a few poems about the Cornish coast (including 'The Companions' (80P) and 'To Zennor' (GA, 1925). In the spring of 1919 he stayed with his old friend Will Harvey at Redlands, Minsterworth and was able to sign on again at the Royal College of Music for the next academic year. The publication of *War's Embers*, Gurney's second book of poetry, by Sidgwick & Jackson in May 1919, must have been a real boost to his confidence. Strangely, perhaps, it was not as well reviewed as the first volume, even though later critics have judged it to contain the superior poetry. But he continued writing and began putting together material for another book of poems. He was composing music as well.

It is surely not coincidence that this surge in creativity corresponds with his discovery of a favourite place – Dryhill Farm under Crickley Hill (Figure 4.2). 'This is just, and just the place would please you,' he wrote to Marion Scott on 22 April 1919.

> An old gray-stone rambling building under a Roman camp near the site of a Roman villa where many things have from time to time been discovered. A place of thorn, oak, ash, elm, clear streams, a 500 feet-up place where one gets a sight of Severn sea, May Hill, and on clear days of the Welsh Hills, by looking out of a window or wandering out of a gate. Here I am set to learn farm business, to become sane and glad for life, with many books, Beethoven, Bach, Mozart, Tristan and the Magelone Lieder★.

★The Magelone Lieder – Brahms op33; fifteen Romances from Tieck's 'Magelone' for voices and piano

Gurney was to be employed as a farm labourer. His letter is full of almost child-like enthusiasm: 'My wages (in money) are to be 5/– a week and keep; but O what a full competence and more of beauty! Aren't I lucky?' (To Marion Scott, 22 April 1919) 'The loveliest place almost that ever was, the widest sweep beauty before one.' (To Marion Scott, late April 1919)

He was convinced he had found a way of life in which the physical exercise of farm labour would keep his depression in check, whilst the landscape with its beauty and ghostly Roman presence would inspire his writing and composing. He threw himself with vigour, into this enterprise: 'Tomorrow to follow the plough, do an hour's Fugue perhaps and hammer out the Sonata on the rickety old piano here.' (To Marion Scott, 22 April 1919)

The farm work could be dreary and laborious as Gurney was only able to do unskilled jobs – clearing brambles, lifting root crops, mending fences – but he was prepared to put up with this for the sake of his sanity and creativity. In 'Above Dryhill' we see him helping with the skilled task of hedge-laying, and recognising some similarities with the craft of interpreting a Bach composition.

> ABOVE DRYHILL (extract)
> And there the high wild hedges saw I tamed
> And cunning woven when the green buds flamed
> With deft inweaving like a player's showing
> Of Bach's fourstranded thought,
> Fixed pattern wrought
> So easy and as cunning to move wonder.
> In April's kindest and her softest day
> I helped, as clumsy two-left-handed may,
> Cutting the green briar from the horrid stem
> And tangling every step in swathy thorn.
>
> (*80 Poems or So*, p.45)

It is significant that about this time he started composing the 'Gloucestershire Rhapsody', an extended orchestral piece, celebrating his Gloucestershire landscapes and history. This work has only recently been played for the first time at the Three Choirs Festival 2010, and the influence of Crickley Hill and the Dryhill area is, I believe, very strong (*see* p.136). During April and May 1919,

Dryhill Farm, 'an old gray-stone rambling building under a Roman camp'. This photograph was taken in 2010 and the house is now a private dwelling.

The view from near Dryhill Farm, showing Chosen Hill, the Severn Vale and the far-off hills of the Welsh borderland.

The site of Dryhill Farm, taken in 2010. The Roman villa site is in the field above the farm.

whilst working at Dryhill, his creativity was high: 'lots of music inside but lots of verse written out and awaiting transcript,' he explained (letter to Marion Scott, 9 May 1919).

In August 1919, he accompanied John Haines on a holiday in the Black Mountains, enjoying the scenery particularly at Llanthony in the Ewyas valley, a place with an interesting connection to Gloucester. Llanthony Priory in the Black Mountains is the original foundation (Llanthony Prima) of 1108, whilst the Gloucester Llanthony is Llanthony Secunda, being built by Milo of Gloucester in 1137 as a refuge for the Augustinian monks when they were attacked by Welsh rebels and forced to leave. In a letter to Marion Scott, August 1919, Gurney feared that his love for Gloucestershire might prejudice him against the original Llanthony. Nevertheless, the poem he wrote is more significant in revealing his dread that his muse might leave him, and his desire to draw on Wordsworth's inspiration. Tintern Abbey, another ruined abbey on the Lower Wye and the place that inspired one of Wordsworth's most famous long poems, was not far from Llanthony. The last few lines of the poem are difficult, partly because Gurney tends to leave out words; however, he is really describing aspects of the technical ('shaped to square') and the creative ('glowed from deep heart out') processes of writing and hoping that he can continue to be inspired.

> Llanthony lay in the hill's hollow and dreamed.
> I who had come from this other Llanthony, there
> Sat awhile and drank tea while sunlight gleamed
> Above roofless choir of the old Abbey.
> Beautiful as peace need ever be it seemed;
> Would I might stay to write there, (O that it may be
> My place of meditating before long! Here to make song!)
> London was a poor sort of companion here;
> O for loved Wordsworth and his Tintern manner!
> Which glowed from deep heart out and was shaped to square
> Achieved verse in a few days, for all men to honour …
> For raptures, truth and beauty in small space.
> Near Gloucester, indeed (might) have been a safer place,
> But Mozart or Chaucer might have been dreamer.
>
>   Llanthony (GA, 1925)

Back in Gloucestershire, and drawn inevitably back to Crickley, he wrote a great deal of music and poetry. In the latter part of 1919, Gurney composed more than forty songs (many judged to be of the highest quality) including several short piano pieces and among them the 'Five Preludes', later published by Winthrop Rogers; a violin sonata; the string quartet in F Major and the beginnings of another in A major, all in addition to working on 'The Gloucestershire Rhapsody'. We know that walking, and especially his night walking, was essential to his creativity. In the pattern set by Margaret Hunt, he would then return home to tidy up the text or musical notation.

> But O that night when after going to see Emmie at Cleeve I walked back by Leckhampton, Shurdington, Brockworth – just missing Crickley. Meteors flashed like sudden inspirations of song down the sky. The air was too still to set firs or beeches sighing, but the grass swished; twigs crackled beneath me, and the occasional stir of wild creatures in the undergrowth set off the peace – O the depth of it. Crickley is a pure joy. (That came another night) It was shameful to leave it, but after making up my mind to do 20 miles, I was foolishly drawn on. Schumann would have stayed there under those royal cliffs in that flood of light, would have gathered the influence of the fire into him, later have given it out.
>
>   (Letter to Marion Scott, September 1919)

When Gurney returned to the Royal College of Music, in the autumn of 1919, he was able to take up lodgings with the Chapman family for a second time and so, for a while, to become part of the relatively normal family life in High Wycombe. But signs of his medical troubles reappeared in 1920. Perhaps indicative of this was his flight from London back to the Gloucestershire countryside in February 1920. He walked from High Wycombe to 'a place near Oxford' (perhaps Thame?), caught a train to 'a place on the Cotswold ridge' (possibly Chipping Campden?) and then walked all along the Cotswolds back to Dryhill Farm (Howell's letter to Marion Scott, GA). Another 1925 poem provides Gurney's own account of this incident and seems to fit the route suggested above. The 'friend' he left at 8 o'clock will be Edward Chapman. It is worth producing the poem in its entirety (even though it is clearly a draft and unedited) since it reveals something of Gurney's state of mind in 1920.

THE LITTLE WAY

At eight o'clock, I had left my friend with appearances
Of walking just so far – taking tram and later
Train; to get home respectably and to books and a matter of a Quartett left half-written…
but the spirit demanding
Said 'So you did not think in your intents [interest?] of France'.
Obedient as ever to the call leftward and south-eastward,
I kept my instinct past trespass. It was an all night chance
Of by? paths and of Roman ways; no hurry – but my body went faster
Than rules. At eleven o'clock, I was lost and in belief steering –
And by divine stars never before it seemed on slants
And azure heights of heaven so ordered (Save Varennes'
Frost stricken fury of beauty) Land in dim smothers.

On and on, I knew not where, till the unknown
Majesty of Leckhampton rose Roman as shield-shape known,
Confirming faith-of-beauty: its best way, spirit
In me – and West and South now after South alone
Moving, the dark land passing like a dream of one
Night (but Cotswold's chiefest). To the spinney I had come
Where at last in the thick growth night unstarred
Gave gloom alone. Where I halted and lay; choosing as always
Tobacco for a friend, but stifled the gaudy match blaze
Hurting the dusk – lay smoked, thought of books and the companies
Of Roman here had travelled, rested, or blundered through brambles
(The camp and little most treasured farm so near.)

                                                                                    (GA, 1925)

This is my own transcription of Gurney's handwriting – question marks indicate unreadable or confusing words.

He was clearly still mulling over his war experiences and needing the soothing rhythms of movement ('obedient as ever to the call' and 'my body went faster than the rules') as well as the promise of Cotswold places ('majesty of Leckhampton' and 'confirming faith-of-beauty') to help him deal with the stress and depression he was experiencing.

Gurney dreamt about having a cottage in the Cotswolds and using this as the base for his creative work. In 1919/20, he was working at Dryhill Farm ('most treasured farm'). and poems of this period see him revelling in the sunsets and dawns seen from the Edge ('Crickley Morning'); watching the farm work with a percipient eye ('The Bramble Patch', 'The Lantern Shine'); wondering about the Romans who lived at Dryhill Villa and whose pottery and coins kept turning up in the fields ('The Coin, Up There'), and describing the wild flowers and animals that frequented the slopes above the farm ('Scabious and Trefoil').

It is easy to imagine how Gurney's attention was drawn to a small cottage at Cold Slad, located about half a mile from the farm and standing empty in 1919/20. He thought he'd found his dream. Acting on an impulse, it seems, he returned from High Wycombe and took over the cottage in May 1920, planning to make enough money, presumably from farmwork, to allow him to stay here.

> Well, in one of my fits of not being able to stand it any longer, I wrote a letter to the chief church-warden at Wycombe, arranged for the service to be taken, and came here – to find out what might be found out. An old Cotswold stone house with one pretty good upper room, but draughty. There are holes in the floor – to be dodged. There are two square places in the roof which will need stopping. The garden was long ago a ruin, the stream dried up, and weeds grew in it; no one came save the curious; and now under the shadow of the great rise of Crickley – here am I. I am a bit afraid, but hope to earn a little somehow enough to carry on.
>
> (Letter, 13 May 1920)

In fact, the attempt to live alone here only lasted a few weeks. By the autumn of 1920 he was back in London and he never lived at the cottage again. Despite the brevity of this experiment, it should be seen as an important indicator of Gurney's growing place-dependence, an addiction that was becoming increasingly difficult to accommodate with life as a London-based musician.

In July 1921 he formally left the Royal College of Music and took up residence back in Gloucestershire, but not at the family home in Barton Street; instead, he stayed with his Aunt Marie in Longford, a small village on the northern outskirts of Gloucester, quite close to the vicarage at Twigworth where his old friend Alfred Cheesman was now based. Even back in Gloucestershire, Gurney didn't seem able to settle to any one activity. The list of attempts over this period is long: he had tried working in a munitions factory (October 1918), doing farm work (April 1919, August 1920 and February 1922), becoming a church organist again (September 1919), working in a cold storage depot (August 1921), playing the piano in cinemas in Bude, Cornwall (December 1921) and in Plumstead, London (January 1922), and joining the civil service in Gloucester tax office (July 1922). No job lasted more than a few weeks (twelve weeks at the tax office was by far the longest). Gurney seemed restless and unable to focus on the realities of an ordinary working life.

In retrospect, this restlessness was not surprising, nor was it unusual. We know that, all over England, returning soldiers and their families were experiencing the immense difficulties of 'coming home'. The men who returned were not the same as those who had left England in 1914, full of hope and patriotism. Their families who had not experienced the war could not imagine the terrible traumas and privations they had suffered, and the men could not talk about them.

At least Gurney had his poetry as a form of release and, despite the personal tribulations, this was a most creative period for him. He wrote many poems and was able to find publication outlets for some of them, with Marion Scott's help. Poems appeared in, for example, *Music and Letters* (October 1920), the *London Mercury* (Oct 1922) and in two poetry collections published by J.C. Squire (1921 and 1922).

Reinventing Poetry

The poetry of this period can be appreciated by looking at the volume entitled *80 Poems or So*, gathered together from archive material by Walter and Thornton and published in 1997. This was the collection that Gurney

1 Westfield terrace, Longford in 2010. Today much of the meadowland, which lay all round the houses, has been built over.

had failed to get published in 1922. Had it been published it would have revealed how Gurney was breaking new ground, dealing directly with the real and the everyday, and trying out new rhythms that suited the way he roamed across the Gloucestershire countryside and related his own experiences to his reading – 'a tantalising glimpse of how Georgian poetry could have re-invented itself,' Walter and Thornton suggest (1997). In this sense, Gurney might be thought of as part of a first wave of modernist writing; in fact, Lucas (2001, p.32) suggests that 'Gurney ought to be seen as at least as valid a presence in post-war poetry as Eliot'. What is fascinating is how many of the poems are about Gloucestershire, either directly about named places or indirectly, but, equally forcefully, about the spirit or sense of the different Gloucestershire places. Walter and Thornton have arranged the poetry in broad themes (the seasons, the Gloucestershire topography, literary and mythic allusions, London sights and crowds). However, for me, an equally interesting way to arrange the poetry of this period would be by place (Figure 4.1). It is possible to trace Gurney's movements and inspiration along the Severn near his Aunt Marie's house at Longford, and further afield in Ashleworth, at Dryhill below Crickley Hill, climbing the Cotswold Edge, and walking the streets of Gloucester. We see him watching the sky, reflecting on the history or the wild flowers and desperately seeking the remedy for his depression: 'I would see the gray church spired again / And then die. / Other things are weariness; I am tired of them altogether. / There I am I.' ('Ashleworth', 80P, p.94) It is nearly always possible to tell which kind of landscape he is inhabiting, whether it is riverside, low-lying vale, scarp edge or high hills. So 1918–22 can be seen as the high point of his direct poetic connection with these places; on the whole a celebratory connection, but even at this stage revealing (as in the poem 'Supposition', 80P, p.97) the suspicion that it may all be taken away: 'Where should I turn, where look, that have / No life save Her's, that Gloucester gave / And shall give still.'

Fig. 4.1: Tentative Suggestions About Places and Poems

Date	Place	Poems	
Autumn 1918 to Spring 1919	**Gloucester (Barton Street) and Severn Meadows** Living in Gloucester at Barton Street; walking the city and the Severn Meadows (apart from Cornwall (Christmas 1918), London (Jan 1919), Black Mountains (August 1919))	**About Gloucester:** Western Sky - Look On a Western City On a Town Blessings Above Maisemore The Town Morning	**About Severn Meadows** Lovely Playthings Brave Carpets Longney Town Thoughts from Severn The Crocus Ring Iliadian April 10 1919 There is a Valley
February 1920, and May to September 1920 (+ brief period at Dryhill Farm April 1919)	**Cotswold Edge and Dryhill** Living at Dryhill Farm and briefly at his cottage at Cold Slad below Crickley; Doing farmwork and walking on the Cotswold Edge	Above Dryhill Change Midnight Quiet Fireshine Common Things	Compensations Late September Alterations Up on Cotswold Supposition
Autumn 1919, Autumn 1920 to February 1921, Jun/July/August 1921	**London** Living in London at various addresses or at High Wycombe or, briefly, Stokenchurch	London Dawn Sights The Road North Woolwich Woolwich or So	Fine Rain London In Town Home Thoughts The Ship

Date	Place	Poems	
Much of 1921 and Feb–April 1922	**Gloucester (Longford) and Severn Meadows** Living at Aunt Marie's house in Longford; walking the Severn Meadows. Special interest in Shakespeare 1922	Western Before Resurrection Good Friday First Spring Coming Dusk Spring Dawn Rainy Midnight April Gale April Mist Dull Afternoon Water Colours Sedges The Change This County Ashleworth Roads The Garden Doom's tongue Moments	**Shakespeare Related** Personages Generations Dursley School Master April 23 1922 Shakespeare's Day April 23 1922 May Day

The poems have been 'placed' by reading the kind of landscape which is featured (e.g. under the Edge of Cotswold, the Roman hill or lanes, elm trees and sedges of Severnside); tying up the poem's themes and concerns with what was happening in Gurney's life at the time (e.g. mention of the Cold Slad cottage or of his aunt and her dog); using information about dates of publication of some individual poems (e.g. 'Crocus Ring' published in *Music and Letters* Oct 1920). Not all of the poems of *80 Poems or So* are here. Sixty-one have been 'placed' above. Another three were written in Cornwall ('The Companions', 'Moor and Ocean', 'Western Light'). The others are more difficult to place.

Some of the poetry of 1918–22 shows a harder social and political edge than earlier writing. Lucas (2001) explains how the poems of this period reveal Gurney's bitterness and growing anger over the plight of those soldiers who returned home to neglect, poverty and humiliation. It is interesting to compare the personal regret and sadness expressed in 'Strange Service' (WE, p.23) – 'None but you can know my heart, its tears and sacrifice' – with the more angry and outspoken criticism on behalf of others written in 'Strange Hells' (B, p.90, also K, 2004, p.141) –'Where are they now, on State-doles, or showing shop-patterns / Or walking town to town sore in borrowed tatterns / Or begged.' It was not only the soldiers Gurney worried about. There are several poems from this period that reveal a wider concern with the state of housing and conditions for the poor. For example, in 'North Woolwich' (80P), the evil dwellings and the lives of the inhabitants are compared with the healthier and more satisfying conditions of ancient Greece, and England is condemned for wasting the strength and talents of its inhabitants. Gurney would have undoubtedly been influenced by the growing tide of political unrest in England (strikes and labour disputes) in the 1920s, and by powerful currents of socialist thinking, particularly amongst the artistic and literary communities. In London, he could claim to be part of a growing literary circle, and Lucas suggests that Gurney's was one of the socialist voices now being heard.

There were also developments in the Cotswolds that Gurney must have known about – a number of utopian community experiments (as at the Tolstoy-inspired Whiteway colony near Bisley) and the Arts and Crafts movement which, influenced by William Morris, was as much a social and educational vision as it was artistic.

One of the most distinctive aspects of Gurney's disturbed life between 1918 and 1922 is his continual movement between places, and particularly between the town and the countryside, between London and Gloucestershire. It was as if he no longer knew where he belonged.

GURNEY'S COTTAGE AND DRYHILL FARM

In Gurney's day, a footpath ran across the fields below Crickley Hill. It led from the cottages on Cold Slad Lane to Dryhill Farm and must have been walked many times by Ivor Gurney. Today, despite appearing on the 2005 map, the footpath has apparently been diverted. Dryhill Farm is a private house, but the smaller of the two cottages on Cold Slad Lane stands uninhabited. Could this have been Gurney's cottage? The small amount of evidence (and I must admit, my own intuition!) suggests that it might be.

The cottage I have discovered fits the description so well. The main part of the building is Cotswold stone, possibly built in the eighteenth century, though there is a newer (possibly early twentieth century) extension and the roof has been renewed at least once. There are windows looking up to the hill (though blinded now by overgrown vegetation), and a small garden crossed by an intermittent stream. Most importantly, the location is perfect, on the ancient trackway between Crickley and Little Shurdington, directly under the nose of Crickley and within a few minutes' walk of Dryhill Farm. The cottage is not inhabited at the time of writing; it waits under the overgrown hedgerow at the side of the track, looking out from its gateway eastwards towards the farm. To reach Dryhill Farm now, it is necessary to take a new bridleway that has been created to link with another ancient track, the Greenway (see Walk 4 On the Roman Hill p. 132).

There are no letters covering May–October 1920 but we do have Gurney's poetry. 'Midnight' sees him rapt in writing, enjoying the sense and sounds of his own creative hideaway, though perhaps already beginning his downward spiral into mental 'pain'.

Midnight

There is no sound within the cottage now,
But my pen and the sound of long rain
Heavy and musical, I must think again
To find so sweet a noise, and cannot anyhow.

The soothingness and deep-toned tinkle, soft
Happenings of night, in pain there's nothing better,
Save tobacco or long most looked for letter…
The different roof sounds. House, shed, loft and scullery.

(*80 Poems or So*, p. 112)

The disused cottage at Cold Slad sited under the steep slope of Crickley Hill. This may be the cottage Gurney lived in for a few months.

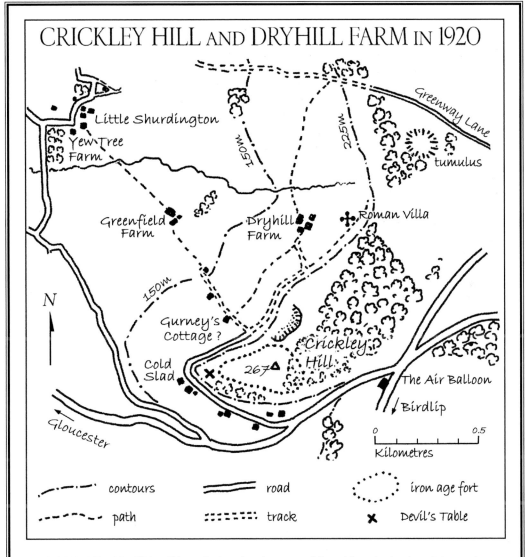

CRICKLEY HILL AND DRYHILL FARM IN 1920

Little Shurdington

Yew Tree Farm

150m

225m

Greenway Lane

tumulus

Greenfield Farm

Dryhill Farm

Roman Villa

N

150m

Gurney's Cottage ?

Cold Slad

267△

Crickley Hill

The Air Balloon

Birdlip

Gloucester

0   0.5

Kilometres

| ·—·—·—· | contours | ══════ | road | ⸰⸰⸰⸰⸰ | iron age fort |
| ---·—·— | path | ::::::: | track | ✖ | Devil's Table |

Fig. 4.2: Crickley Hill and Dryhill Farm. This map has been based on current OS map information, but the scale is approximate only. (Map by Roger Ellis, 2010)

Did he intend to live here permanently or in the holidays from London? Was it a potential answer to Gurney's problems, as he thought then? Or was it an impossible dream, given his fragile mental condition and difficulty in holding down even the farm job on a permanent basis? All answers are conjectural only. What we do know is that in October 1920 he was back in London, and in Spring 1921 he was living with his aunt at Longford. The only further mention of the cottage that I can find (apart from the poetry) is in a letter to Marion Scott, 9 September 1921:

> No, I am not yet well; in spite of a journey to Crickley yesterday, where I found Cold Slad occupied, renewing, with two new, welcome windows looking up on the Hill. Mr Masefield was running Iphigenia in Tauris at Stroud yesterday, and wrote to ask me over; but not being well and having a chance of Crickley, decided not to go.

The dream was over. He couldn't live with Crickley but he couldn't live without it.

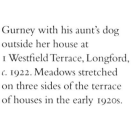

Gurney with his aunt's dog
outside her house at
1 Westfield Terrace, Longford,
c. 1922. Meadows stretched
on three sides of the terrace
of houses in the early 1920s.

Ronald Gurney at 19 Barton Street,
1915.

Ronald Gurney's house at 52
Worcester Street, Gloucester. It was
here that Gurney was lodging in
1922 when he was taken away to be
committed to Barnwood Asylum.

His identification with Gloucestershire had been kept alive all through the years of war – a countryside in his mind being built on the foundations of his memories of childhood and young adulthood. Being well was linked with being in Gloucestershire; being creative was intimately connected with the physical act of moving out and about in this countryside. And yet, his professional life was based in London at the Royal College of Music or with his literary colleagues. When Gurney was away from Gloucestershire, he wanted to return and did so, often by walking long distances. His walk from High Wycombe to Dryhill Farm (February 1920), and his attempt to live at Cold Slad, take on great significance in retrospect. It was as if this place represented a last chance to achieve stability and independence. When it failed, the restlessness increased; he needed the physical connection of walking the countryside to help him settle.

Walking the countryside soon became a way of life and a way of keeping the worst aspects of depression at bay. Harvey's family worried about Gurney, apparently leaving their dining room window open at Redlands so that he could climb in, help himself from the pantry and sleep in a chair after one of his night walks. Aunt Marie in Longford must also have been very tolerant of Gurney; he could not have been an easy lodger in 1921–22. He did not eat at normal hours, he frequently went off walking for a whole day and often the night too, sleeping under hedges or coming back at dawn and raiding the larder like a naughty schoolboy. At other times he would sit up all night composing music and poetry. 'My aunt who lives here – indeed owns the house – is a dear, and spoils me,' he told Marion Scott (Letter, 26 April 1921).

All this instability and hyper-activity came to an abrupt end in 1922. The job at the Tax Office, arranged for him by Edward Marsh, was never going to work. In August 1922, Gurney left his post; he imagined that electrical tricks were being played on him and, finally, he left Aunt Marie's house and turned up unannounced to stay with his brother Ronald and his wife, newly married and living in Worcester Street, Gloucester. Ronald, already bitter about what he saw as Ivor's special treatment because of his music and poetry, found the unstable Gurney too much to deal with. Not surprisingly, he called the police when his brother wielded a gun and threatened to kill himself. The upshot was that Gurney was eventually certified insane and committed to the Barnwood House private asylum in October 1922.

A Dark Wind Blowing

For the next fifteen years until his death in 1937, Ivor Gurney was locked away from Gloucestershire, the countryside he identified with so strongly and which had provided him with joy, inspiration, peace and the opportunities for physical exercise and work.

The shock of entry into the asylum in 1922 provoked a rush of letters from Gurney to many of his friends and family, revealing his confused mental state and distress. 'I hope for release and a chance of death successful,' he wrote to Haines and Harvey (Letter, 4 November 1922); 'I pray in the Name of God to be taken out of electrical influence,' he requested of the Mayor of Gloucester (Letter, October 1922). Gurney believed he was subject to some electrical treatment, seemingly mistakenly for there is no evidence that such treatment was ever used with him. To Ralph Vaughan Williams, he wrote: '...get me term of imprisonment, dangerous public service, work, freedom to go on tramp, but chance of death always – rather than be left here...' (Letter, November 1922)

An unsuccessful escape attempt on 8 November, in which Gurney escaped out of a window, led the authorities to believe that it was essential to move Gurney from Gloucestershire and, after negotiations by Marion Scott, who wanted him near enough to London for her to visit, he was moved in December to the City of London Mental Hospital, Dartford, Kent. According to the reports of his friends, he was initially unsettled in 1923, writing distressing letters of appeal to everyone he knew (and to some, like the Metropolitan Police, that he didn't!) and once even escaping and making for Vaughan Williams' house in London. Eventually he seems to have come to endure, though not accept, his incarceration, a sentence which lasted for another fourteen years.

Gurney's friends visited him, at least in the early years, though they did not find it easy. Herbert Howells would only visit if Marion Scott accompanied him and, after one particularly distressing visit, refused to go again. Florence Gurney, Ivor's mother, made efforts to keep in touch, writing letters to Ivor himself and to Marion Scott, but she only visited him once. She complained that she couldn't visit often and that she feared her son would think she didn't care about him – life was 'so trying I can't save much money' (letters of Florence Gurney to Marion Scott, GA). Even Will Harvey, though saddened by Gurney's fate, seems to have been unable to maintain visits, either for family reasons or perhaps because of his own depression and memories of his long imprisonment. Marion Scott was the one person who steadfastly stood by Gurney. She visited regularly, she took him gifts of books, music and cigarettes. She encouraged him to play the piano that stood in the ward and she arranged to take him out of the asylum for car drives. Just as important, Scott was the one person who collected and kept safe all Gurney's poetry and music. She was active in promoting his work, and it was largely due to her efforts that some poems were published in journals and magazines in the 1920s.

The hospital records show that Ivor Gurney was generally a quiet and solitary inmate, not aggressive but prone, perhaps not surprisingly, to occasional violent outbursts of anger and frustration. The diagnosis, such as it was, suggested that Gurney suffered from 'delusional insanity', a term later translated as schizophrenia, though more recently it has been suggested that he was bipolar (Hipp, 2005; Blevins, 2007). Bipolar illness is a severe mood disorder caused by chemical imbalance, in which the sufferer experiences dramatic mood swings. It does not affect the cognitive or thinking processes in the way that schizophrenia does. This seems to fit Gurney's condition; he had always been prone to creative highs and deep lows or depressions – what he called his neurasthenia. His recuperation at Framilode in 1913 followed one such severe low mood. If he was bipolar, then the periods of relative normality and more settled mood must have been even harder for him to bear, wanting desperately to write and compose but finding himself shut away from his inspiration. On occasions, particularly in the later years at the asylum, he often believed he was Beethoven, Whitman or Shakespeare and even took to correcting the work of these artists. Such delusions are one consequence of an untreated bipolar condition and we know now that the patient has little control over their occurrence. Gurney had previously turned naturally to physical exercise, such as farm-work and walking, to regulate his moods. Such activities were now denied to him although, significantly, Gurney's mother Florence wrote to the authorities in 1933 suggesting that he be brought back to Coney Hill hospital, Gloucester where there was an attached farm and surrounding rural countryside. 'I think he would be better with something to do,' she told them (letter to City of London Mental Hospital, 1933, GA). In hindsight, she might well have been right.

In his better periods, Gurney was quite capable of acting normally, holding lucid conversations – particularly about music and literature – and continuing to write with passion and discipline. Between 1922 and 1926, Gurney wrote literally hundreds of poems. Despite the refusal of his *80 Poems or So* collection in 1922, Gurney had started almost immediately gathering together material for another collection, which he had entitled *Rewards of Wonder* – the subtitle was 'Poems of Cotswold, France and London'. This was effectively finished and sent to Marion Scott in 1924, and he had titles ready for at least another six books. According to a document in the archives (GA), the books he had been preparing included 'Dayspaces and Takings'; 'Ridge Clay, Limestone'; 'La Flandre and By Norton'; 'Roman Gone East'; 'London Seen Clear'; and 'Fatigues and Magnificences' – the names themselves offering a tantalising glimpse of the poet's interest in landscape, geography and history. Recently, in sorting the archives, it has become clear that in the two years 1925 and 1926, Gurney wrote at least 750 poems, most of which are coherent and worthy of publishing (*see* Lancaster, 2010). The music did not come quite so easily to him and yet, in 1925, he seems to have had an outburst of composing. The forty to fifty songs written then are, however, of variable quality.

Despite Marion Scott's efforts to ameliorate his conditions, the one thing that Gurney could never regain was Gloucestershire. Dartford was to remain his home for the rest of his life. Although conditions were improving for mental patients in the twentieth century, this was certainly not a place of home comforts; nor was Gurney going to be able to find any stimulation in a professional sense or in the natural surroundings of Dartford. Apparently, when encouraged to go outside in the hospital grounds one day, Gurney retorted that it was not his idea of countryside! Effectively, he was being condemned to a non-place, somewhere that held no memories, no spark of inspiration and no sense of his own identity. Given the lack of understanding of conditions such as Gurney's in those days, it is not clear exactly how he could have been treated differently, although one wonders whether sending him back to Gloucestershire might have been a more humane response. What is clear is that in losing Gloucestershire, Ivor Gurney was losing his creative muse. This is not to say that he was unable to write poetry or music any more. As we have seen, there was quite an outpouring of poetry, in particular, in the 1922–26 period, and much of it is of very high quality. The *Rewards of Wonder* collection, now gathered together and published by (Walter 2000) has a strong focus on Gloucestershire places. Gurney revels in the sights, sounds and sense impressions of the Severn Meadows and the Cotswold Edge. He is particularly eloquent about the magic blue line of the Cotswolds seen from afar: 'Cotswold Edge shines out at morning in gold' ('Cotswold', p.63); 'Long shines the thin light of the day to north-east, / The line of blue faint known' ('Early Spring Dawn', B, p.79 and RW, p.62); 'Sheer falls of green slope against setting sun' ('Sheer Falls of Green Slope', RW, p.69). He relives the changing day and weather conditions: 'One could not see or think, the heat overcame one, / with a dazzle of square road to challenge and blind one' ('The Cloud', B, p.78 and RW, p.52); 'Smudgy dawn scarfed with military colours / Northward, and flowing wider like slow sea water' ('Smudgy Dawn', B, p.84 and RW, p.59). These are some of his best poems for the sheer intimacy of involvement with a loved place, despite the fact that he was no longer there. As he himself wrote in 'Dawn' (p.79, RW), 'To see the dawn soak darkness, look out now, / Open window, smell the air, and be happy though / The day but one acted routine is known.' In the first few years, Gurney is able to remember and re-imagine his place experiences, to smell the air and be happy despite the acted routines of his everyday life in the asylum. Nevertheless, the last poem in the

Rewards of Wonder collection, significantly entitled 'Poem for End', seems to me to be telling us how difficult this process of living on memory became.

> And all the dawns that set my thoughts new to making;
> Or Crickley dusk that the beech leaves stirred to shaking
> Are put aside – there is a book ended; heart aching.
>
> (B, p. 104; RW, p. 100)

What else is Gurney saying but that he fears he is losing Gloucestershire, and that the direct creative input from his own place is now going? Without the immediate contact, without being there, memory can only last so long and he fears that this book represents the end. He did go on to write many more poems, some of which we are only just beginning to discover because they have lain in the archives for many years. And he did write many more about Gloucestershire, but it seems to me that, for example, in those poems that are available in *Best Poems and The Book of Five Makings* (Thornton and Walter, 1995), we can no longer feel the poet directly in contact with his countryside and even his memory is fading. The writing is more distant, using Gloucestershire places as a conduit for his musings about his childhood, the war, France, the Romans and the Elizabethans. In 'The County's Bastion' (K, 2004, p.248), Gurney writes of 'Bredon, and Nottingham Hill, Cleeve, Crickley and those / Sudden with new beauty, day after unlooked for day'. But he reminds the reader that 'the poet might weep to have such thoughts, but well knows / Earth's poetry calls his pen; nothing his own poetry'. Gurney believed that his role was to express the meaning pouring out of the natural world – it was not his own poetry, but Earth's poetry. Denied his presence in Gloucestershire, the Earth could not speak.

Equally telling are some of the many poems from 1925, gathered in the archives in collections relating to America (e.g. 'Six Poems of the North American States'; 'Poems in Praise of Poets'; 'Poems to the States'; 'Poems of Gloucesters, Gloucester and of Virginia'). The group as a whole explores the American Civil War, American writers and Gloucester's connections with the New World (there was a Gloucester, Massachusetts); but several are distinctive because of their strange format. Despite titles that recall American place-names, particularly Civil War battlefields, the poems are not about the Civil War or historical commentary. 'Rappahannock', 'Culpeper', 'Petersburg', 'Cedar Mountains', 'Wilderness', 'Harper's Ferry', 'Front Royal', 'Salem' – are some examples. The names are all Civil War sites but (in the same order as the list above) as poems they are actually about his early life and war memories, his knowledge of the wild flowers, his father in Gloucestershire, Crickley Hill, Cooper's Hill, Ashleworth ferry, Severn Meadows villages, and Gloucester Cathedral. He rarely explains the connection his mind has made but I suggest that many of them are to do with the way he is trying to unravel what place means to him and how his own intimate connection with Gloucestershire developed. So, for example, looking at the beginning of 'Rappahannock' (p.106), Gurney provides the linking object 'tobacco', of Virginian fame but also a reminder of his memories of smoking while sailing as a young man on the river at Framilode. 'Culpeper' (p.125) reminds him of a poem, in Kipling's *Rewards and Fairies*, that drew on the work of Nicholas Culpeper, seventeenth-century botanist, and listed the medicinal plants growing wild in England; this leads on to his own experience of learning about Gloucestershire

'There is a coppice on Cotswold Edge.' A late autumn scene at dusk on the Cotswold Edge at Leckhampton Hill.

plants as a child, in the meadows and woodlands of home. 'Petersburg' (p.20) suggests Russia, which reminds him of Leo Tolstoy who shares his birth date (28 August), and so his own birth brings him to his father who hoped for a son who would 'say, what he had never never, been able to say or sing of such beloved Earth', i.e. Gloucestershire.

Other writers (Scott, 1998; Scott and Walter, 1998) have investigated the American poetry and suggested that one thing that comes out of it is the connection between the two wars and Gurney's desire to examine this. Whilst this may well be the case for some poems, it is not the case for all. It seems that when examining his atlas, Gurney's mind began to roam back to Gloucestershire. Indeed, in a poem entitled 'Maps' (BP) he tells us how 'one's blood warms' to the lists of names, the location of towns and rivers and the allusions that arise. He needed to understand why and how the meadows and the high hills of Gloucestershire had come to be the centre of his life, and why and how he was losing the connection. These poems are narrative and explanatory, not involved and intimate; they run over past experience rather than burn with present joy. They are not the passionate outpouring of the person who is there on the hilltop at Crickley or in the sailing boat at Framilode. They are the reflections of a detached viewer; the place is 'out there', not 'in here'. Paradoxically, then, Gurney's late asylum poetry is still about place but it is a poetry of absence; the poet is out-of-place.

Some poems of the mid and later 1920s reveal the mental agonies Gurney suffered. There are bitter words that show he felt betrayed: 'betrayed to a hell of anguish without any quiet' ('Rappahannock'); there are some searing lines that are awful to read: 'why have you made my life so intolerable and set me between four walls' and 'I am merely crying and trembling in heart / For Death and cannot get it' ('To God', K, 2004); 'Here no dreams touch me to colour / Sodden state of all-dolour' ('The Depths', K, 2004); 'and I write thus at the year's end, in nine hell-depths, with such memories' ('The Coppice', K, 2004). But most of all there is intense sadness at the Gloucestershire countryside being as lost and unfulfilled without him as he is without it. In 'The Coppice', he speaks of the woodland 'that longs for me tonight as if my name were great / And owner of that swift fall, that wind-beaten swerve; / Were sayer of what the wood's heart could never forget'.

After 1926, the poetry dried up, the poet became silent. Gurney lived on at Dartford, attended always by the faithful Marion Scott. His health was failing; he had problems with his digestion and with his teeth and he began to lose weight in the 1930s. But there are glimpses of the old Gurney. Scott took him out in the car whenever she could and, on one occasion, they visited Dover beach and the Kent coast. In her article 'Recollections of Ivor Gurney' (Scott, 1938),

she recalls that it was a 'day of racing wind and sun, the Channel full of moving colour'. Gurney stood at the water's edge, looking across to France and watching the restless movements of the sea. Perhaps he thought of his war experiences in France or remembered his sailing jaunts on the Severn. This may have been the moment that inspired the poem 'Sea Marge' (or was he remembering Cornwall in 1918?). In any case, 'Sea Marge' is one of his last coherent poems and not only a wonderful and clear evocation of the sounds and patterns at the sea's edge, but a cry of longing for the freedom that the sea represents – to create the 'patterns' and 'glorious music', and to be part of creating new things, in the way that the water is doing at the sea marge.

Gurney standing on the pebbly beach at Dover, 1926.

Sea Marge

Pebbles are beneath, but we stand softly
On them, as on sand, and watch the lacy edge
Of the swift sea.

Which patterns and with glorious music the
Sands and round stones. It talks ever
Of new patterns.

And by the cliff-edge, there, the oakwood throws
A shadow deeper to watch what new thing
Happens at the marge.

(B, p.59)

Another telling incident occurred in 1932, when Gurney was visited by Helen Thomas, the widow of the poet Edward Thomas who had been killed at Arras. Initially shocked by Gurney's appearance and passivity, Helen realised that he was missing the Gloucestershire countryside. She explains what happened (Thomas, 1978):

> Ivor Gurney longed more than anything to go back to his beloved Gloucestershire, but this was not allowed for fear he should try to take his own life. I said 'But surely it would be more humane to let him go there even if it meant no more than an hour of happiness before he killed himself'. But the authorities could not look at it in that way.
>
> The next time I went with Miss Scott I took with me one of Edward's own well-used ordnance maps of Gloucester where he had often walked. This proved to have been a sort of inspiration, for Ivor Gurney at once spread them out on his bed and he and I spent the whole time I was there tracing with our fingers the lanes and byways and villages of which he knew every step and over which Edward had walked. He spent that hour in revisiting his beloved home, in spotting a village or a track, a hill or a wood and seeing it all in his mind's eye, a mental vision sharper and more actual for his heightened intensity. He trod in a way we who were sane could not emulate, the lanes and fields he knew and loved so well, his guide being his finger tracing the way on a map. It was most deeply moving and I knew that I had hit on an idea that gave him more pleasure than anything else I could have thought.
>
> (p.111)

Fig. 4.3: Edward Thomas' Map.

N.b. The map extract is taken from the 1 inch to 1 mile map of 1896, sheet 216, NW Gloucestershire (by kind permission of Alan Godfrey Maps, UK). This is almost certainly the map that Edward Thomas would have used to walk in the area between Dymock and the Severn.

Above: St Matthew's Church at Twigworth, where Gurney was buried in 1937.

Right: Gurney's gravestone at Twigworth church.

For this brief spell, the map (Figure 4.3) became Gurney's memory. He was not only able to reconstruct the landscape, but to place himself there and identify with these places.

Throughout the remaining five years, Gurney's condition declined further. Given his restricted life at Dartford and the delusions that he suffered, it is not surprising that his creativity declined and that he gave up writing both music and poetry. According to the records, Gurney became more bitter and aggressive, occasionally abusive to other patients and asylum staff. Although he continued writing, his later 'poems' and letters seem rambling, disjointed and fragmented. It seems that 'The Wind', with its vivid image of 'Time like a dark wind blowing / All days, all lives, all memories / Down empty endless skies' might have been the last coherent poem he wrote. One can feel the terrible sadness and despair of the man who saw his life's work apparently disregarded, 'a blind wind strowing / Bright leaves of life's torn tree / Through blank eternity.' Ironically, even as his faculties declined, Gurney was, at last, beginning to receive more recognition as a poet and musician. Marion Scott had arranged for a special edition of *Music and Letters* to be focused on Ivor Gurney, and Oxford University Press was to publish twenty of his songs. But, by November 1937, Gurney weighed only 7 stone and was found to be suffering from tuberculosis. As Gurney commented when the proofs of the songs were brought to him, 'It is too late.' He died on 26 December 1937 and then, and only then, was he returned to Gloucester. He was buried in Twigworth church, with the music played by Herbert Howells and his old friend and mentor Alfred Cheesman conducting the service.

THE WIND (extract)
All night the fierce wind blew,
All night I knew
Time, like a dark wind, blowing
All days, all lives, all memories
Down empty endless skies –

A blind wind strowing
Bright leaves of life's torn tree
Through blank eternity:
Dreadfully swift. Time blew.
All night I knew
The outrush of its going.

(K, 2004, p.317)

5

THE OLD CITY: GLOUCESTER

She is a city still and the centuries drape her yet;
Something in the air or light cannot or will not forget
The past ages of her, and the toil which made her

('Time to Come', K, 2004, p.101)

Citizens of Gloucester are justly proud of the home in which their lot has fallen – proud of the beauty of its situation and the grandeur of its cathedral, and proud that they are denizens of an ancient city, rich in historic associations; but perhaps only a few fully realise how good a cause they have for pride. At first sight Gloucester does not appear very differently circumstanced from other county towns. They too, for most part, can boast stately minsters, lovely sites or pre-historic foundations ... but if we look only a little closer we shall find many a difference, and even among our cities whose past has been most eventful, not half a dozen have played so prominent a part on the stage of national history as Gloucester. It shared with York, Colchester and Lincoln, the honour of being one of the four British 'colonia' in the days of the Roman Empire; it was one of the three cities in which our Norman kings held annually a national council; parliaments in the days of the Plantagenets met within its walls; its actions decided, on two occasions, the fate of dynasties; and it has kept its name, wholly in sense and partially in form, for two thousand years.

(F.A. Hyett, *Gloucester in National History*, pp.1-2, 1906)

Ivor Gurney's Gloucester

At the dawn of the twentieth century, Gloucester was a city intensely proud of its history. For Gurney, the city was his home but also a strong presence that influenced his writing in many direct and indirect ways. It is not just that he made continual reference to the city's historic periods (Romans, Saxons, Danes, Normans, Elizabethans, Georgians) and personalities (such as William Rufus, Duke Humphrey, Bishop Hooper), but also that the character and historic presence of the town (referred to in 'Time to Come' (K, 2004, p.101) as 'a shapely fulness of being drawn maybe from the air') seemed to convince him that he was destined to be her chronicler – the 'true child of that dear City – one worthy one'. In 'The Poet Walking' he is proud to think that he is the one chosen to 'marvel at street and stone'. The location mentioned 'where Eastway meets with old Roman Wall' is in Eastgate Street near the present-day Boots store, and very close to the site of Gurney's birthplace at 3 Queen Street (*see* Figure 5.1).

THE POET WALKING
I saw people
Thronging the streets
Where the Eastway with the old
Roman Wall meets –
But none though of old
Gloucester blood brought,
Loved so the city
As I – the poet unthought.
And I exulted there
To think that but one
Of all that City
Had pride or equity
Enough for the marvelling
At street and stone,
Or the age of Briton,
Dane, Roman, Elizabethan –
One grateful one – true child
Of that dear City – one worthy one.

(K, 2004, p. 118)

There were many significant periods of Gloucester's history which exerted influence on the layout, character and buildings of the city (*see* Figures 5.1 and 5.2), the evidence of the past probably more apparent in Gurney's day than at the present time. The earliest settlement seems to have been the Iron Age Caer Glow (favoured place), occupying a dry site above the flood plain near to present-day Longford, where Gurney's aunt lived. There is little left to inform us about this settlement, although finds of decorated pottery suggest that Caer Glow was a relatively civilised place even before the Romans arrived. In the late AD 40s, Gloucester began life as a Roman military fort (at present-day Kingsholm) located at the strategic Severn crossing and providing a base from which the Roman troops could defend their possessions from the hostile Celtic tribes.

By AD 68, the fort was abandoned and the main Roman settlement was moved south-westwards to the current site of Gloucester. The street plan of the central area, based on the four main roads (Eastgate, Southgate, Westgate, Northgate) meeting at the Cross, is one of the Romans' more lasting legacies (*see* Figure 5.1).

In AD 96–98, although the legion moved west to Caerleon, the Romans did not disband Glevum, as they called it, but turned it into one of only four 'colonia' or centres of Roman civilisation in Britain (the other three were Colchester, Lincoln and York). In the following three centuries, Glevum grew to become a fine Roman town, boasting baths, a forum, a basilica and many large houses with courtyards, mosaics and piped water.

Growing up in Gloucester, in a house that straddled the old Roman wall, within sight of the historic cross-roads established by the Romans, and near to the city's main museum, the young Gurney was, not surprisingly, steeped in Roman history. Many of his poems refer to the villas, roads and forts, particularly of the Cotswold Edge (*see* Chapter 7). His poems of Gloucester rarely focus on the Romans as the main topic – more often it is the Normans, the Elizabethans, the Civil War and, of course, his beloved cathedral (St Peter's Abbey) that receive pride of mention. Nevertheless, there is a continual awareness of the legacy owed to Rome and a harking back to the power and prestige of the times ('these four most ancient ways come in', in 'The Old City'; 'Rome, Florence, the bare names are spoken power', in 'On a Town'). It is as if Gurney's Gloucester poetry is forever framed by the order and regularity of Roman roads, streets and buildings.

In the immediate aftermath of Roman withdrawal, Gloucester's fortunes declined and the many fine buildings and roads were abandoned, but the Anglo-Saxons re-settled the place in the sixth century, using the Roman street plan as the basis for their town. By the ninth century, the city was relatively prosperous as a result of its strategic location on the Severn and, although there were

Fig. 5.1: Gloucester in 1901. This is an extract from the Ordnance Survey 1:2500 Gloucestershire Sheet 25.15. Revised 1901, published 1902. The map will no longer be at 1:2500 scale but the linear scale on the map will be correct. (Reproduced by kind permission of the Trustees of the National Library of Scotland)

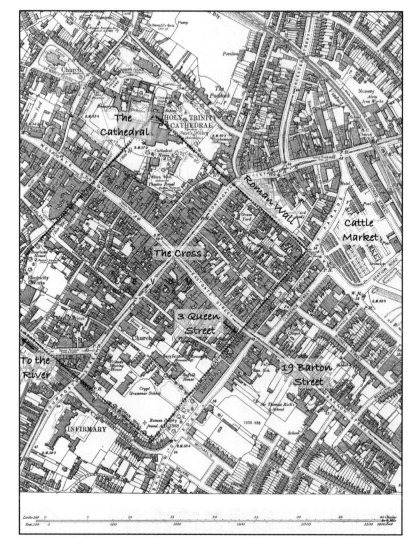

periods of difficulty due to attacks by the Danes, Gloucester was significant enough to warrant a castle being built after the Norman conquest (Gloucester Gaol is now on the former castle site).

The eleventh century was a time of growth and expansion. William the Conqueror held a great court in Gloucester in 1085 where he commissioned the Domesday Book, St Peter's Abbey was founded in 1089, and many churches and monastic houses appeared alongside the densely populated and narrow alleyways of the city. Events of national significance helped to confirm Gloucester's status as one of the major cities of England. These include the crowning of Henry III in St Peter's Abbey in 1216 and the establishment of three great monasteries (Greyfriars, Blackfriars and Whitefriars) in the thirteenth century. The burial of the murdered King Edward II at St Peter's Abbey in 1327, after other abbeys had refused, proved to be particularly advantageous for Gloucester, as it quickly became a place of pilgrimage, creating wealth for the city and cathedral.

In 1541, Henry VIII granted cathedral status to the abbey, so saving it from the destruction suffered by other abbeys. Gloucester flourished as a mercantile city and grew to prosperity under both Henry and Elizabeth. In the reign of Queen Mary (Bloody Mary), Gloucester witnessed one of its less glorious moments when the Bishop of Gloucester, Bishop Hooper, was burnt to death outside Mary de Lode Church, as a punishment for his Protestant leanings – or, as Gurney describes it, 'here Hooper, Bishop, burnt in scorn / While Mary watched his agonies.'

The seventeenth century was a period in which Gloucester's role as a market town developed rapidly. Cattle, sheep, grain and other farm produce were traded in the city's many markets, and professional and commercial services grew up alongside. Politically, progress was less peaceful. Gloucester's role on the Parliamentarian side in the Civil War meant that it suffered from a Royalist siege (1643) and large areas of the city were damaged in the fighting. It is clear that Gurney applauded the more radical and rebellious Parliamentarian side, perhaps seeing an echo of this spirit in the Gloucester of the early twentieth century. In his poem 'The Old City' (K, 2004, p.31), he is convinced that 'here and now I see the strength / in passing faces, that held at bay / Proud Rupert in an arrogant day / Till Essex's train-bands came at length, / And King's Power passed like mist away'. The Parliamentarians, under Colonel Massie, successfully resisted the siege until they were rescued by the Earl of Essex's forces, although the victory was double-edged for Gloucester as the city's Roman walls were destroyed afterwards by a vengeful Charles II. The only stretches of wall still visible in the twentieth century are located under the City Museum and the town centre branch of Boots.

In the eighteenth and nineteenth centuries, the city experienced a vigorous revival as a result of commercial growth connected initially to the roads, river and docks. By 1800, the main industries were flax-making, shipbuilding, pin-making and bell-founding. Although the last two declined by mid-century, those industries connected with transport and trade were given a great boost by the opening of the Gloucester & Sharpness Canal in 1827 and the coming of the railway in the 1840s. The docks and associated warehouses and mills grew rapidly. The city itself expanded across adjacent villages and meadow land, and new facilities like street lamps, drains, hospitals, prisons and libraries were established. By 1891 the city's population had grown to nearly 40,000. This was the period when Gloucester was being refashioned to produce the urban landscape that Gurney saw. New buildings were made of brick and stone, unlike the earlier timber structures. Some grand new buildings were constructed, a good example being the Custom House with its classical façade, opened in 1845 to cope with the anticipated growth in foreign trade. Gurney would have been well aware of this building since it overlooks Commercial Road, the street running down the quayside, about which he wrote in his poem. Significantly, the Custom House

Bishop Hooper's Monument.

The cathedral: 'who says Gloucester sees a tall / Fair fashioned shape of stone arise.'

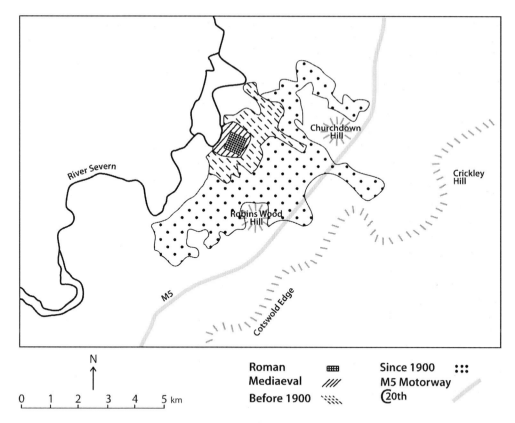

Fig. 5.2: The Growth of Gloucester. This map has been based on information in various historical sources, including Darrell Kirby's *Gloucester* (2007) and on various OS maps of Gloucester and the surrounding area in the nineteenth, twentieth and twenty-first centuries.

became the Soldiers of Gloucester Museum in 1987, and so it is in this building that the records of Gurney's regiment (then called the 1st and 2nd Battalions of the Gloucestershire Regiment) can now be found.

In the nineteenth century, many of the city's older wooden buildings were being refaced with brick. John Clarke, writing in 1850, regretted the loss of the ornamental carvings for which Gloucester's craftsmen were renowned and was anxious about the 'modern fronts of brick, compo and plate glass'. Echoes of this anxiety are found in Gurney's poem, 'Time to Come', in which Gurney worries that 'the respectable and red-brick will rule all' and that 'queerness and untidiness will be ruled out'. Roads were also widened to make way for heavier traffic and, according to Kirby (2007), it was at this time that Gloucester lost its High Cross at the junction of the four main roads, its unusual churches and buildings in the middle of Westgate Street, and the East, North and South Gates themselves.

'The Old City – Gloucester' is one of the poems which best describes the way in which, for Gurney, Gloucester's history was an integral part of its sense of place and a special attraction to him: 'Yet walking Gloucester history seems / A living thing …' The poem moves from making historical references in the first two stanzas to describing the surrounding landscape and setting of the city in the fourth stanza, because, for Gurney, these two features were inextricably interwoven – time and place merged, particularly for the walker. Gloucester is so steeped in its history that the place is alive with these sensations; even the present-day inhabitants ('The passing faces') hold within them the same spirit that prevailed in the sixteenth and seventeenth centuries. Gurney picks out the eras he sees as particularly glorious for Gloucester and England – the Elizabethans withstanding the Spanish Armada; Gloucester holding out against the Royalist siege in the Civil War.

THE OLD CITY – GLOUCESTER (extract)

Who says 'Gloucester' sees a tall
Fair fashioned shape of stone arise,
That changes with the changing skies
From joy to gloom funereal,
Then quick again to joy; and sees
Those four most ancient ways come in
To mix their folk and dust and din
With the keen scent of the sea-breeze.
Here Rome held sway for centuries;
Here Tom Jones slept,
Here Rufus kept
His court, and here was Domesday born,
Here Hooper, Bishop, burned in scorn
While Mary watched his agonies.

Time out of mind these things were dreams,
Mere tales, not touching the quick sense,
Yet walking Gloucester history seems
A living thing and an intense.
For here and now I see the strength
In passing faces, that held at bay
Proud Rupert in an arrogant day
Till Essex' train-bands came at length,
And King's power passed like mist away.
Courage and wisdom that made good
Each tiny freedom, and withstood
The cunning or the strength of great
Unscrupulous lords; and here, elate,
The spirit that sprang to height again
When Philip would conquer the wide Main
And England, and her tigerish queen.

(K, 2004, p.31)

Gloucester's history has been strongly influenced by its site and situation, and these features are also alluded to by Gurney in 'The Old City', including the river bridge at Over, the meadows, ('the surprising, the enormous Severn Plain / So wide, so fair') and the constant backdrop of hills. Lying at a natural crossing point over the river, Gloucester was, until 1966 and the building of the first Severn Bridge at Aust, the lowest bridging point on the Severn. The river has provided fish and fertile meadow land, and drier patches of river terrace to use for settlement above the flood plain. The site meant that Gloucester has always been a meeting point, not only between Roman and Briton, Celt and Saxon, English and Welsh, but also between the younger landscapes and softer rocks of the English Midlands supporting arable and dairy farming, and the older, harder rocks of the Welsh uplands and mountains mainly used as grazing. As Hurd has described it (1978, p.18), Gloucester 'is in every sense a crossroads; a place of arrival and departure, of mingling, sifting, blending and separating'. Hurd explains how significant all this was for Gurney. Gloucester was a place which offered immense variety and stimulus for a young poet and musician.

It is not one city; it is several. And at the turn of the century its different faces would have been more obvious than they are perhaps today. Down from the hills and up from the Severn plain came sheep and cattle, wheat and vegetables, all heading for Gloucester the market town. Along the roads, along the Gloucester-Berkeley canal, along the Midland railway and the Great Western (for here the narrow gauge and the broad gauge had met in bitter rivalry) went goods from Gloucester the industrial centre. Up and down that canal floated barges and sailing ships to the Port of Gloucester – the furthest inland of the whole country. Magnificent and serene above the bustle, stood the great Cathedral Church of St Peter. In Gloucester town met country and country met sea.

(Hurd, p.18)

The Fascinating City

Figure 5.3 presents twenty-six poems written directly about Gloucester or its features and it attempts to illuminate some of the themes that interested Gurney. There are, of course, many other poems in which there are hints and references to Gurney's home city if the reader is alert to find them, and there will almost certainly be more Gloucester poems still in the archives awaiting publication. Those Gloucester poems written directly about the city from within (e.g. 'The Old City', 'The Poet Walking', 'Time to Come') do not evoke the same involuntary rush of joy that characterises Gurney's roaming of the wilder countryside of the Cotswolds and Severn Meadows. They are more measured and ordered, revealing a deep fascination and respect for the history and shaping of the urban landscape. One gets the impression that, whilst he strode rapidly across the countryside, soaking up the sense impressions ('O up in height, O snatcht up, O swiftly going...' in 'Old Thought'), in Gloucester he walked more carefully and wonderingly, observing and reflecting on people and events ('I saw the people thronging the streets...' in 'The Poet Walking').

Fig. 5.3: Poems of Gloucester.

Title of Poem	Theme or Occasion
Down Commercial Road Day-boys and Choristers The Vicarage	Poems about memories of childhood and youth in Gloucester. 'Down Commercial Road' recalls walking as a child with his mother down to the docks; 'Day-boys and Choristers' is a memory of school days; 'The Vicarage' refers to a stay with Canon Alfred Cheesman in Twigworth village on the edge of Gloucester. All written 1915–18.
The Old City Saturday's Comings The Poet Walking Blessings The Day of Victory On a Two Hundredth Birthday The Tax Office	'The Old City', originally written at Buire au Bois, France in 1917. Others are poems about living, walking and working in Gloucester in the period between the end of the war and incarceration in mental hospitals (1918–22). 'Blessings' was originally entitled 'Under Robinswood Hill' (1918) but was later placed in the *80 Poems or So* collection. 'Saturday's Comings' describes the livestock market, then in Kings' Square, Gloucester. 'The Tax Office' refers to the office where Gurney briefly worked in 1922. 'The Day of Victory' and 'On a Two Hundredth Birthday' are both poems written for occasions – the first on the day the 1914–18 war ended and the second on the 200th anniversary of founding the city's first newspaper, the *Gloucester Journal* (9 April 1722).
Above Maisemore There Was Such Beauty Smudgy Dawn Longford Dawns On a Western City Gloucester	Poems about the setting of Gloucester in its surrounding country-side and the beauty revealed in the 'long view'. 'There Was Such Beauty' and 'Smudgy Dawn' (also known as 'Spring Dawn' and published in *London Mercury*, 1924) do not mention Gloucester by name, but there are many clues which suggest that it is Gloucester to which the first refers and that the second was written when Gurney was staying with his aunt in Langford. Despite its title, 'Gloucester', this poem is mainly about the daffodils that characterised the meadows around the city every spring in the early twentieth century. All written in the early 1920s.

Title of Poem	Theme or Occasion
The Town On A Town Time to Come	Poems written for Gurney's proposed third volume of poetry – *80 Poems or So* – revealing Gurney's interest in 'realty' or the physical, everyday reality of common activities and events. Each poem regrets unthinking change and praises the mix of past and present, old and new. The publisher turned down *80 Poems or So* in 1922.
The Abbey The House of Stone From the Meadows – The Abbey The Tower Ship Over Meadows (Gurney archives) Salem (Gurney archives)	Poems about the cathedral (St Peter's Abbey) 1920–26. Many references to the cathedral appear in other poems, where the cathedral is really a symbol for Gloucester's historic significance and beauty. 'The Tower' (*War's Embers*) recounts seeing the cathedral tower from the west and is dedicated to Margaret Hunt. 'The Abbey' talks of the Cotswold Edge quarries 'where these stones grew' – *see* p.89 for more detail. Duke Humphrey, mentioned in 'The House of Stone', was Duke of Gloucester in the mid-fifteenth century. Kavanagh (2004) suggests that 'From the Meadows – The Abbey' is about Tewkesbury Abbey but I am sure it is Gloucester. 'Ship Over Meadows' and 'Salem' are both formerly unpublished. 'Salem' is one of the New England poems; the name is an American Civil War battle site though the content is mainly Gloucester-based (*see* p.71).
The Bridge	This poem, written in 1926, is seen by Kavanagh as Gurney saying goodbye to Gloucester. Its reference to the half-haggard lady (the River Severn) and the changes that have taken place in the city make it one of the saddest poems he wrote, suggests Kavanagh (2004, p.xxv).

N.b. This is not intended to be an exhaustive list of Gloucester poems, either published or unpublished. It is a selection and the comments are my own, unless attributed.

A small number of poems look back to his childhood and were published in *War's Embers* in 1919. 'Down Commercial Road' and 'Day Boys and Choristers' both present sentimental views of growing up in Gloucester, the first remembering walking with his mother down Commercial Road to the docks, and the second, written about his school days at the King's School, Gloucester. In the King's School poem, the song-like format of the piece with its rousing chorus – 'So here's to the room where the dark beams cross over, / And here's to the cupboard where hides the cane' – provides a poignant counterpoint to the reminder that most of the school boys ended up fighting in Flanders: 'When Fritz stops his fooling we'll see them again.'

These are early Gurney, in which his memories are relatively unscathed by the doubts, depression and resentment that occur in later work. They are descriptive and nostalgic; he recalls his fascination with the sea and sailors in 'Down Commercial Road', and can still pronounce confidently in 'Day Boys and Choristers' that Europe will honour his old school mates and 'a whole world praise them' after they return from the battlefields. In later poems, he was bitter that this had not happened. 'Twigworth Vicarage', also in *War's Embers*, is dedicated to Alfred Cheesman, who first agreed to be Gurney's godfather when vicar at All Saints' Church, Gloucester but later (1914) became vicar at Twigworth church. The poem refers to occasions when Gurney would stay at the vicarage, and it recalls his delight in the peace and beauty of Gloucester's surrounding countryside visible from Twigworth – May Hill, Maisemore's delightful ridge, Wainlode's and Ashleworth.

Some Gloucester poems observe Gloucester's history, buildings and activities in the period 1918–22. 'Saturday's Comings' is a colourful evocation of the Gloucester cattle market, in

The King's School, Gloucester, which Gurney attended. (2010)   The Cattle Market in the mid-twentieth century. (Gloucestershire Archives)

Gurney's day held in King's Square since 1823. The cattle and sheep were driven into town along the main streets, causing much noise and excitement and the provision of local stalls and events to cash in on the increased business. Gurney's poem sets the scene with early-morning mist rising off the Severn, and moves on to the detail of the 'traffic marks' (cart wheels and hooves), 'dapper farmers', and 'bookstalls past paupers' resisting'.

SATURDAY'S COMINGS

The horses of day plunge and are restrained,
Dawn broadens to quarter height, and the meadow mists
Drift like gauze veilings, the roadway ingrained
With traffic marks shows so, Saturday enters the lists

To show like a panorama – cattle brought in
And dapper farmers bargaining in white spats,
Cross crowded, bookstalls past paupers' resisting
And as ever the Cathedral masterfully blessing the flats.

(B, p.39; K, 2004, p.77)

Several Gloucester poems appear in the innovative *80 Poems or So* collection that was eventually published in 1997 (Walter and Thornton). Three of these poems reveal that one of the new themes that Gurney was interested in was that of 'realty'. Originally a legal term, used for example in wills, realty means the physical, direct world of the present. Gerard Manley Hopkins, another poet who influenced Gurney, used the term in his poem 'Dun Scotus' Oxford'. In the three poems ('The Town', 'On a Town' and 'Time to Come') Gurney praises the common everyday features and activities of Gloucester. In 'The Town' (80P, p.81), he talks of 'homely cities with plain Georgian look'. He draws attention to alleyways and 'queer, inconsequent marble, hoop, skipping playgrounds of the ragged', to girls 'learned in flower names' and to boys who 'go leagues for flowers and know foxes' lairs, swim and get fish from out their border river'. All these are to be celebrated: 'downnoted in a book, / Before progress has marched them out of door.' In 'On A Town' (80P, p.78), he refers to Gloucester as the 'Western City' in which 'realty holds so strong the actual hour' and where there is an 'undercurrent of deep strength' seen 'in casual day-business of fold or pen'. 'Time to Come' (80P, p.83) talks of 'small shops', 'skip games in the gutter', 'ten o'clock flirtings' and contrasts all these with the dullness and uniformity likely to result if 'queerness and untidiness' are smoothed out. Gurney was keen to preserve traditions, attitudes and physical symbols of a town's (and nation's) history. The last three lines of 'The Town', which apparently Gurney rewrote several times (Walter

Narrow alleyways of
Gloucester; College Court
near the cathedral in 2010.

The Westgate Street tram terminus in the late nineteenth century.
(Gloucestershire Archives)

and Thornton, p.138), have a distinct flavour of the kind of patriotism characterised in John Major's speech of 1992: 'Where trams are rattly and a losing game / And 'England' is a thought of fields outside, / And Cricket, or strange journeys at Whitsuntide.'

But Gurney was not perpetuating a rosy, sentimental view of England and his home town. He saw all the problems of poverty, poor housing and lack of employment for returning soldiers and was eloquent about the social improvements that needed to be done (e.g. in the poem 'North Woolwich'). What the Gloucester poems show is that he realised how crucial to England was the mix of past and present, town and country, modern and traditional. Rebuilding new but drab houses and disconnecting people completely from their rural origins was not, for him, an acceptable approach. Gurney, unknowingly anticipating one of the greatest concerns of the twenty-first century, feared that in times to come, the sons of our great grandsons 'will know no reason for the old love of the land'. The last verse of 'Time to Come' expounds Gurney's belief in the potential that cities like Gloucester provided for a satisfying future life.

> We see her well, and should have great thanksgiving,
> Living in sight and form of more than common living.

> (K, 2004, p.101)

'The Bridge', written in 1926, needs to be considered alone. It seems to deal with the ending of some traditional ceremony that had always taken place on Westgate Bridge ('ceremony that the boys loved is no more'). Perhaps Gurney had heard about this from a Gloucester visitor or his mother's letters? The poem is also a sad reflection on Gurney's state of mind in Dartford Asylum at that time, revealing as it does his feeling of betrayal and despair. It may have been the last Gloucester poem written. In his mind, the history of the city is being forgotten – the old gates, the old bridges, the historic ceremonies and personalities (such as Duke Humphrey). Now he envisages the river constrained by man's developments ('a dirty water drifts between crampt borders'), whilst looking down from the Cotswold slopes he imagines 'in far ravines and on heights love delights in / The trees will pity the haggard half-lady / Of crystal-sprung Severn / The flowers beneath accuse angels betraying.' (K, 2004, p.308) Remember that the man who wrote this had not seen Gloucester for four years; the horror was mainly in his mind, images of Gloucester being used to project his personal and creative despair.

Gloucester in its Setting

Several poems (*see* Figure 5.3) can be selected to show how Gurney appreciated the site and setting of Gloucester and its closeness to the land. 'Above Maisemore' and 'There Was Such Beauty' both date from the 1918–19 period when, despite illness and difficulties following his discharge from the army, Gurney was writing prolifically. The similarity of vision in these poems is striking. It is almost a painterly view of Gloucester that Gurney presents, dominated by St Peter's Abbey (the cathedral) and, nestling harmoniously next to the river, 'town, tower, trees'. In both poems, one senses the sky and the clouds of a spring or early summer day (dim azure in 'Above Maisemore', royal azure in 'There Was Such Beauty') and is aware of the green meadows and pasturelands skirting the city. Gurney makes much of the sense of this place: 'sober and glorious city of the plain'; 'the gathered loveliness of all the years'; 'the power felt of the day'. For me, these poems recall Wordsworth's sonnet 'On Westminster Bridge' (*see* Figure 5.4), not only in the way the poet is observing a beloved city from a vantage point, but even more directly in the wording and sentiments aroused. Like Wordsworth, Gurney feels the deep sense of contentment and happiness deriving from the sense of place: 'Harbour of peace, haven for contented and high art, / Desire is satisfied, sorrow finds salve in you' he writes in 'There was such Beauty'; 'no beast no clod so dull / But the power felt of the day and of the giver / Was glad for life, humble at once and proud' he echoes in 'Above Maisemore'. Both sentiments recall Wordsworth's famous lines from 'On Westminster Bridge': 'Ne'er saw I, never felt a calm so deep.' We know that Gurney had read Wordsworth and was influenced by his philosophy of reflecting on beautiful scenes in tranquillity after the immediate event that had inspired joy. In a letter to Matilda Chapman, October 1915, Gurney wrote: 'My mind gradually tranquillises itself and more and more I see that splendid teacher Wordsworth is for all sorts of men.' It is clear that he knew the Westminster Bridge sonnet very well. Writing to Marion Scott in 1917, he adapts a line from this sonnet as an ironic comment on the fact that each year of wartime seems bloodier than the last: 'Dear houses, the very God does seem asleep.' (29 November 1917)

Fig. 5.4: Wordsworth and Gurney; visions of a city.

Composed Upon Westminster Bridge (London) William Wordsworth, 1803 (full poem)	Above Maisemore (AM) and There Was Such Beauty (TWSB) (Gloucester) Ivor Gurney, 1918–19 (extracts only – you are advised to read full versions in B pp. 52 and 30 as below, also in K, 2004, pp. 43 and 45 – slightly different)
Earth has not anything to show more fair: Dull would he be of soul who could pass by A sight so touching in its majesty:	There was such beauty in the dappled valley As hurt the sight, as stabbed the heart to tears (TWSB)
This city now doth like a garment wear The beauty of the morning, silent, bare, Ships domes theatres and temples lie Open unto the fields and to the sky; All bright and glittering in the smokeless air.	Oh lovely city! All the valley blue Covers thee like a garment of soft art (AM) Town, tower, trees, river Under a royal azure sky for ever Up-piled with snowy, towering bulks of cloud: (TWSB)
Never did sun more beautifully steep In his first splendor valley, rock or hill;	A herald day of spring more wonderful Than her true own. Trumpets cried aloud In sky, earth, blood: (TWSB)

Ne'er saw I, never felt a calm so deep! The river glideth at his own sweet will: Dear God! The very houses seem asleep; And all that mighty heart is lying still!	Harbour of peace; haven for contented and high heart, Desire is satisfied, sorrow finds salve in you (AM) … no beast, no clod so dull But of the day, and of the giver Was glad for life, humble at once and proud (TWSB)

It is interesting to note that although the Gurney poems are not classic sonnets – each has fifteen lines, as printed in Blunden and Kavanagh 2004, instead of fourteen lines – in the original manuscript version of 'Above Maisemore' in the archives, the poem has no line 9 and is therefore a regular sonnet. Wordsworth's sonnet was written after the event and drew on the notes made by his sister Dorothy. In Gurney's case, he described one occasion, in a letter to Marion Scott dated 17 March 1919, when he felt such joy at the sight of Gloucester: 'O but you should have seen last Thursday! The whole world seemed to exult and glory in mere being! A Beethoven day by the Lord!'

There are many of Gurney's poems that conjure up images of the Severn Meadows at different seasons and in diverse conditions (*see* Chapter 6), but three are located by the wording or title, so that we know the poet was observing from within or on the edge of Gloucester. 'Smudgy Dawn' and 'Longford Dawns' were, I believe, written at about the same time (*see* Figure 5.3). They probably refer to the period from February 1921 to August 1922 when, apart from being away over December and January, Gurney was living with his aunt Marie in Longford. Longford is now a suburb on the northern edge of Gloucester; in Gurney's day it was still a relatively separate village straddling the road leading northward to Tewkesbury. To the west were open meadowlands and the broad meandering River Severn; to the east and north-east were views of the Cotswold Edge. Gurney tried various jobs, including farm labouring, as he explained in letters to Marion Scott at this time, but he was also writing poetry and music and reading widely. Apparently, he often worked late, frequently abandoning the writing to walk out into the dark countryside, rarely returning before dawn. In 'Smudgy Dawn' (RW), he describes a sunrise as he looks northward and eastward; the mention of 'railings' seem to place him in a settlement – he is possibly walking out along the main Tewkesbury road from his aunt's house. The skies are grey to the west but there are glorious colours observed in the north-east and the sun (the imaginatively-named 'fire-swinger') is beginning to appear 'behind the elm pillars'. All these promise a day worthy of such beginnings. The line 'waves readied for laughter' brings to mind the sparkling low sunlight sending ripples of light across the water as the sun gains height. Gurney is inspired by the dawn display to return to his room and work again. 'Longford Dawns' (K, 2004), clearly located in the village by the title, compares Gloucester dawns with those in London, where Gurney recently spent several weeks (December 1921 to January 1922). He notes that, even though it happens everywhere ('time's duty to lift light's curtain up and down'), dawn does not seem to be such a striking event in the city of London, as it does here in the Gloucester meadows. A letter to Marion Scott (10 May 1922) tells her about 'the chief luck of living out at Longford where the neighbor [*sic*] meadows are matchless – such arrangement of trees, such light, and levelness never known'.

'Blessings' is a short piece consisting of rhyming couplets, which gives it a jaunty air. Nevertheless, it has significance in giving us a picture of the poet standing, looking down on Gloucester in its wider setting. A first version with the title 'Under Robinswood Hill' was written from that vantage point in 1918 (a 1926 version was called 'From Robinswood Hill'). We can imagine Gurney standing on that small hill a couple of miles to the south-west of the city centre, surveying the churches and cathedral he knew and loved, whilst ever aware of the surrounding hills of the Cotswold Edge and the landscapes of the Severn valley below him.

The poem 'Gloucester' is all about daffodils ('dancers'). Perhaps Gurney is referring to Wordsworth's famous poem 'Daffodils' when he talks of the many who have praised 'dancers', but his imaginative reconstruction of the daffodil fields is quite distinctive to him and to the Gloucestershire landscape. In the early springtime, the meadows around the city and surrounding villages of Maisemore, Newent and Minsterworth were well known for the magnificent show of native daffodils ('princesses' as opposed to 'foreigners' that were non-native species). Local people had always picked bunches to sell in Gloucester market and, by the early twentieth century, lorry loads of flowers were being sent to London as well. Gurney draws a sharp visual image, mentioning the distinctive red soils of the area ('ruddy lit lands'), the green of the spring grass bright and clear after the bleakness of winter, and the far off shapes of the Cotswold Hills.

GLOUCESTER

Many have praised dancers
As folk of fine pride –
And I have seen foreigners
Dance, beauty revealed.

But on sombre ruddy
Lit lands of Gloucester –
Suddenly in March, suddenly
Gold princesses were master

Of lovely and emerald lit fields
Winter saw desolate…
They sang to far hills melodies
Like Easter water in spate.

They were like young children come
To a century-lonely house –
Heralds of glory should soon foam
And glitter beside the hedgerows.

(K, 2004, p.276)

The poem, 'On a Western City' (80P, p.76), also talks of the daffodil trade and comments on how strange it is to realise that Gloucester's daffodils are being sold amidst the 'jostling business-people, rush of cab and petrol-car' in London. Gurney seems to be making a case for young people to have the full experience of living close to nature and seeing the daffodils grow wild (as Gloucester boys do who 'go out to gather / (a half day travel) daffodils on red pastures; / Of hidden byways and lone copses are they masters'). Nothing can compare to the sight of 'Daffodils sprung like flames from red lands bleeding'. In London, the daffodil has become a mere symbol – 'This Eastertide, the London Churches will fill / With children who should seek the daffodil / And anthems will mouths sing that dumb should be / Before the sudden store under the ringed tree.'

The House of Stone; Gloucester Cathedral (*see* colour illustrations 2 and 3)

As a King's School boy, chorister and later an articled pupil of Herbert Brewer, the organist at the cathedral, Gurney had a special affection for and understanding of Gloucester Cathedral. Generally acknowledged to be one of the finest cathedrals in England, the original St Peter's Abbey, built of wood, was founded in 681 by Osric, ruler of the Saxon Hwicce tribe. Over the centuries that followed, the abbey's fortunes rose and fell according to the politics and personalities of the time, being rebuilt and extended in the good times and left to stagnate in the bad times. Notable periods of growth were in the eleventh century under the patronage of the Norman Abbot Serlo, and in the fourteenth century when a major reconstruction followed the burial in the Abbey Church of the murdered King Edward II. His son, Edward III, provided funds to transform the area around the tomb, and pilgrims flocked to see and donate money to the abbey. The result, according to Mead (2003), 'was one of the finest Perpendicular sections of any

Gloucester Cathedral in its setting; a view
from Cooper's Hill, 2010. (Philip Wade)

The cathedral; the East End and
the Crecy Window.

English cathedral and – largely due to the influx of pilgrims – the city of Gloucester became the
15th wealthiest town in the country.' (p.91)

During the Reformation, St Peter's Abbey was dissolved by Henry VIII but, although some
minor monastic buildings were destroyed, the Abbey Church was lucky enough to be made
a cathedral in its own right in 1541. So, Gloucester Cathedral survived to prosper in later
generations. The last big period of expansion was in Victorian times, when the presbytery and
choir were paved, the choir sub-stalls and Bishop's throne established, a new high altar reredos
designed and a substantial amount of new glass installed. At that time, the cathedral was the
substantial and elegant building that still attracts tourists today, bearing within it the signs of all
these eras of growth. Notable is the contrast between the predominantly Norman nave with
its massive Norman columns and rounded arches, and the fine Perpendicular architecture of
the East End presenting delicate vaulting, the Lady Chapel and the huge East Window. The
latter dates from about 1350 and commemorates those who fought at the battle of Crécy (1346).
The cloisters, built 1351–1412, form a square walkway which originally connected all the
monastic buildings, and are noted for their mediaeval atmosphere and fine fan vaulting.

We know that the cathedral was a strong presence in the young Gurney's life and that he
was thrilled, as a choir boy and cathedral scholar, to be part of the historic narrative of the
ancient building. An unfinished fragment in one of his notebooks (mentioned by Kavanagh,
2004, p.xxxiii) explains that:

> The squareness of west Gloucester pleases me.
> The spires and square places and the supremacy
> Peter's Place has above that white-looked stretch,
> The river meadows…

Given this, it is perhaps surprising that there are not more published poems about the cathedral
itself. Judging by poem titles, there are only four short pieces directly focused on Gloucester
Cathedral – 'The Tower' (*War's Embers*),'The Abbey' (*Rewards of Wonder*), 'From the Meadows –
The Abbey', and 'The House of Stone' (the last two published in Kavanagh, 2004); however,
there are almost certainly more in the unpublished material, and two ('Ship Over Meadows' and
'Salem') will be mentioned later.

In each case, the poem is using the cathedral as a symbol of some important idea or emotion.
In 'The Tower' (WE, p.93), written at an early stage in Gurney's war service, he is still convinced

that the war is a noble cause and the big idea behind this poem is patriotism. Looking at the cathedral tower from the west, he exclaims, 'And then I knew, I knew why men must choose / Rather the dangerous path of arms than let / Beauty be broken.'

In 'From the Meadows – The Abbey', bitterness and depression are at the fore. This is a poem reflecting one of Gurney's depressive periods, before he entered Barnwood Mental Hospital. It is as if, seeing the familiar view of the cathedral from afar, Gurney realises the extent of his pain and misery. He can no longer enjoy even this sight – 'What sorrow raised you mighty, for I have forgotten joy / And know only sufficient urge of black pain,' he writes (K, 2004, p. 182).

According to Kavanagh's notes (2004, p. 377), the abbey refers to Tewkesbury Abbey; but I wonder on what this statement is based, as the description and tone seem to suggest Gloucester. Gurney frequently viewed the cathedral from the meadows to the west. However, such simple analyses may hide the deeper significance of the cathedral to Gurney. It is a symbol of Gloucestershire and, as such, represents a deep sense of history and identity; it is the place he loved and through which he expressed his creativity. In the unpublished poems, 'Salem' and 'Ship Over Meadows', Gurney examines the way in which the cathedral not only 'ruled the meadows' ('Salem') or 'rules the plain' ('Ship') but also stands for stability: 'One never feared it would alter or change' ('Salem') and 'guards a deeper peace' ('Ship') and represents English history and identity. The image of the cathedral as a 'ship' in its 'sea' of meadows is perfect, as anyone who has glimpsed the cathedral when driving in from the west will know (*see* illustrated map), although the twentieth century did its best to close in the view with railway lines and electricity pylons, as Gurney feared.

Ship over Meadows

Like any ship over green peaceful seas
But mightier, more full of peace the Abbey stands.
Segovia they say lifts up ceremonial hands.
This rules the plain, and guards a deeper peace
Than is known on the main.
Whether the centuries shall close that out
With factory chimneys or high railway walls
None knows, but meanwhile the quaker quivers its veils
And the moondaisy boasts, and its pretences found out.

(GA, 1922)

'The Abbey' and 'The House of Stone' celebrate a sense of history. 'The Abbey' (RW, p. 96) is interesting because it links the cathedral with its rural hinterland, wondering about the stones from Cranham and Cooper's Hill quarries that were used in building. It also mirrors Gurney's own explorations up the scarp slope to the east of Gloucester. This poem probably needs to be read alongside an unpublished piece entitled 'Twyver Begins' (GA, 1925), because this explains the historic significance of the tiny Twyver stream, a tributary of the Severn flowing in from the Cotswold Edge. According to Gurney, the Twyver was used to float rafts of stone from the quarries of Cooper's Hill down to the abbey site, probably in the eleventh and twelfth centuries (*see* Figure 5.5).

The Abbey

If I could know the quarry where these stones grew
A thousand years ago: I would turn east now
And climb Portway with my blood fretted all grew
With the frightened beeches with that strange wind-kindled rough row.

And there, grown over with blackberry and perhaps stray ferns
Willowherb, tansy, horehound, other wonders (here to come)
I should find a wide pit fit for a masque★ (if the turns
Of such should ever again) with tree screens and robing room.

(RW, p. 96)

★ Gurney is thinking of an Elizabethan masque or short play, being performed outdoors. *See* also 'By Severn' p. 97)

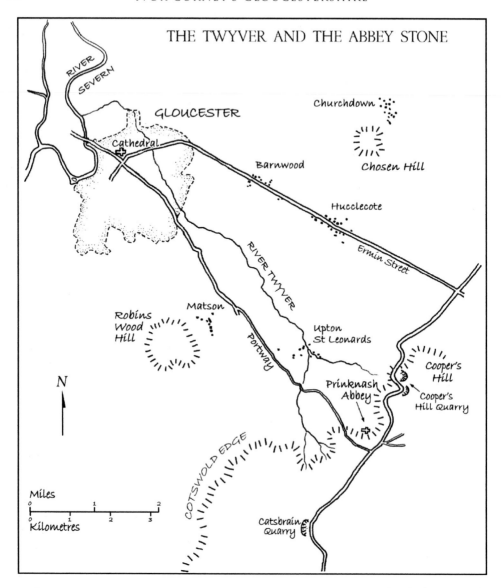

Fig. 5.5: The Twyver and the Abbey Stone. (Map by Roger Ellis, 2010)

TWYVER BEGINS

Twyver or another begins in a little copse
Beneath the Roman height where the road bends abrupt,
So as to be loved by Springtime, the violet shaft
And mantle of purple delicate for the rapt
Walker by roads long sacred from many worships.
In pretty swaddling clothes indeed is she lapt,
The tiny Twyver who bore down to Gloucester the raft
Or rafts of stone built Abbey high in April to be caught
By the far distant watcher on other land, the tops,
The tiny Twyver with harebells and such like mapped
With Coopers, and with Prinknash, has history wrapt
Round Her, not many miles does she sparkle and lapse,
The Severn receives Her, Her one life is soon absorbed.

(GA, 1925)

The cathedral
through an archway.

The shape and atmosphere of the cathedral are present in many of Gurney's poems, even when the cathedral is not directly mentioned. He frequently talks, for example, of 'the tower', 'fair fashioned shape of stone', 'St Peter's', 'the Abbey', remembering its glory and the promise of return, when in France or London, or otherwise alienated from his home places. What is more, the architecture seems to be an important influence on his writing. For those who read Gurney for the first time, there are frequent and mysterious references to words such as square, square-shaping, square-making and framing. In the cathedral and the churches of Gloucester he was surrounded, from an early age, by the square shapes of towers, the framed windows and archways, and the precise placing of columns and cloisters. Not only were these visual images of solidity, and square or perfect form, they were also the magnificent products of craftsmanship that Gurney admired. One meaning of 'squaring' seems to derive from such craftsmanship; it refers to the idea of estimating, predicting and measuring precisely so that carpentry, architecture, stone working and design can be finished off to perfection. Interestingly, Seamus Heaney refers to squarings in a poem with this title: 'In the game of marbles, squarings / Were all those anglings, aimings, feints and squints / You were allowed before you'd shot.' So there is a similar emphasis on aiming for perfection and accuracy.

Gurney saw himself as a craftsman, his words and his music requiring him to exercise skill and judgment, following on from the initial and less controllable sources of inspiration. In 'Compensations', he explains this sequence of creativity: 'Spring larch should set the body shaking / In masterless pleasure, [i.e. the inspiration] / But virtue lies in a square-making' (the craftsmanship). In 'Masterpiece'(K, 2004, p.214), a whole poem about the process of creating music, he refers to the 'night worker writing his square work out' as the necessary stage once the creative thought has arisen 'like dark fires'. He uses the term squaring when referring to other creative artists as well – for example, William Byrd 'master and squarer of sound' (K, 2004, p.335). Seen in this way, it is not fanciful to suggest that Gurney's sense of form in poetry and music was influenced by the ecclesiastical architecture all around him. Edmund Blunden, in the *Introduction to Poems of Ivor Gurney* (1973, p.26) speaks of Gurney's 'quick sensibilities awakening among ancient buildings, especially country churches; he grew up with instances of old craftsmanship in carved work, wood or stone, ever in view'. For Blunden, Gurney's poetry consequently 'has its sweetness' but also has 'sharpness and severity' and 'something of the high-poised gargoyle against the flying cloud'.

Finally, no discussion of the role of the cathedral in Gurney's poetry could fail to mention the church music. I do not have the musical expertise to trace the influence of musical form on the patterns and rhythms of his writing – though others have done so (Lancaster, 2007). It is, however, clear from Gurney's letters, writings and poetry that the beauty of the music in which he was immersed as a boy and young man, growing up and studying in Gloucester, made a huge impact on his creative development. In Gurney's essay 'The Springs of Music', he explains that, for him, 'the springs of music are identical with those of the springs of all beauty remembered by the heart' and that poetry arises from these same springs, often serving to stir the musician to 'height of music'. Essentially, Gurney was saying that music, poetry and the creative emotions are all linked with the experience of beauty, whether found in natural landscape, culture or craftmanship. He recognised that 'in Bach is fairy tale, firelight, cathedral space (of this a great deal), much human friendliness'. The sight of Gloucester Cathedral symbolised home and country, but it also brought to mind music: 'To see Great Peter's like 'Leonora' over Severn meadows,' he writes in 'The Elements'(K, 2004, p.255), as he describes his writing and walking routine while staying with his aunt at Longford. 'Leonora' is the Beethoven overture; the cathedral moves him to inspiration and music. The fine building, the peaceful meadows, the River Severn, the magnificent music are all intimately connected in his mind. Indeed, it may be suggested that the best of Gurney's Gloucester poems are those which invoke the town in its wider setting ('Above Maisemore', 'There Was Such Beauty', 'Smudgy Dawn'). Although he was born in the city, those who listen to his poetry and music sense that Gurney's greatest inspiration came from the natural world, from the hills, the beech-woods and the river meadows. But these are essential to Gloucester as well as the streets and houses and docklands. Gurney's vision was of countryside and town both being necessary for the good life. What is more, as this chapter has aimed to show, the city of Gloucester made a huge impact on his sense of history, on his understanding of craftsmanship and on his belief in the social welfare of the working man.

6

THE SEVERN MEADOWS

And so to Minsterworth meadows where Ivor Gurney's ghost
walks in sunlight, unforgotten;

('Severn Bore', Catherine Fisher:
Between the Severn and the Wye, 1993, p.113)

Of all significant things, the most striking, poignant, passioning, is the sight of a great valley at the end of the day – such as the Severn Valley which lies hushed and dark, infinitely full of meaning, while yet the far Welsh hills are touched with living and ecstatic gold. The first breakings of the air of night, the remembrance of the glory not all yet faded; the meeting of the two pageants of day and night so powerfully stir the heart that music alone may assuage its thirst, or satisfy that longing told by Wordsworth in the 'Prelude'; but that telling and outpouring of his is but the shadow and faint far-off indication of what Music might do – the chief use of Poetry seeming to be, to one, perhaps mistaken, musician, to stir his spirit to the height of music, the maker to create, the listener worthily to receive or remember.

('The Springs of Music', Ivor Gurney, 1922)

Ivor Gurney's Severn Meadows

The great valley of the River Severn above and below Gloucester was the first area, outside the city itself, to be explored by the young Ivor Gurney. He was born a town boy but almost effortlessly developed a rapport with the countryside. As we have seen in Chapter 2, his parents, David and Florence Gurney, were both country people, hailing from the Severn Meadows and Cotswold Hills respectively. Walking out into the Severn Meadows would have been one of young Ivor's earliest memories when the Gurney family visited the children's paternal grandmother at Maisemore. The poem 'Petersburg' (Chapter 2) recognises the immense debt that Gurney owes his father in learning country lore: 'his was the friendliness of every hill and tree in all West Gloucestershire.' It also makes clear his father's expectation that Ivor, the first son, was destined to speak out for Gloucestershire.

Walks with his family were soon augmented by his own explorations of Gloucester, upstream to the open meadows, farmlands and orchards of Longford, Twigworth, Sandhurst, Norton and Apperley and, on the other side of the river, Highnam, Lassington, Woolridge, Hartpury, Ashleworth, Hasfield and Corse. 'Too much food, too few hours, yet sunrise I saw / Brighten sweet Highnam woods,' Gurney writes in the first few lines describing his boyhood in 'Chance to Work' (K, 2004, p.349).

Downstream from Gloucester, the river widens as it flows into the estuary and the two banks seem like separate lands. Here are the east bank villages of Hempsted, Elmore, Elmore Back, Farleys End, Wickgreen, Longney, Epney, Upper Framilode, Framilode, Fretherne, Saul and Arlingham, whilst on the west bank are Minsterworth, Oakle Street, Chaxhill, Bollo, Rodley,

Left: Church and manor house at Maisemore, the home village of Gurney's paternal grandmother.

Right: Hock Cliff at Fretherne, 2010. (*See* also Figure 6.1)

Cleeve, Westbury on Severn, Broadoak and Newnham. One of Gurney's early poems, 'The Fisherman of Newnham', recalls his fascination with the river tides, the Severn Bore ('swift on its way to Bollo') and fishing beneath the river cliff at Hock Cliff, Fretherne, with his father (Figure 6.1).

Significantly for Gurney's later development, however, all this active physical involvement with the Severn Meadows was given a new slant because of the efforts of Alfred Cheesman, Gurney's godfather, and the Hunt sisters to introduce him to literature and music. As he roamed the riverside paths and the pasturelands, the physical world of his senses was increasingly refracted through a developing intellectual framework and a growing awareness of his own musical talents. This is beautifully explained in the poem 'There is a Valley', in which Gurney speaks of 'breathing lovely sense of songs and books', mentioning the historical novel *The Cloister and the Hearth* by Charles Reade, Wordsworth's 'The Prelude', and the music of Brahms. The phrase 'half discord' is not meant to record unease, but to recognise how the different media of book learning, music and nature can charmingly create a new meaning in the poet's mind:

> THERE IS A VALLEY
> There is a valley soaked in with memories,
> Cloister and Hearth, The Prelude, and Brahms' mellow –
> A river loiters downward in rich ease,
> To salmon and the Easter Bore's low bellow;
> Meadows I think in plain land without fellow
> And breathing lovely sense of songs and books,
> Charming half discord with its level looks;
> Palm grows there, kingcups shall, and tansy yellow.

(80P, p.88)

In this way, the Severn Meadows was the place that became intertwined with his creative growth. His attachment to the cathedral, both as a choir boy after 1900 and a musical scholar from 1906, enhanced his experience yet again, as if the musical skills and techniques gave him a language and a wider vocabulary with which to express himself. He began seriously writing music some time after about 1906 and, although early attempts are not judged of any great quality, it is interesting to note that he often chose pastoral themes in poems by Housman or Bridges as the basis for his song settings.

In the period 1906 to 1911, Gurney's friendship with Howells and Harvey provided the opportunity to reflect on the different aspects of his life with like-minded young men as they walked on the riverside, played and listened to music together. The activity of sailing assumed a

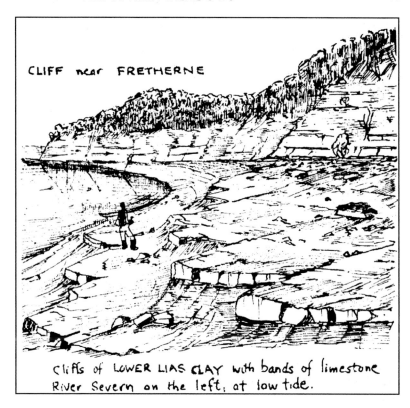

CLIFF near FRETHERNE

Cliffs of LOWER LIAS CLAY with bands of limestone
River Severn on the left; at low tide.

Fig. 6.1: Hock Cliff
near Fretherne.
(W. Dreghorn, 1967)

growing importance. Gurney had learnt to sail as a boy with the Harris family at Framilode lock, and had purchased his own boat in 1907. It was here, with Harvey in particular, that sailing opened up a whole new perspective on the Severn Meadows; the landscape was now experienced along with the ever-changing movements and light conditions of the river.

So the Severn Meadows was an integral part of Gurney's growth and development and, as such, it was the first place he turned to in his poetry and music. Gurney's first poetry collection (*Severn & Somme*) was mostly written in France, but bore the name of the River Severn and focused on Gloucestershire 'whose images of beauty' were always on his mind, as he claimed in the introduction. Even the second volume, *War's Embers*, continually harked back to the riverine meadows and landscapes of his childhood, with poems about the river itself, Minsterworth, Will Harvey and the lock-keeper at Framilode. Perhaps even more significant is the fact that after the war, in his confused and often depressed state of the 1918–22 years, his poetry shows that he was continually turning to the Severn Meadows to walk and find solace, but also to reflect and reconsider what the place meant to him. The collection *80 Poems or So*, which we know covered poetry of the 1918–22 period, is a revelation in this respect. About two thirds of the poems in this collection are about the Severn Meadows. He writes of the sedges, the pastures and the wild flowers; he records the mists, the dawns, the cold late spring of 1921; he revisits Maisemore, Wainlode Cliff and Ashleworth; and he draws on his love of Shakespeare and the Elizabethans to deepen his understanding. But it is not just a collection of poems about the Severn Meadows. Gurney's poetry *is* the Severn Meadows. It is in this collection that we see how the music, the poetry, the Severn Meadows and the poet himself have become too closely interweaved to separate out which is the source and which the creation. Looking at the extracts below, the landscape is 'like music eager curving or narrowing / From here to there', the experience of watching a sunset produces a sensation 'something like love', and it is only the poet's difficulty in finding words, 'dumbness', which 'mocks his search for speech' and so denies him access to the full intensity of the dawn's beauty.

Like music eager curving or narrowing
From here to there. Strange how no mist can dull
Wholly the silver edge of April song
Though the air's a blanket weighing on like wool.

('Dull Afternoon')

After the halt of dawn comes the slow moving of
Time, till the sun's hidden rush and the day is admitted;
Sunset dies out in a smother of something like love
With dew and the elm-hung stars and owl outcries half-witted.

('Lovely Playthings')

Dawn pales the stars a brief while earlier, day
By bright day and the stars take new array.
Only my dumbness mocks my search for speech,
Only the thing-accomplished makes delay.

('First Spring')

Creating poetry or music was not, for Gurney, a two-stage process of seeing a beautiful view and then creating a piece of music or poem to celebrate it; as the extract from 'The Springs of Music' at the start of this chapter makes clear, in the Severn valley, the music was already there waiting in the landscapes 'infinitely full of meaning'. It was Gurney, the musician and poet who, with his sensitivity to and experience of this 'place music', could begin to express it and, in so doing, satisfy that longing told of by Wordsworth.

The Great Valley above Gloucester

The area defined as the Severn Meadows for the purposes of this book includes the river and its valley from Tewkesbury in the north to Newnham and Fretherne in the south, and extends from the Forest of Dean in the west to the steep Cotswold Edge in the east. As explained in Chapter 2, this relatively narrow strip of land is more diverse in landscape than might be expected, partly because of the underlying geology of Liassic and Triassic rocks. Gurney's poetic response to this area was sensitive to these differences and, in particular, to the distinction between the country upstream and downstream of Gloucester.

William Dreghorn's book about Gloucestershire's landscapes (*see* p.30) picks out the Wainlode Hill area upstream of Gloucester, where there is an impressive river cliff. Dreghorn emphasises the geology/landscape relationship.

> To reach Wainlode Cliff it is best to take the turning to Haw Bridge, branching off to the left before reaching the bridge itself. Here the river swings along fine red cliffs by the Red Lion Inn, in front of which green meadows stretch down to the river's edge. This is Gloucester's 'Lido', which becomes quite crowded on sunny weekends, and is no place to go after heavy winter rains. For then, the surrounding fields become flooded, parts of the road are impassable and, when the flood waters subside, thin coats of mud are left behind...
>
> (Dreghorn, 1967, p.18)

The July 2007 flood height is marked on the wall of the Red Lion, showing that this flood surpassed even that of 1947; in Gurney's day, the greatest flood still remembered was that of 1916. Dreghorn's description of the river as a bathing area no longer holds true, as bathing is forbidden and the site bears a neater more managed appearance. But the description would have held true in Gurney's day and he probably swum here as a boy. He certainly walked along the river banks at Wainlode and Ashleworth and knew the red cliffs well.

1 A Locational Map of the northern part of Gloucestershire, covering places named in the text. (Ordnance Survey data © Crown Copyright and database right 2010)

2 Gloucester Cathedral; the South Porch. *Who says 'Gloucester' sees a tall / Fair fashioned shape of stone arise,* 'The Old City'. (Photograph, Philip Wade)

3 The Cloisters at Gloucester Cathedral, built 1351–1412 and forming a square walkway which originally connected all the monastic buildings.

4 Minsterworth; orchards and the church at this village beside the River Severn. Gurney's great friend, Will Harvey, lived at Minsterworth and is buried in the graveyard here.

5 Portway. One of Gurney's 'Cotswold Ways', climbing to *dim wood lengths without end*. This view looks down on Gloucester on a June day.

6 *The dead land oppressed me; / I turned my thoughts away / And went where hill and meadow / Are shadowless and gay,*
'Trees'. This image of desolation on the Western Front is entitled 'We are Making a New World' by Paul Nash,
1918. (Produced by kind permission of the Imperial War Museum, London)

7 *Where Coopers stands by Cranham.* Cranham Woods in early autumn – the place to which Gurney turned in his
imagination to find *Trees worthy of all worship* in comparison with the desolation of northern France, 'Trees'.

8 Barrow Hill above Ashleworth. One of Gurney's favourite places, where he often stood to admire the view of the Cotswold Edge. In France he remembered the place *Where eyes and heart and soul may drink their fill*, 'Above Ashleworth'. (Photograph, Greig Simms)

9 The Boat Inn, Ashleworth Quay, looking, as it did in Gurney's day, more like an old red-brick cottage than a public house. (Photograph, Greig Simms)

10 The wide reaches of the River Severn at Framilode. *When I saw Framilode first she was a blowy / Severn tided place under azure sky*, 'First Framilode'.

11 The path alongside the disused Stroudwater Canal in Framilode. The seating area of the Ship Inn is in the foreground, to the right.

IVOR GURNEY'S GLOUCESTERSHIRE

Early 1900s: looking east towards Gloucester Cathedral with the Cotswold escarpment behind. Old Gloucester cattle graze in the water meadows.

Cruck-framed cottage near Ashleworth

Gurney sails the 'Dorothy' up river on the Severn with an incoming tide

Malvern Hills

Pendock

Redmarley

Staunton

RIVER LEADON

Ashle

NEWENT

May Hill

Maisemore

Huntley

Highnam

GLOUCESTER

Minsterworth

Westbury on Severn

Robi

Newnham

Upper Framlode

Fretherne

Awre

Ha

Frampton on Severn

Coaley Peak

Miles

Kilometres

12 An interpretation of 'Ivor Gurney's Gloucestershire'. This map was created by Roger Ellis, map artist, working with the author. (Roger Ellis Studios)

Kestrel

TEWKESBURY

Deerhurst

pperley

Nottingham
Hill

Langley
Hill

WINCHCOMBE

CHELT

Cleeve
Hill

Southam

CHELTENHAM

Leckhampton

Chosen
Hill

Leckhampton
Hill

Crickley
Hill

ston
Leonards

4

Witcombe   Birdlip

Coopers
Hill

TWA

Cranham

3

Briapsfield

Syde

nswick

Slad

Bisley

Brimscombe

FROME

VALKS

Perennial
Cornflower

Bee Orchid

The Devil's Chimney at
Leckhampton overlooking Cheltenham.

An ancient sunken lane in the Cotswolds

Gloucestershire tithe barn and Cotswold dry stone wall

Left: 13 A view of the wooded slopes of Cooper's Hill in June 2010, with the Cheese Roll clearly visible in the middle of the slope. Cooper's Hill was one of the 'ideal places' to which Gurney turned during the noise and fear of trench warfare in 1916–17.

'That Centre of Old'

And Cooper's Hill showed plain almost as experience.
Soft winter's mornings of kind innocence, high June's
Girl's air of untouched purity, and on Cooper's Hill
Or autumn Cranham with its boom of colour…
Not anyway does ever Cotswold's fail – Her dear blue long dark
    slope fail –
Of the imagining promise in full exile.

Right: 14 Looking out from Witcombe Woods to the site of the Witcombe Roman Villa. This photograph was taken in May 2010. Gurney's poem was written in early autumn; the willowherb is not in evidence now but the sense of place and sense of the Romans remains. (Photograph, Philip Wade)

'Above the Villa'

The wind of autumn has touched there, the beech leaves have changed.
All the willowherb of all the world falling steep to the Villa
Where once the Romans ranged, is a wonder of light chanced
Upon … O friend are you not drunken with the sea of far lost mystic colour?

A LIDAR image of Cooper's Hill and High Brotheridge.

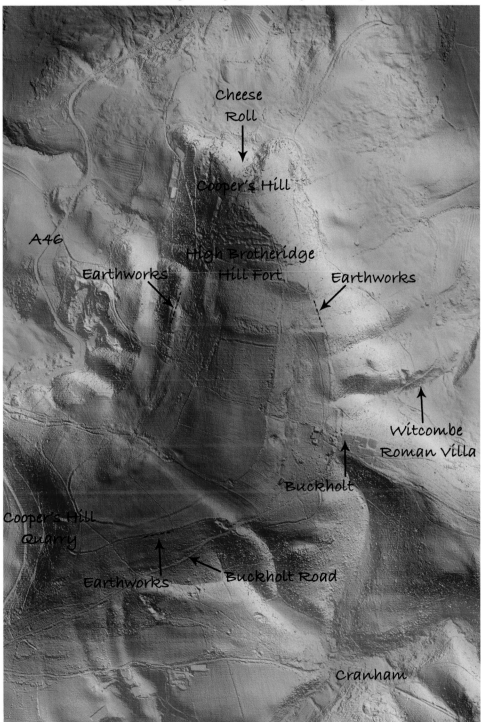

Cheese Roll

Cooper's Hill

A46

Earthworks

High Brotheridge Hill Fort

Earthworks

Witcombe Roman Villa

Buckholt

Cooper's Hill Quarry

Earthworks

Buckholt Road

Cranham

15 Light Detection and ranging (LIDAR) is a relatively new technology. The false colours are: red for high land, and green and blue for lower areas. The false colour lighting is from the north-east. Two sets of pulses were measured – one from the tree tops and one from the ground level. The two sets of data can be separated out and so this image shows the area without its heavy tree cover, allowing archaeological and other features to be seen more easily. Some features of Walk 3, which runs across this area, have been noted and see also figure 7.1. (Produced here by permission of Precision Terrain Surveys Ltd)

16 Crickley Hill. *If only this fear would leave me I could dream of Crickley Hill / And a hundred thousand thoughts of home would visit my heart in sleep.* 'De Profundis'

17 Devil's Table on the walk down Crickley Hill. There was a local legend that early people used this rock as a sacrificial table. This view looks towards Cooper's Hill, with Witcombe Reservoir below and the modern dual carriageway A417 in the immediate foreground.

18 The view north-westwards from Chosen Hill, looking towards the Malvern Hills. Gurney and Howells frequently walked on Chosen Hill. *What Malvern is the day is, and its touchstone / Gray velvet or moon-marked; rich or bare as bone.*

19 Lord's and Lady's Woods near Sheepscombe. *Autumn dear to walkers with your streaks and carpets / Of bright colour, 'Autumn'.*

20 *Stream sources happened upon in unlikely places.* Ducks on the spring at Bisley on the high Cotswolds. (Photograph, Philip Wade)

21 The Old Vicarage, Ashleworth, built in the sixteenth century. *A Manor's bones spied in the frame of some wisteria'd house.*

22 *Fragments of Abbey tithe barns.* The mediaeval tithe barn at Ashleworth. 'The barn is about 40 yards long, magnificent with buttressed walls, fine old roofs, and two projecting entrances with great beams supporting their stone gables.' (Extract from Arthur Mee, *The King's England*)

23 *Old troughs.* This stone drinking trough catches the waters of the spring that flows in the field above Dryhill Farm.

24 Spring woodland growing on the slopes of Wainlode's Hill. Bluebells can be seen in the foreground and a glimpse of the River Severn through the trees.

25 The Cotswold Edge in snow, February 2010. Looking from Barrow Wake towards Cooper's Hill. Robinswood Hill can be seen in the far right of the photograph.

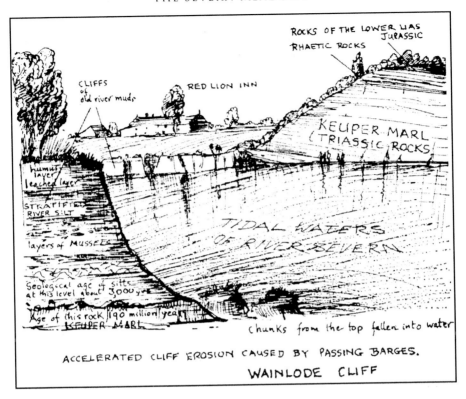

Fig. 6.2: Simplified geology of Wainlode Cliff. (W. Dreghorn, 1967)

Visitors to Wainlode Cliffs can actually hear and see erosion [of the red cliff deposits] taking, particularly on summer evenings after a fine day when the sun has been shining on the cliffs. As the temperature drops in the evening there is expansion and contraction of the cliff surface and little pieces of rock come tumbling down.

(Dreghorn, p.21)

By Severn

If England, her spirit lives anywhere, anywhere
It is by Severn, by hawthorns and those grand willows ...
Earth heaves up there twice a hundred feet in clear air,
And muddy clay falls sheer or scooped out to the shallows,
There in the breaks of Maytime Spring has her chambers –
Robing-rooms of hawthorn, cowslip cuckoo flowers
Wonder complete changes for each square hour of the hours,
Past thought miracles are there and beyond numbers.
If for the atmospheres and master managed lighting,
In London town, Oriana's playwrights had there
Wainlode her theatre and coppice clad dear
Hill for her ground of sauntering and slow waiting ...
Why, then I think, our chiefest glory of poetry's pride,
Would nothing of its meeding be denied, little denied,
Her sons' praises from England's mouth be outcried.

As dear Chaucer prayed.

(GA, 1925; also slightly different version in K, p.121)

The natural amphitheatre at Wainlode Cliff. The Red Lion Inn is in the distance beyond the cliff. (2010)

It is clear that the natural amphitheatre that lies beneath Wainlode Cliff and the 86m (283ft) eminence of Norton Hill are exactly what Gurney had in mind when he wrote 'Earth heaves up twice a hundred feet in air / And ruddy clay falls scooped out to the weedy shallows.' (Figure 6.2) He even mentions the red cliffs ('ruddy clay') with 'falls' possibly referring both to the steepness and to the pieces that fall to the river beach. He likens the natural stage set of this site to the theatres of London town in the Elizabethan era, claiming that the Elizabethan playwrights ('Oriana's playwrights') would glory in this natural theatre. This is a real place – the Wainlode Cliff recognised by the geomorphologist, Dreghorn, with its peculiarities of rock type and formation, but it is also a creation of the poet's mind, in which Gurney, the walker, has crossed time and space to elicit a richly-layered 'spirit' of England.

This layering of experience is also noticeable in Gurney's treatment of the Severn's terraces. The Severn, like many mature rivers, has features known as river terraces which now form significant elements of the Gloucestershire landscape. In the quite recent geological past (about one million years ago), the Severn was a much bigger river, fed by melting water from the ice sheets to the north and carrying a large load of gravel and debris in its waters. All this was laid down in a wide valley appropriate to the size of the river, but during the ice age there were alternate periods of advance and retreat of the ice, and of fast and slow-flowing rivers. When the Severn flowed more powerfully, or sea levels fell, the river cut into its old valley floor and left remnants of this high and dry on either side of the river. When sea levels rose, or the river flowed more slowly and was filled with debris, then there was deposition across the valley plain. In the case of the River Severn, this process has happened several times so that a sequence of at least three sets of river terraces can be seen.

Figure 6.3 presents Dreghorn's three diagrams, showing that there are three main terraces recognised here – at roughly 80-100ft (24–31 m), 120-150ft (37–46 m) and 250ft (76 m)– and the result is the distinctive landscape of low hills and gentle farmland seen to the north of Gloucester, where these superficial or 'drift' deposits cover the underlying solid geology of Liassic and Triassic rocks. The terraces comprise fertile river deposits and a mix of rock material from the local area, as well as material brought by the river from places outside the local area. They lie above the present flood plain and so are well-drained and safe from flooding. Not surprisingly, they make good settlement sites and rich farmland – orchards, arable land and dairy pasture with extra grazing down on the floodplain itself.

In 1967, Dreghorn explained that 'this terrace region is a quiet backwater, a softly pleasant land rather like the Constable country of Essex and Suffolk, where fertile fields are interspersed with sleepy villages – Apperley, Tirley, Norton, Deerhurst, Hasfield, Ashleworth, Sandhurst and Maisemore.' (p.55) Although the region has changed considerably in function and lifestyle, and many of the settlements now house commuters to Gloucester and Cheltenham, visually, the landscape would almost fit this description today – at least in the middle of the day before the bustle of homecoming motor cars. It can be seen from Figure 6.3 that Wainlode Hill is on the lower terrace, Sandhurst Hill and Hasfield Hill are on the middle terrace and Wooldridge

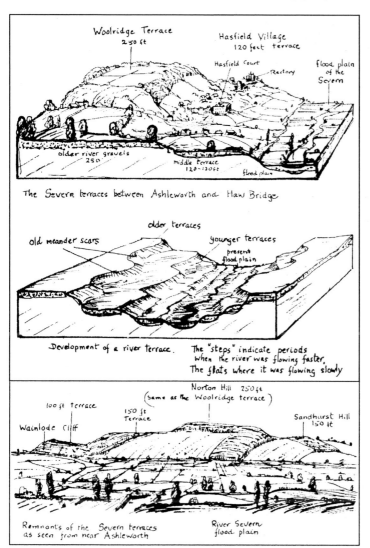

1. Severn Terraces looking west.

2. Terrace formation.

3. Severn Terraces looking east.

Fig. 6.3: The Severn Terraces. (W. Dreghorn, 1967)

Hill and Norton Hill are on the highest terrace (so is Gurney's Barrow Hill, near Ashleworth). In Gurney's poetry, we are aware of the joy he found in walking in this area, observing the villages with their long-established churches and manor houses (e.g. Ashleworth, Norton), enjoying the play of light and dark on the river (e.g. in the poem 'Water Colours'), and reaching the summits of these small hills (e.g. in 'Foscombe Hill', 'Above Ashleworth') to revel in the views across to the Cotswold Edge and the Forest of Dean. And, nearly always, he makes references to past ages (Saxons, Normans, Elizabethans), past reading (Wordsworth, Whitman) and past experience (the war, childhood, sailing).

The walk, **Above Ashleworth** (p.102-103), traces a route across this sleepy Severn Meadows countryside, visiting one of Gurney's favourite Severnside villages and drawing on his poetry and experience. Follow the route as you read the commentary – best of all, find the relevant OS maps and walk it in person, with the commentary by your side.

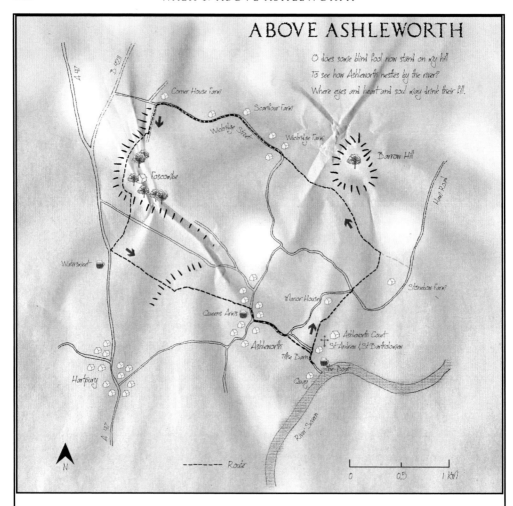

ABOVE ASHLEWORTH

O does some blind fool now stand on my hill
To see how Ashleworth nestles by the river?
Where eyes and heart and soul may drink their fill.

(See colour illustrations 8 and 9)

Route Facts:

Distance/time
8km (5 miles) 2½-3 hours.

Map
OS Explorer 179 1:25,000 Gloucester, Cheltenham and Stroud.
OS Landranger 162 1:50,000 Gloucester and Forest of Dean.
Note that Ashleworth Parish Council also publishes a leaflet of walks in this area, available from the church.

Start and Parking
The walk starts at Ashleworth Quay next to the Boat Inn (GR818251). Cars can only be parked there when using the inn. Or park in the village hall car park.

Refreshment
The Boat Inn at Ashleworth Quay. Not open on Mondays or Wednesday lunchtime. Check on www.boat-inn.co.uk; Queen's Head, Ashleworth; Watersmeet, Hartpury.

O does some blind fool now stand on my hill
To see how Ashleworth nestles by the river?
Where eyes and heart and soul may drink their fill.

(K, p.38)

This walk will take you deeply into Gurney's Severn Meadows, an area that is not, as its name might suggest, a mere expanse of grassy riverside pastures but an enchanted world of settled villages, hidden manor houses, ancient churches, narrow lanes and sudden hilly heights. The walk begins by the River Severn at Ashleworth Quay, heading through the edge of the village past the tithe barn, church and big house before climbing up Barrow Hill (see photo below), the hill featuring in the poem 'Above Ashleworth'. A particular attraction to Gurney was the amazing view of virtually all Gloucestershire from the top. The return journey takes in Foscombe Hill, with its woodland and grand Gothic house, and the old Waggons Lane leading back to Ashleworth. Gurney frequently walked and cycled in this area, heading out from Gloucester whenever he could get away to find peace and creative inspiration. He was a regular visitor at the Boat Inn, and was known to the barge men, fishermen and farmers who frequented the bar. Ashleworth and Severn Meadows became an 'ideal place' to which he longed to return when in exile in France and in Dartford Asylum.

Barrow Hill at Ashleworth, representing the highest (76m) river terrace deposited over an underlying layer of Blue Lias limestone. The hill is viewed from Ashleworth Quay, 2010.

WALK 1
ABOVE ASHLEWORTH

1. The Boat Inn, Ashleworth Quay, looks like an old red-brick cottage rather than a public house. In Gurney's day it was a busy ferry point and coal quay (Forest of Dean coal). The present owners are descendants of the original Jelf family, who were granted rights to the ferry crossing, probably in 1651 by King Charles II. Across the river, you will see Rodway Lane, the landing point on the other bank. Nowadays the river is peaceful and the Severn Way runs beside the water's edge. Imagine Gurney arriving by ferry after walking or cycling from Gloucester ('the city once all Roman') – it is not just a river landscape that he is describing but a place alive with the ghosts of those who have gone this way before him (Britons, Romans, Saxons, Danes).

HARPER'S FERRY★

Since Roman had gone there, Dane also gone
Surely it was before the old path of Briton –
Many had gone before me, with music had foregone.
And I who had passed from the city once all Roman,
By ways of Dane, by a church named of Saxon,
Looked over to Ferry, hailed and shouted on
Till the boat came – and where Harpers had often ferried;
I also was rowed on Severn, Severn me bore and carried;
(who had writ verse at Dane Rouen, music near Roman Vermand,)
To see the tithe barn so noble, the church by time scarred;
But praise both of Divinity and the making hand.
★★Ashelworth, name as musical as any in the wide Severn-land.
★(see p. 71)
(GA, 1925) ★★Gurney's mis-spelling of Ashleworth

2. Turn your back on the inn and walk up the lane away from the quay. According to Arthur Mee:

If we come to old Ashleworth's orchards and meadows from Sandhurst, using the ferry where the silver Severn swings round a great bend, our first acquaintance is with a delightful company of old neighbours, church, house, and tithe barn. They are part of a group of monastic buildings belonging once to St Augustine's of Bristol.
The King's England: Gloucestershire (1938, p.29)

The church provides a cross-section of architecture from Norman to Victorian; the house is a beautiful timber-framed fortified Tudor dwelling and was originally thatched; and the tithe barn is a massive (125'x25') structure originally owned by the Abbot of Gloucester, now part of a working farm and managed by the National Trust. They are all built of the local blue lias stone. When the road bends left, take the footpath straight on and follow the field edge path round to the right (ignore a gate straight ahead). Ashleworth Manor, to the left, was built in 1460 as a summer residence for Abbot Newberry of the abbey at Bristol. Sandhurst Hill (86m) should be visible on the east bank of the river and, as you walk, views of Barrow Hill (78m), its twin on the west bank, will appear ahead. On reaching the road at a T-junction, cross over to find a footpath.

3. Follow the footpath across fields, heading towards the lower slopes of Barrow Hill with Stonebow Farm to your right. In less than a kilometre, at a small bridge over a ditch, your path meets a bridleway. Turn left and follow this often muddy and rutted track until it crosses pasture land and you find yourself on the lower edge of the field containing Barrow Hill summit. The public footpath continues contouring at this height, but the summit is up to the right and the landowner is usually happy to let visitors see the view.

At the top of Barrow Hill you are greeted by a clump of trees and, if it is clear, you can enjoy the magnificent 360° view. Highlights include (moving anti-clockwise from the east) Wainlode's Cliff with Sandhurst and Norton Hills behind it; the Cotswold Edge from Haresfield Beacon to Cleeve Hill, 'as if never / A curve of them the hand of Time might change' ('Above Ashleworth'); Bredon Hill, Tirley and the woodland of Corse and Hasfield; the Malvern Hills, May Hill and, in the distance, the Forest of Dean. For Gurney, Barrow Hill was a special refuge.

ABOVE ASHLEWORTH

O does some blind fool now stand on my hill
To see how Ashleworth nestles by the river?
Where eyes and heart and soul may drink their fill.

The Cotswolds stand out eastward as if never
A curve of them the hand of Time might change;
Beauty sleeps most confidently for ever.

The blind fool stands, his dull eyes free to range
Endlessly almost, and finds no word to say:
Not that the sense of wonder is too strange

Too great for speech. Naught touches him; the day
Blows its glad trumpets, breathes rich-odoured breath;
Glory after glory passes away.

(And I'm in France!) He looks and sees beneath
The clouds in steady Severn silver and grey
But dead he is and comfortable in Death.

(K, 2004, p.38)

Is Gurney contrasting the viewing of this scene by an insensitive person ('some blind fool') who cannot partake of the richness even though he is present, with the appreciative response Gurney himself would have made had he not been in France? Or is Gurney himself the 'blind fool' who, by his absence in France, is dead to these glories seen from Barrow Hill?

4. Return to the bridleway and leave the field at the south-west corner through a muddy gateway. Follow the hedgerow down to another gate and go into the next field. Take a path that runs first downhill but then bears to the right through (or round) some shrubs to exit at the corner of the field beside Wickridge Farm. Now walk up the pleasant country lane through the hamlet of Wickridge Street. 'Riez Bailleul' was the first place the 2/5th Glosters were stationed in France. Gurney was only a few weeks away from England, but was already hanging on to images of the Severn lanes of home:

RIEZ BAILLEUL

Riez Bailleul in blue tea-time
Called back the Severn lanes, and roads
Where the small ash leaves lie, and floods
Of hawthorn leaves turned with night's rime,
No Severn though nor great valley clouds.

(RW, p.57, first stanza only)

After Wickridge Farm, the route lies along lanes, passing Berrow Farmhouse, Yew Tree Farm (formerly Scarifour Farm) and Limekiln Farm, presumably on the site of an old limekiln. In 'Kilns', Gurney wrote that 'Severn has kilns set all along her banks / Where the thin reeds grow and rushes in banks' and then he talks of local brick-making. After 1km of lane walking, turn left through some iron gates. It is signposted Whitmore Way.

5. Walk along this small roadway. In the spring you will be surrounded by bluebells, wild garlic and cowslips, while away to your left you will catch sight of Barrow Hill again. The path turns right to avoid Foscombe House, but you will catch glimpses of the Victorian Gothic house, built from local blue lias stone by Thomas Fulljames, who, at the time, was resident architect to Gloucester Cathedral. To your right, a view opens out to the south – the small but prominent Catsbury Hill in the foreground and the

higher wooded slopes of Woolridge Hill behind it. Gurney's poem 'On Foscombe Hill' focuses on the small stream ('talking water') that rises in a spring near the house and runs in an easterly direction down into Ashleworth and eventually the Severn.

ON FOSCOMBE HILL

O exquisite
And talking water, are you not more glad
To be sole daughter and one comfort bright
Of this small hill lone-guarding its delight,
Than unconsidered to be
Some waif of Cotswold or the Malvern height?
Your name a speck of glory in so many.
You are the silver of a dreaming mound
That likes the quiet way of thought and sound,
Moists tussocks with a sunken influence,
Collects and runs one way down to farm yard
Sheds, house, standing up there by soft sward,
Green of thorn, green of sorrel and age-old heath,
Of South-West's lovely breath.

(K, 2004, p.179)

For an easy stroll down the ridge back to Ashleworth, go straight ahead on the main path. The more interesting route (but involving a steep and potentially muddy slope downhill) turns right off the main path when Foscombe House is behind you. Go steeply down this tiny path, which emerges in a field, before crossing the road and continuing on down another field to reach the A417 Ledbury Road. If you need some refreshment, the Watersmeet Inn is a few metres down the (busy) road.

6. From the A417 at the footpath junction, turn at right angles to take another signposted footpath running south-east, at first along the edge of two fields, then climbing up a river terrace. Near the top of the ridge, turn right and immediately left up some wooden steps to cross another stile. Look out for views of Gloucester Cathedral before taking a path diagonally to the left; this is Wagons Lane, an ancient cart track, deeply hidden in the wooded slope. Join the tarmac road in Ashleworth, turn right past the Queen's Arms and walk to the village green where there is a fifteenth-century preaching cross. Here turn left down the road signposted 'the village church and tithe barn'. You can either walk back via the road, taking a right at the next junction or, on the gentle bend before the junction, take a footpath leading across a field and aiming directly at the church tower. You come out by the tithe barn and so make your way back to the start at Ashleworth Quay.

Will Harvey and Minsterworth

Before moving downstream to the pastures and estuary lands below Gloucester, it is necessary to pause awhile, as Gurney often did, at Minsterworth. Just 4 miles downstream from Gloucester, Minsterworth was the location of the Harvey household at Redlands and, for Gurney, the Severn Meadows was always associated with Will Harvey. The poem 'After-Glow' (S&S) is dedicated to 'F W Harvey' and contains memories of Redlands: 'the little room with tea-talk loud and laughter of happy boys.' 'The Farm', another poem, is dedicated to 'Mrs Harvey and Those Others'; Gurney tells how during the war 'when in queer holes of chance, bedraggled, wet, / Lousy I lay; to think how by Severn-side / A house of steadfastness and quiet pride / Kept faith to friends (when hope of mine had died almost to ash)' (WE, p.15). Redlands still stands beside the A48 today, now hidden behind tall trees. Crossing the road to the lane beside the Apple Tree public house, one can walk down to the banks of the Severn and along the riverside path towards the church where Harvey is buried.

In August 1916, Harvey was reported missing and Gurney, also in France, believed him to be dead until October 1916, when the news came that Harvey was not dead but a prisoner of war. The poem 'To His Love' clearly refers to this initial terrible news, although the poem was revised many times after its initial creation and was eventually finished at the army camp at Seaton Delaval, Northumberland, 1918. A second poem, 'Ypres-Minsterworth', was written sometime after the first draft of 'To His Love' and is dedicated to Harvey in prison. In both these poems, memories of Harvey are inextricably mixed with the Gloucestershire places that the two knew so well. 'Ypres-Minsterworth' begins with the orchards, shaken by autumn winds, and the leaves strewn on pastures. 'To His Love' remembers Cotswold walks and sailing on the Severn, 'driving our small boat through'. The two poems are quite different, however. 'Ypres-MInsterworth' has a sadness and a longing for the 'boy' languishing in the German prison, but its final message is one of optimism, talking of comrades safely returned, of friendly greetings and good wishes. 'To His Love' is much more intense and even shocking, because of the last stanza and the 'red, wet / Thing I must somehow forget'. The 'thing', emphasised by being placed as the first word on the last line, may refer to the bloodied wound or to the mangled corpse, both images which Gurney might have imagined if Harvey had died. For Gurney, the horror of his friend's death, as he then thought, would have been something raw and emotional, and he would have wished to avoid conjuring up the precise details of this and just remember his friend, walking on the Cotswolds and sailing their boat. By the time Gurney revised and finished the poem, he would have known that Harvey was alive and so this is why it is not dedicated to F.W. Harvey. The use of different pronouns ('he', 'you', 'I', 'our') may suggest that Gurney is also talking to another person – Sarah Kane, the woman who Harvey eventually married, is the obvious choice. However, all the references in the poem are to the life that Gurney and Harvey shared – right down to the detail of 'our small boat', but, as it appears in *War's Embers*, it seems to be an elegy for any soldier who died in the war, away from home. Gurney and Harvey had a very close and intense friendship, born of a love of music, poetry and the Severn Meadows, and this piece strikes a real note of tenderness. The same depth of feeling can be seen in a letter to Marion Scott from France on 22 March 1917, which included another song-like poem, 'June-to-Come'. The 'him' is clearly Will Harvey and the place is inextricably linked with the emotions.

> JUNE-TO-COME (extract)
> When the sun's fire and gold
> Sets the bee humming,
> I will not write to tell
> Him that I'm coming,
>
> But ride out unawares
> On that old road
> Of Minsterworth, of Peace,
> Of Framilode,

(S&S, p.57)

The Great Valley Below Gloucester

The soft and varied terraced landscape of the Severn Meadows above Gloucester gives way eventually below the city to a wilder and more open vista of wide expanses of water, mud flats, and reed beds – a typical estuary landscape. The change-over from river to estuary seems to the walker to take place somewhere near Framilode and the Newnham bend. Upstream the Severn is undoubtedly a river, with each bank nodding acquaintance to its fellow across a winding channel; downstream the channel widens until it becomes a vast sea, and the shorelines are lost to each other in mist and distance. Dreghorn describes the riverine landscape of the Westbury on Severn area:

> The cliffs by the river are the same rocks in age and type as those at Wainlode Cliff – the red Triassic rocks and Keuper Marl – but the rocks of the Garden Cliff at Westbury are even more striking in appearance. This is no place like Wainlode Cliff for bucolic merriment and cheerful curiosity about the past. The late afternoon sunshine glints on broad reaches of the Severn and on wide expanses of sand- and mud-flats, and the visitor is awed by the remote and melancholy grandeur of the cliffs of the Keuper Marl.
>
> (p.25)

If the estuary seemed remote in the sixties, how much more mysterious and lonely it would have appeared in the early twentieth century – the huge stretches of water, the low horizons, the marshy reed-beds, bird calls, fishermen and boats. In many ways, the estuary area is a strange transitional country where one is aware of the changing relationship of land and water, the mixing of seawater and river water, plants and fish adapted to salty water, the vagaries of tides and currents and the ever-changing skyscapes. Gurney's poem, 'First Framilode', explains the mysterious beauty he found here and, as so often happens with Gurney, the place brings to mind other writers – R.L. Stevenson, Walt Whitman, William Shakespeare. It seems that he recognises both the drama and adventure (the 'boy') and the beauty and romance (the 'girl') aroused by this watery landscape.

FIRST FRAMILODE

When I saw Framilode first she was a blowy
Severn tided place under azure sky.
Able to take care of Herself, less girl than boy.
But since that time passed, many times the extreme
Of mystery of beauty and last possibility
Of colour, sea breathed romance far past any may dream.
With 'Treasure Island', 'Leaves of Grass' and Shakespeare all there,
Adventure stirring the blood like threat of thunder,
With the never forgotten soft beauty of the Frome,
One evening when elver-lights made the river like a stall-road to see

(GA, also Gurney, 2009)

In Gurney's day, a popular activity was elver fishing (last line of poem) – elvers being young eels which were prized as a special dish by Gloucestershire folk. Elvers were gathered laboriously by elver fishermen, usually at night by candle lamplight, sold in the town markets and eaten fried in butter. They are still gathered today and command high prices as a speciality food for London markets. A newly-discovered essay written by Gurney (*The Ivor Gurney Society Journal*, 2009), when he was staying at the house of his aunt Marie in Longford, describes how he watched the elver fishermen on one of his night-time walks. Although the scene described is located 'By Ashleworth' (i.e. upstream of Gloucester), elver fishing took place all along the lower Severn, and particularly in the upper estuary region below Gloucester, as 'First Framilode' suggests. As Gurney explains, it was an activity that came with …

'The silver edge of April's song'
– the Severn's gleaming waters
looking from Fretherne to Awre.

... the great tides to Gloucester, and only at the height of those at the equinox, with the Severn Bore and the daffodils or in the run of leaf, when the long sunsets come. Watching the fisher men one feels the centuries and lives again by the side of those men who fished so ages ago, talked of Black Death or of Tewkesbury battle by candlelight, and swore or rejoiced over the catch together.

More recently, other poets have been fascinated by the Severn. Both Alice Oswald and Philip Gross remind us of the mysterious and transitory quality of the estuary environment. Alice Oswald wrote a long poem, 'A Sleepwalk on the Severn', for the 2009 Festival of the Severn. The poem follows the different phases of the moon watched from the Severn estuary area by the fishermen, bird watchers and river wardens. The initial words of the poem are:

> Flat stone sometimes lit sometimes not
> One among the many moodswung creatures
> That have settled in this beautiful
> Uncountry of an Estuary

> (Oswald, p.3, Prologue)

In his book *The Water Table*, Philip Gross, winner of the T.S. Eliot Prize 2009, writes a series of ten poems, each with the name 'Betweenland' and each painting a sensual image of the river estuary. 'Betweenland VII', for example, likens the estuary to an ear, calling on shape and sound to confirm this image: 'the estuary's battered pewter hearing-trumpet / amplifying distance – closer, suddenly, / a frisson of unaccustomed languages.' Gross's term 'Betweenland' evokes the same kind of transitional character as Oswald's 'uncountry'. The final poem in his book confirms this vision: 'The Severn was brown, the Severn was blue / not this-then-that, not either-or / no mixture. Two things can be true. / The hills were clouds and the mist was a shore.' ('Severn Song', 2009, p.64) Gurney would, no doubt, still recognise this place.

On Sailing a Boat

Whereas walking and cycling were Gurney's preferred modes of transport in the meadows above Gloucester, below the city he frequently took to his sailing boat, the *Dorothy*. Sailing alone was a joy to him, though he was usually accompanied by his cigarettes: 'With tobacco I have sailed Severn rivers, seen filled / In channel on by Bollo its great height whitening / Above the green water, and the boat white-riding.' ('Rappahannock', GA, 1925) Sailing also meant Harvey's companionship, and the two friends were always rushing to escape to the river. Herbert Howells recalls how on one

The *Dorothy* –
Gurney's sailing
boat, bought for £5
from James Harris,
the lock-keeper, and
named after Gurney's
youngest sister. (GA)

occasion, in Gloucester Cathedral, Gurney was unable to continue playing for the morning service
while the sun was shining gloriously outside. 'Oh God, I must go to Framilode,' he announced,
throwing down his books and rushing out to the river (Hurd, 1978, p.21). It is fortunate that we
have several sources from which we can reconstruct Gurney's river adventures and their significance
to him. These are: a short essay written by Gurney sometime between 1920 and 1922, explaining
his enjoyment of sailing a boat on the Severn; a photograph of the *Dorothy* on the Severn; mention
of sailing in his letters; and several poems, including 'Sailor', 'March', 'The Grove' (unpublished),
and 'Rappahannock' (unpublished) – all written in the 1920s in Dartford Asylum. In addition, Will
Harvey wrote his own poem called 'Ballade of River Sailing' (*Collected Poems*, 1983).

On Sailing a Boat on the Severn by Ivor Gurney

When the great tides change a channel twice a week one needs a rough-and-tumble affair, no expensive
toy, to get fun out of Severn. If there are shallows on the left hand, stones and stakes on the right, and a
sand-bank somewhere, one's pleasure is spiced, and always a furious gust may come down from the left
of Barrow Hill.

But there are orchards and spits of pasture, far Cotswold with white scars to look at, the best clouds in
England, and a chance of elver fishing at the Equinoxes; to say nothing of eeling in summer.

If one lays lines one may catch flounders also, and mullet, having been trapped by receding water, are
also known to have tasted well in that one happy village. The best game, however, is to have gone up river
on half-tide as far as impetus went, or on the stillness even of meeting tide and current, and then to return
in comparative certainty, with above-Newnham in sight and a headwind of which the return of water
makes no account. This is, indeed, worth doing, though the baler be more in use than the rudder almost.

Since there are three o[r] four public-houses within four miles of the river there is no danger of any
common thirst being made to suffer, and certainly there are two bakers.

The chief trouble is that this side of the river there are many stones, on the other smooth sand enough,
but one does not wish to be ferried across to one's boat – the thing seems absurd – and in big tides the
anchor drags; but there is no non-chargeable way of managing the affair. Making friends is not always a
cheap arrangement, and beer is a most dangerous equivalent for favours. Cheaper often to purchase an
empty barrel and float out to the boat in that.

River-dangers are not serious. River worries not too many to prevent pleasure. Almost always one can
sail, save in sultry summer, and the sight of bank objects always delighted myself. One likes to see Wick
Farm draw itself out of line of the landing stage. Food and drink are easy to obtain. One can never be
becalmed, and there are explorations on the hither shore that one does not get at proper sailing.

(The Ivor Gurney Society Journal, Vol. 15, 2009)

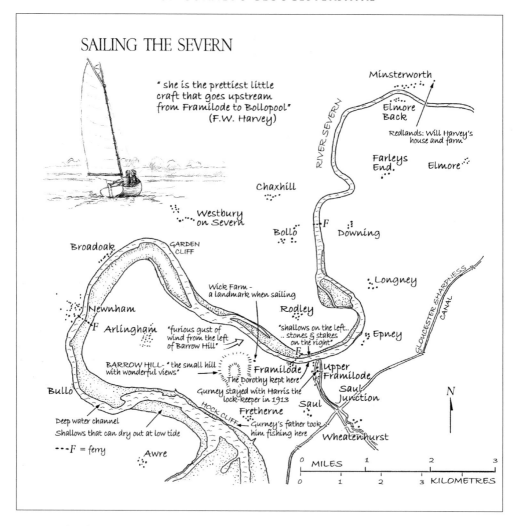

Fig. 6.4: Sailing the Severn. (Map by Roger Ellis, 2010)

Looking at the map (Figure 6.4) and the various written sources, it is relatively easy to find the locations mentioned and reconstruct the voyages made by Gurney. The boat was kept at Framilode, probably Upper Framilode, since that was where Gurney's friend James Harris, the lock-keeper, lived. The navigable channel stays close to the river bank on the southern Framilode side and, as Harvey describes, they would have paddled in the mud and shallow water to push the boat off from the shore. The most usual trip was 'Upstream from Framilode to Bollopool' (Harvey) and it was necessary to avoid the sand banks on the northern bank and to maintain a clear route along the deeper water upstream, around the Longney bend. Gurney explains how, as well as missing the sand banks, the sailors had to avoid the stones and stakes on the other side. The prevailing wind was westerly, which helped the sailors move upstream, although sometimes the wind was stronger than expected and 'a furious gust may come down from the left of Barrow Hill' (the small hill already mentioned in Gurney's letter to Marion Scott, *see* Chapter 3, p.43).

Sailing was sometimes a peaceful activity when Gurney and Harvey were able to enjoy a sunset, look on a summer sky or gaze at the far-off white scars of the Cotswold Edge. At other times, Gurney revelled in the risk and uncertainty of wilder weather or tides. In 'On Sailing', he explains how 'one's pleasure is spiced' by the dangers and how it is possible to play off the tides which move upstream and the normal river currents which move downstream.

The best game however, is to have gone up river on half-tide as far as impetus went, or on the stillness even of meeting tide and current, and then to return in comparative certainty, with above Newnham in sight and a headwind of which the return of water makes no account.

Inevitably, there were occasions when the boat was damaged or capsized and Gurney recounts (in 'Sailor') the 'painful care' of mending leaks with tar and oakum. An amusing comment in the penultimate paragraph of the essay explains the decision to be made about anchoring the boat. Although at Framilode, the western bank was more sandy, as Gurney explains: 'one does not wish to be ferried across to one's boat – the thing seems absurd'; on the other hand, relying on friends to help usually meant buying them a beer, 'a most dangerous equivalent for favours'. Presumably tongue-in-cheek, Gurney suggests that it is 'cheaper often to purchase an empty barrel and float out to the boat in that'.

On the map (Figure 6.4) it is possible to locate all of the various places mentioned by Gurney and Harvey – the change from deep water to sands and shallows on the south and east bank above Priding; Wick Farm, which Gurney used as a landmark to check on the journey upstream ('one likes to see Wick Farm draw itself out of the line of the landing stage'); Barrow Hill, which tended to funnel the westerly wind up the river; the many public houses easily accessible from the river at Priding, Framilode, Upper Framilode, Rodley, Epney and Downing (some of which have now closed); and the existence of ferries (also discontinued), which could be useful to stranded sailors.

Walking the Severn Way at the present time, along this very stretch of river, it is possible to experience the sights and sounds of the river very much as it was in the early twentieth century, and to imagine the white sail of the little boat and the glorious feeling of freedom that this must have given Gurney. All around him on a fine day, he would have seen the hills of Gloucestershire – the Forest of Dean to the north and west, and the curved edge of the Cotswolds to south and east. Beneath him were the ever-changing patterns and flows of moving water. Whereas in the Cotswolds it was the joy of walking and climbing the hills that heightened the experience, here it was the movement of boat upon water. As Gurney explains in 'March' (Walk 2), 'My boat moves and I with her delighting, / Feeling the water slide past, and watching white fashion / Of water, as she moves ever whitening.' The reader appreciates the same hypnotic effect produced by watching the water, hears with the poet the 'sound of Severn water dashing' and even raises one's head to glimpse the azure sky. Both poems, 'March' and 'The Grove', express delight and wonder in the place, as produced through the activity of sailing. The place is speaking through the poet and the movement is crucial to all this.

The walk, **A Blowy Severn Tided Place** (p.110-113), introduces the lower Severn and will enable you to experience the open horizons and river landscapes of the Framilode area. Follow the route as you read the commentary – best of all, find the relevant OS maps and go and walk it in person, with the commentary by your side.

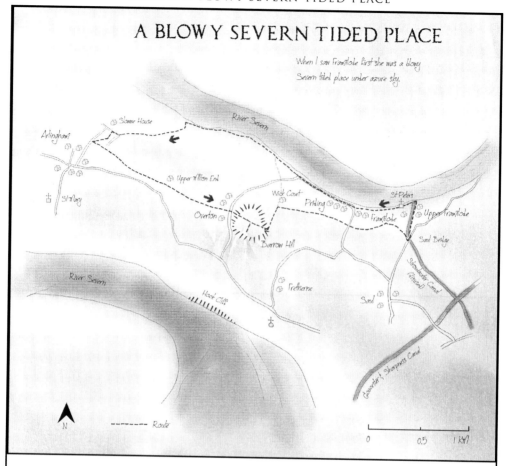

A BLOWY SEVERN TIDED PLACE

When I saw Framilode first she was a blowy Severn tided place under azure sky.

(See colour illustrations 10 and 11)

Route Facts:

Distance/time
9.5km (6m) if include Arlingham/3-3½ hours OR a shorter walk of about 6.5km (4m)/2-2½ hours.

Map
OS Outdoor Leisure Map 14, 1:25,000 Wye Valley and Forest of Dean.
OS Landranger 162, 1:50,000 Gloucester and Forest of Dean area.
Also useful is the Arlingham Walk Leaflet, available from the Arlingham Parish Council and the Red Lion Inn.

Start and Parking
The walk starts at St Peter's Church, Upper Framilode (750104). Cars can be parked right next to the church.

Refreshment
The Ship Inn at Upper Framilode.
The Red Lion at Arlingham (0.5km off route).

When I saw Framilode first she was a blowy
Severn tided place under azure sky,
Able to take care of herself, less girl than boy.

('First Framilode', GA, 1925)

This walk introduces Gurney's second home, the place where he often stayed with James Harris, the lock keeper, and where he kept his sailing boat, the Dorothy. Although on the Severn like Ashleworth, Framilode is a quite different place. Here the Severn is wide and expansive, occupying the foreground with its long gleaming stretches of water and yellowy-grey sandbanks, while the Cotswold Edge to the east and the Forest of Dean to the west provide a permanent backdrop of hill shapes. This walk begins at St Peter's Church, Upper Framilode, before heading downstream alongside the Severn. It leaves the riverside to climb up to the village of Arlingham, sited on the raised ground in the middle of the Severn's horseshoe bend, then meanders through pleasant pastureland and ascends the second Barrow Hill (we have already met one Barrow Hill in walk 1). From this 'small hill not a mile away from where I stayed' (Gurney's letter, June 1913), there is a wonderful view of the river and all the surrounding hills of the Forest of Dean and the Cotswolds. The descent of the hill takes you through the copse where Gurney heard the nightingales sing. Field paths take you back to the village, passing the Ship Inn, the old canal and the lock-keeper's house, before returning to the church.

Wide expanses of sand- and mud-flats near Westbury on Severn.

WALK 2

A BLOWY SEVERN TIDED PLACE

FIRST FRAMILODE

When I saw Framilode first she was a blowy
Severn tided place under azure sky.
Able to take care of Herself, less girl than boy.
But since that time passed, many times the extreme
Of mystery of beauty and last possibility
Of colour, sea breathed romance far past any may
dream.
With 'Treasure Island', 'Leaves of Grass' and
Shakespeare all there,
Adventure stirring the blood like threat of thunder,
With the never forgotten soft beauty of the Frome,
One evening when elver-lights made the river like a
stall-road to see

(GA, 1925)

1. Start at St Peter's Church. In Gurney's day, the Stroudwater Canal, now disused, met the Severn just upstream of this point, and the lock-keeper's house (Lock House) is situated a few metres up the village street. From the church, follow the Severn Way signs westward beside the river. Looking back upstream, you are seeing the main stretch of river along which Gurney and Harvey sailed the *Dorothy* 'upstream from Framilode to Bollopool' (Harvey).

Reading 'March' (GA, 1925), you will feel the joyful rush of energy as Gurney experienced the river with all his senses fully engaged.

MARCH

My boat moves and I with her delighting,
Feeling the water slide past, and watching white
fashion
Of water, as she moves faster ever more whitening;
Till up at the white sail in that great sky heightening
Of fine cloth spread against azure and cloud
commotion
My face looks, and there is joy in the eyes that asking
Fulfilment of the heart's true and golden passion
(Long dimmed) now gets hold of a truth and an
action...
The ears take the sound of Severn water dashing.
The great spirit remembers Ulysses with his
courage lighting
Before the danger of sea water, in a rocky passion
Of surges – and over Bollow comes the wind I've
been waiting.

In less than a kilometre you reach Framilode. The first large half-timbered house on the left is the former Darell Arms, an inn which flourished in the nineteenth and early twentieth centuries as the servicing point for ferry passengers from Rodley. The Darell Arms closed in the 1980s but the private house still has the iron balcony designed for spectators to view the comings and goings as they drank their beer. Walk on through Framilode, take the right turn and proceed on down the road, passing the long line of houses known as Priding –'The river makes its fall / With murmurous still sound, / Past Pridings faery ground' ('Near Midsummer'). The views of the Cotswold Edge are always changing behind you.

2. Where the road turns sharp left just after Pridings House, take the Severn Way footpath straight on across fields. This is one of the Arlingham circular walks, and for the next 3kms you will be following the Gloucester Cattle Walk marked by a brown cow sign! Cross two fields, a coppice and a third field. Ahead of you the Forest of Dean is often visible; behind you Painswick Beacon and the Cotswold Edge appear. After the third field, there is a path junction; the left turn can be taken if you wish to shorten the walk via Overton and Barrow Hill (point 4). For the full walk, go straight ahead on a broad pathway across rough grazing land, with a pylon to your left and views of the Forest of Dean ahead. After passing the pylon, go through one gate and, just before the next gate, leave the Severn Way, turn left up a track and through another gate on your right. Keep the hedge on your right until you reach a small bridge over a stream. Cross it and continue straight ahead until you reach a road (Silver Street) and a pond.

3. Follow the road until you reach Slowwe House. Opposite the house, turn left through a gate and follow this signed path through three gates. If you wish to stop for refreshment at the Red Lion, you should now continue ahead to join Friday Street, and follow it to the left to find the pub in the middle of Arlingham. (Poem GA, 1925)

ARLINGHAM

The road led straight for a mile towards a blue
river –
A noble road to a West England beauty white going.
For long after, I had not read how its history was
Roman truly –nor guessed – so uncouth the
unknowing
To one whose thought of Rome was the high hills
place;
Or the ford-guarding city still Roman showing
After a thousand years and half a thousand
Of misty time – but since the knowledge had true
coming,

It was well to fit in somehow the thought of
legionaires [*sic*]
As on high Cotswold marching these valley ways –
And to imagine a new gleam of steel across new
land.

To continue the walk, go back down Friday Street to
the last 'middle-of-the-field' gate, and turn the other
way to follow Arlingham's Skylark Walk. Follow the
blue skylark signs through a succession of fields with
gates and, at one point, crossing a lane. Eventually
you will reach Overton Lane.

4. Cross Overton Lane and follow the footpath signs
to the top of Barrow Hill. The trig point at 62m is
slightly off the path to the right. Pause at the top of
the hill to enjoy the view on all sides, including the
river (on three sides), the Forest of Dean, May Hill,
the Cotswolds, the Malvern Hills and, if you are lucky,
a glimpse of Gloucester Cathedral. Gurney loved this
hill: 'Oh what a place! Blue river and golden sand, and
blue-black hills – in fine weather, of course' (Letter to
Marion Scott, June 1913).

From the top, retrace your steps to the path
before descending the hill to a gate at the entrance
to a wood on your left. Take this path and you are
now in the copse, written about by Ivor Gurney in
the poem 'The Nightingales'. Imagine the darkening
woods 'with a slip of moon, in a sort of dusk' as he
heard not one, but three nightingales sing. In fact, this
is not a sentimental poem. Gurney seems to prefer
the song of the linnet he had heard in Fretherne Lane!

THE NIGHTINGALES

Three I heard once together in Barrow Hill copse –
At midnight, with a slip of moon, in a sort of dusk.
They were not shy, heard us, and continued uttering
their notes.

But after 'Adelaïde'★ and the poets' ages of praise
How could I think such beautiful; or utter false the lies
Fit for verse? It was only bird song, a midnight
strange new noise.

But a month before a laughing linnet in the gold
had sung,
(And green) as if poet or musician had never before
true tongue
To tell out nature's magic with any truth kept for
long…

By Fretherne Lane the linnet (in the green) I shall
not forget
(Nor gold) the start of wonder – the joy to be so
in debt

To beauty – to the hidden bird there in spring elms
elate.

Should I lie then, because at midnight one had
nightingales,
Singing a mile off in the young oaks that wake to
look to Wales,
Dream and watch Severn – like me, will tell no false
adoration in tales?

> (K, 2004, p.229)
> (★Adelaïde – a song by Beethoven)

At the end of the wood, continue straight ahead
through a wooden gate, walk across a meadow by the
hedgerow and reach another gate. Halfway through
the next field, turn right through a gate in the hedge.

5. From here, head back eastwards across fields
towards Upper Framilode. Follow the footpath signs
through four fields, across the Saul/Framilode Road
and through another four fields to join a track. Go
right up this track to Saul Bridge over the disused
Stroudwater Canal. After all the fields, the path
alongside the canal is a welcome change, with small
cottages on your right and the reedy, overgrown
canal to your left. Follow this back into Upper
Framilode, perhaps pausing at the Ship Inn for
refreshment. At Framilode Bridge, turn left to walk
along the road past Lock House, behind tall hedges.
As you pass the gateway, you may catch a glimpse
of this handsome red-brick house, with its close
connections to Ivor Gurney, who stayed with the
Harris family when he had his breakdown in 1913.
There are two versions of his poem about Harris, for
whom he had a deep love and respect.. The extract
below, extolling the lock-keeper's knowledge, is from
the long version (B, K, 2004, p.84).

THE LOCK KEEPER (fourth stanza of six)

The nights of winter netting birds in hedges;
The stalking wild duck by down-river sedges;
The tricks of sailing; fashions of salmon netting:
Cunning of practice, the finding, doing, the getting –
Wisdom of every season or light –
Fish running, tide running, plant learning and bird
flight.
Short cuts and watercress beds, and all snaring
touches,
Angling and line laying and wild beast brushes:
Badgers, stoats, foxes, the few snakes, care of ferrets,
Exactly known and judged of on their merits.
Bee swarming, wasp exterminating and bird stuffing.
There was nothing he did not know; there was
nothing, nothing.

Ashleworth church and tithe barn, built of Blue Lias stone. (Greig Simms)

View from Barrow Hill looking across to Stinchcombe Hill and Cam Long Down on the Cotswold Edge.

THE HIGH HILLS

The Cotswolds stand out Eastward as if never
A curve of them the hand of Time might change;
Beauty sleeps most confidently for ever.

('Above Ashleworth', K, 2004, p.38)

It is a May morning and I am standing on the high edge of the Cotswolds at Cooper's Hill, my child-hood home. The house – still mine in the hidden folds of my memory – stands proudly on the extreme western promontory of the Cooper's Hill outcrop, with long views stretching away to north, west and south. Here I stood as a child, surveying the amazing wonderland of meadows to run across, woodland to make hideouts in, and steep grassy slopes for scrambling up. As Ivor Gurney was later to write, 'a beauty out of beauty suddenly thrust unasked upon a heart that dared not want more; had not dreamed of asking more, and was suddenly given completely eternal right' to (in my case) Cooper's Hill, Cranham, Sheepscombe and Birdlip. Immediately to the east, my eye travels across the cowslips and thistles of the meadow below the house, and then round the densely beech-clad hillsides of Cooper's Hill, as I reach back in time for the memories of riding my pony through the lemon-green beech leaves of early May. Looking northward, I can survey the prominent curve of the Cotswolds evoked so poignantly by Ivor Gurney as he gazed up at the edge from Ashleworth. Straight ahead is the sharp cliff face of Crickley Hill, and I try to keep my eyes on the limestone scars, the rough grassland and the woodland running away behind the edge. If possible, I want to avoid seeing the grey streak of the modern A417 dual car-riageway road. In Gurney's day, this did not exist. Ermin Street, legacy of the Roman Empire, ran straight as a sword across the vale from Gloucester then up Birdlip Hill, taking a breath, as it were, with what Gurney called 'a crook in the road', before climbing the scarp slope directly and making its unhindered way on towards Cirencester. A minor country road left Ermin Street at Witcombe and wound its way more respectfully up Crickley Hill, following the line of the Witcombe embayment. Now its modern replacement, the A417, is a traffic engineer's dream, efficiently planned and boldly drawn, designed without too much concern for the micro-landscape, to carry an endless stream of vehicles between South Wales and Oxford. The 'hand of time' has already changed Gurney's beautiful Cotswold curve.

Author, 2011

Ivor Gurney's High Hills

For Ivor Gurney, this stretch of the Cotswold Edge centred on Crickley Hill was his 'High Hills', and this was the place that inspired and claimed him (*see* map. Colour illustration 12). Many of his poems are filled with his unique 'sense of this place', of its beauty and of its importance to him. Although the Severn Meadows was the place that naturally entered his blood and filled his being, I would suggest that the 'High Hills', as an idea, can claim to be a more gradual and

The hand of time has already changed Gurney's Cotswold Edge. Looking from Cooper's Hill over the factories and houses of Brockworth in 2010. Note the Malvern Hills in the distance.

Walking at 'cold dusk' on Leckhampton common.

personal creation. His attachment to the Severn Meadows was forged out of the companionship of family, Will Harvey, Herbert Howells and James Harris the lock-keeper. He then made it his own in poetry and music. The sense of the High Hills grew from his own more solitary explorations. He grew up in sight of the steep Cotswold Edge that lines the skyline seen from the Severn Vale; he sought it out as a child and young man, climbing Portway by foot and on bicycle; and in France he found that the chalk landscapes of the Somme brought to mind more peaceful days and nights on the limestone Cotswold Edge, particularly when fear and discomfort were all that was available.

It was in the post-war period, however, that Gurney really intensified his relationship with the High Hills. In 1918, he was back in Gloucestershire trying to rebuild his life. Amidst the struggle of trying to restart his Royal College of Music work, find paid employment, decide where to live and hold back the depression that kept returning, he turned again and again to the Cotswold countryside to lift his mood. Howells was now busy with his musical career, Harvey was becoming more established as a lawyer and was soon to be a married man – the old friendships were no longer in existence in quite the same way; war had changed all that and Gurney seemed to find it hardest to recover and adapt. This was also the time when Gurney worked on the land at Dryhill, finding solace in the hard manual labour and the ghostly presence of the Romans.

Significantly, it was in 1920 that Gurney's dream of having his own cottage and 'writer's den' nearly came to fruition and it was Cold Slad, under the steep slopes of Crickley, that was chosen as the location (*see* p.66-67). In *80 Poems or So*, as well as a strong focus on the Severn Meadows, there is a whole group of poems that clearly belong, inspirationally, to this period and reveal his growing attachment to the white scars, the Roman-looking hills, the copses of the edge and the habit of walking alone to experience the changing moods of the landscape.

COLD DUSK
Now the red sun goes under
To a thousand foemen,
And dusk brings mystery
To all that Roman
Camp, height and common.

I am the trespasser
With thistles and waste things.
It is right to fear.
An owl cries warnings
From the dim copse near.

(80P, p.60)

THE HIGH HILLS

A 'white flash of lucky places' on the Cotswold Edge at Barrow Wake.

Another poem of this period (but not part of the *80 Poems or So* collection) is the short but intensely moving piece entitled 'The High Hills', with its first two lines: 'The high hills have a bitterness / Now they are not known' (*see* p.137). Written at a time of low mood sometime between 1920 and 1922, it is clearly both the cry of the blocked writer who cannot express his feelings, and, perhaps, a premonition of the anguish of leaving the High Hills, and so of losing the inspiration and passion from his life. Later poems written in the asylum, including the collection *Rewards of Wonder*, show that his mind was still working over the question of what the High Hills were, and of what they meant to him. Many of these poems are filled with movement – the poet and composer pacing the hillside to feel the sense of place; the walker soaking up the landscape and atmosphere as in 'Cotswold Slopes'; the motion ever stirring up joy and creativity as in 'Crickley Morning'.

Although the region known as the Cotswolds is quite large, normally seen as extending from Chipping Campden in the north to Bath in the south, and from the scarp edge in the west to the more gentle slopes dipping away towards Oxford in the east, Gurney's 'High Hills' is quite limited in extent if one is guided by the places mentioned in the poems. Gurney's Cotswolds are strongly focused on the scarp edge at Crickley Hill, about midway between Dursley and Chipping Campden. Surrounding this is a line of favoured places – Cranham, Painswick Beacon, Cooper's Hill, Birdlip, Shurdington Hill, and Leckhampton Hill. Beyond this core area, Gurney mentions other places radiating from the centre and including Cleeve Hill, Nottingham Hill and Bredon Hill in the north; Dursley, Brimscombe, Randwick, Horsepools and Stroud in the south; and occasional mentions of other places such as the Windrush Valley and Northleach, in the eastern Cotswolds. The limited extent of Gurney's 'High Hills' is a surprise because the depth and range of the poetry gives the impression that Gurney has introduced the reader to the whole Cotswold region, summarised its essential features and opened our eyes to its distinctive landscapes. Susan Hill (1988) suggests that this is because in Gurney's poetry, 'an odd stanza, a single line or image … encapsulates and evokes not just his own region of Gloucestershire, but the whole countryside of which the Cotswolds are the heart'. The poem 'Cotswold Slopes', for example, presents a journey or cross-section from the scarp edge onto the high plateau regions. With a deft economy of words, Gurney uses the first four lines to paint a picture of the steep edge in all its guises, whether road, quarry or grassland:

> ### COTSWOLD SLOPES
> Wonderful falls makes Cotswold edge, it drops
> From the roadway, or quarry or young beech copse
> It gestures, and is below in a white flash
> Of lucky places …

And later in the poem, he introduces us to the high but flatter Cotswold plateau:

> And the flat thousand foot up plain, whose barns
> Front light like Thebes' self or strength of Timgad★
> Runs on to waterless, treeless gray spaces,
> And to acre ploughlands square with gray walls – Cotswold walls –
> And light mists on commons and fallow sad places
> With some change seen in the grass colours and farm faces.

(RW, p.50)

★Note the references to Thebes, an ancient Egyptian city of about 3500 BC located on the eastern bank of the Nile, and to Timgad, a Roman colonial town of AD 100 sited in modern-day Algeria. In both cases, there are remains of buildings, temples and walls to be seen. The allusion creates a glow of grandeur and mystery.

Left: The rough and uneven hill slope at Crickley Hill.

Right: Glimpses of the ragstone rock face at Leckhampton.

As argued in Chapter 2, the Oolitic limestone of the Jurassic period is, and always has been, one of the main factors giving this part of Gloucestershire its distinctiveness. Gurney was keenly aware of the impact of the rocks on the landscape – in many ways he was a good amateur geologist, with a sharp eye for detail. To those who understand the geology/landscape link, there is no doubt that Gurney is describing limestone scenery and, specifically, the Jurassic limestone of this part of Southern England. His poetry gives us a complete set of typical features of the Middle Jurassic, such as the steep scarp where the Liassic clays and sands are followed by the Inferior Oolite limestones in 'Crickley Hill' ('O sudden steep! O hill towering above! / Chasm from the road falling suddenly away!'); the stepped nature of the slope, and frequent landslips, where the different types of limestone that make up the Inferior Oolite reveal their different strengths and characteristics, as in 'East Wind' ('Naked landslips show, away down hill mist-shades cover / The land'); the spring line at the junction of permeable limestones and impermeable clays meaning that springs seem to suddenly appear ('stream sources happened upon in unlikely places', in 'Cotswold Ways'); the glimpses of the blocky and creamy-white rock face (the freestones much loved by quarrymen because of their ease of cutting) and the more ragged and gritty upper slopes (the so-called Grits) of the Upper Inferior Oolite seen around Crickley and Leckhampton ('the pieces of limestone scattered in the spaces white', in 'Quietitude' [*sic*]); the grey-white stone of the Cotswold cottages and walls, and the ubiquitous white limestone dust on the lanes ('the white Cotswold scars, / Or sheets spread white against the hazel tree', in 'Cotswold Ways').

In the early years of the nineteenth century, many geographers searched for a deeper link between geology, landscape and human activity, believing that it should be possible to recognise a unique 'sense of place' for each small region. In France, the geographer Paul Vidal de La Blache introduced the term 'pays' to describe the small regions where people and nature achieved a degree of harmony. Alison Murray, in her 1930s' book entitled *The Cotswolds*, was in no doubt that she could sense 'an almost mystical integrity' or spirit of place here in the Gloucestershire Cotswolds (p. 12). Henry Massingham, in *Cotswold Country* in 1937, pointed out that although he saw himself as a more scientific writer, he could not describe the character of the limestone belt without recourse to what he calls 'improper psychological terms'. 'By using his eyes,' he wrote, 'any traveller can see for himself that, like the chalk and the granite and the more primeval Carboniferous limestone of the Mendips, the limestone has a psychology of its own.' (p. 10)

Gurney recognised, almost intuitively, the psychology of the area – its distinctive moods and the atmosphere of the place. He knew the scarp edge in sunshine and in wind and rain; he commented on the mist hanging on the upper slopes or filling the vale like a mysterious sea;

and some of his most effective poetry draws pictures of the amazing hues of dawn and dusk. Massingham makes much of the play of light on the limestone: 'there is no stone that retains the light as this limestone does,' he argues, 'and so reciprocates the moods of the day.' (p.6) Ten or so years before he wrote this, Gurney had captured the idea in a more poetic manner in 'Crickley Morning', as he described the play of changing light as the dawn breaks over Crickley Hill:

> CRICKLEY MORNING (extract)
> Morning struck the first steel of cloud light,
> And steel and armour changed to flooding oceans
> Of light, with infinite slow cautions and motions;
> Full power awaiting and signals of full delight.
> Faded away strength to sea-shells of fashion exquisite;
> Delicate; to tiny sea-shell trinkets of waves
> Touched with unmatched separate pallors of light;
> Rose-coloured, ocean-matching; the last spirit to delight of music.
>
> (RW, p.82)

The Delectable Mountains

Further investigation reveals the specific landscape features of the Cotswolds that Gurney was able to describe. Many of his poems (such as the one quoted at the head of this chapter) describe the shape and character of the scarp edge, as seen from below. This is not surprising since the edge is quite distinctive in the middle section of the Cotswolds, and Gurney could see it from his childhood home in Gloucester and from the many Severnside villages and walks that he frequented. Massingham (1937) spoke of the 'great adventure of the Edge' and described it as the point at which the rising plateau lands suddenly come to a climax: 'headland after headland suddenly stops short in space and all become a cliff line scalloped by its series of bays and overlooking the Severn sea.' Alison Murray is even more outspoken about the impact this landscape feature makes:

> There is something peculiarly fascinating about that undulating line of steep, sheer, peakless hills when viewed from the plain below. They invite exploration like the Delectable Mountains of the immortal Dream. They arouse a desire to tramp through the intervening woods and fields of the vale, straight across to the foot of the Edge, climb its face and discover the region that lies on the other side of that clear-cut skyline.
>
> (Murray, 1930, p.6)

Gurney clearly shared the fascination of these writers and was moved by the same desire as Alison Murray to walk and climb the edge. In 'Yesterday Lost' the reader is standing with the poet, looking up at the edge and sharing his joy at seeing the familiar line of the scarp at the same time as noting how 'the seeing of it each new time is a miracle'.

> YESTERDAY LOST
> What things I have missed today, I know very well,
> But the seeing of them each new time is miracle.
> Nothing between Bredon and Dursley has
> Any day yesterday's precise unpraiséd grace.
> The changed light, or curve changed mistily,
> Coppice, now bold cut, yesterday's mystery.
> A sense of mornings, once seen, for ever gone,
> Its own for ever: alive, dead, and my possession.
>
> (K, 2004, p.79)

Gurney marvels at 'the changed light, or curve changed mistily' – sometimes he sees it on a clear, sunlit day, sometimes the slopes are shrouded in mist and rain clouds, so that the coppice of trees on one occasion prominently displayed has, on another occasion, mysteriously disappeared from view. The poem is given greater poignancy because it was written in the 1920–22 period, just before Gurney entered Barnwood House private asylum, never to have the freedom of his Cotswolds again. It reads as if he is foreseeing his banishment and the need to hold the memories close ('once seen, forever gone, / Its own for ever: alive, dead and my possession'). In a poem entitled 'The County's Bastion' (K, 2004, p.248), the Cotswold Edge is 'azure and noble' and Gurney picks out 'Bredon, and Nottingham Hill, Cleeve, Crickley' as being the familiar shapes he seeks out 'day after unlooked-for day', as he looks northwards from Dryhill Farm.

It was not just the general shape of the edge that drew Gurney's interest. He had a sharp eye for detail and was able to describe those features that sparked his curiosity both accurately and with a poet's sensitivity to any deeper meanings or connotations. Most obviously, perhaps, he noted the changing seasons; in 'That Centre of Old', for instance, he charted images of dew-laden or perhaps snow-covered grass on Cooper's Hill in winter, the fresh sparkle of a June day and the colourful blast of autumn leaves at Cranham. Such descriptions call on touch, sight, sound and smell to form a complete image. In 'The Bronze Sounding', he reiterates the metaphor from 'That Centre of Old', explaining how 'Autumn would clang a gong of colour between Cranham and the Birdlip curve'. This is a powerful evocation of the bold line of red and orange that strikes the observer approaching the edge from the Severn Vale in late September and early October. In 'Old Thought', the autumn beech-woods 'set music on glowing in my mind' – somehow the mixed images of glowing colour and a warm, mellow sound summon up the sight and sense of those woods exactly. Indeed, this was not just poetic licence. As we have seen in Chapter 6, Gurney, the musician, found the natural beauty all around him to be what he called his 'springs of music', so that trees, high cliffs, winding roads and peaceful valleys all evoked a different kind of music in his mind.

In the essay entitled 'Springs of Music', he writes:

> Autumn is strongest in memory of all the seasons. To think of autumn is to be smitten through most powerfully with an F sharp minor chord that stops the breath, wrings the heart with unmeasurable power. On Brahms it is so strong, this royal season; has given him so much, worthily and truly translated. What! Do you not know the Clarinet Quintet, the Handel variations, the C minor symphony? And do you not smell Autumn air keen in the nostrils, touch and wonder at leaves fallen or about to fall? Have you not hastened to the woods of the F minor Quintet?
>
> (Gurney, 1922)

It is not surprising that the language of his poetry is so musical, presenting pleasing patterns and unusual rhymes that illuminate the natural world.

As well as the seasonal changes, Gurney was inspired by the daily and hourly changes of weather and light, experienced so starkly on, or looking up at, the Cotswold Edge. 'Cotswold Edge shines out at morning in gold,' he says in 'Cotswold'. As someone who was always looking up to the hills from his Gloucester home, he saw the edge in all its manifestations. Night walking brought him particular satisfaction; he revelled in the quietness, the mysterious shapes and forms made in the darkness, and the rustling of wild creatures. In 'Brimscombe', he arrives at the village east of Stroud 'at one lucky hour'. Walking out from under the pine trees, he sees the stars 'like steady candles gleam / Above and through them Brimscombe wrapped (past life) in sleep' (K, 2004, p.125). Early morning was much loved, as he frequently rose early to walk or write. Indeed sometimes, having walked at night, he was still out as day dawned.

> A night walk brought me at dawn to Birdlip; I had done 6 hours digging that day, and still am sick. It is a beastly thing. And one feels *such* a great musician at that time! If only I were well! ...
> The woods were very calm and pierced through with stars of the quietest. And Crickley looked magical enough against the 6 o'clock light.
>
> (Letter, 26 April 1921)

Left: 'The line of the Edge' from Leckhampton Hill looking north towards Cleeve Hill and Nottingham Hill. Cheltenham lies in the embayment below.

Right: 'Stream sources happened upon in unlikely places.' The Bisley spring.

This was the text of a letter to Marion Scott, written in April 1921. He frequently found that hard walking helped to relieve his depression and mental instability, but on this occasion it does not seem to have worked to his satisfaction. He regrets that he does not feel well enough to use the inspiration from the landscape in order to write music. 'Dawns I Have Seen' (K, 2004, p.230) reveals Gurney immersed in the changing display of light and sensual stimulation as experienced by a watcher below the edge. 'Terrible for mystery or glory dawns have arisen / Over Cotswold in great light, or beginning of colour / And my body at them has trembled, for beauty enraptured shaken.' Since this poem ends with the sadness that he finds 'no music in me to fit that great life-in-flood awakening', but finds only that he must walk 'in other men's poetry' (i.e. reading aloud Shakepeare or Milton), it may well refer to an occasion such as the letter described (or even that precise occasion) when Gurney's depressive illness inhibited his creativity.

When Gurney was out on the steep scarp slopes, or on the high tops, he was not just a passive observer of the scene. He was always an active participant, walking and running along the paths, interrogating the landscape and immersing himself in the sounds, sights and feelings aroused. We know from his letters and from the reminiscences of his family and friends that he was a great walker, not just as a pleasant hobby but because this was an important source of mental well-being and creativity. He needed to be out moving in the landscape, whether it was in the Gloucester streets, along the riverside paths or on the high Cotswold tracks. This is how his creativity ('speed of thought') was aroused:

OLD TIMES
Out in the morning
For a speed of thought I went,
And a clear thought of scorning
For home-keeping; while downward bent
Grass blades with dewdrops
Heavy on those delicate
Sword shapes, wonder thereat
Brightening my first hopes.

A four hours tramping
With brisk blood flowing
And life worth knowing
For all that something
Which let happiness then –
Sometimes, not always,
Breath-on-mirror of days –
And all now gone, since when?

(K, 2004, p.204)

He recognised this need in himself – 'I could walk 20 miles a day for weeks, and take pleasure in music or verse after that, but I must have work and movement not to be badly depressed.' (Letter to Mrs Voynich, December 1915) By work, he meant in this case intellectual 'brainwork', although in other writings he also expressed pleasure in hard physical labour helping his mood. Once one starts looking, it is clear that many poems have either a direct reference to walking, or reveal the rhythms and shapes of movement in the actual verse. 'One comes across the strangest things in walks'; 'Miles go sliding by under my steady feet'; 'Autumn that name of creeper falling and tea-time loving, / Was once for me the thought of High Cotswold noon-air', are some first lines that take us straight out onto the pathways to his happiness and his inspiration.

As he walked, he noticed small things: strange tree shapes, 'old troughs, great stone cisterns bishops might have blessed', stream sources, and wild flowers always mentioned by name – bryony, orchis, speedwell, creeper, wisteria. The poem 'Cotswold Ways' draws on a mixture of images from vale and high hills, but the last ten lines are pure Cotswold, summoning up the landscape of the high edge, in a way that all walkers will recognise. We are taken along as Gurney looks curiously and sympathetically around him, and we are listening to our walking companion as he reflects on the different characters of the roads and trackways climbing the scarp. 'Cotswold Ways' also reveals Gurney's interest in the landscape's history. The poem explains how the landscape is a palimpsest in which, if we keep our eyes open, we can find the layered hints of past histories – Roman, Saxon, Tudor, Victorian, modern. This is not the great sweep of political history but the features of everyday life, such as the stream sources (springs), mill falls, mounting stones, timber frames and houses of brick and stone (see colour illustrations 20-23).

COTSWOLD WAYS

One comes across the strangest things in walks:
Fragments of Abbey tithe-barns fixed in modern
And Dutch-sort houses where the water baulks
Weired up, and brick kilns broken among fern,
Old troughs, great stone cisterns bishops might have blessed
Ceremonially, and worthy mounting stones;
Black timber in red brick, queerly placed
Where Hill stone was looked for – and a manor's bones
Spied in the frame of some wisteria'd house
And mill falls and sedge pools and Saxon faces
Stream sources happened upon in unlikely places,
And Roman-looking hills of small degree
And the surprise of dignity of poplars
At a road end, or the white Cotswold scars,
Or sheets spread white against the hazel tree.
Strange the large difference of Up-Cotswold ways:
Birdlip climbs bold and treeless to a bend,
Portway to dim woodlengths without end,
And Crickley goes to cliffs are the crown of days.

(B, p.23; K, 2004, p.71)

The suggestion that Gurney sometimes ran may be surprising, since running for pleasure or sport is, of course, a late twentieth century and twenty-first century activity, and I am not suggesting that Gurney ran in this sense. Nevertheless, there is also the natural outpouring of joy and energy displayed by children and some adults, who retain a childlike enthusiasm for the outdoor and for movement. This is what one senses in Gurney's poetry – a joyful exuberance and uprising of joy. 'O up in height, O snatcht up, O swiftly going' – the arrangement of each statement in 'Old Thought' (Chapter 1, p.8) forces us to breathe faster, like a runner on the steep hillside. We can hear each breath he takes but this is not begrudged effort; the whole experience is welcomed, longed for even: 'breathing is loving'. We are taken along at this fast pace, smelling the leafy earth, pushing aside brambles, glimpsing with Gurney the high cirrus clouds above the Cotswold Edge and feeling the ecstasy of movement in this glorious environment. 'The wind frightens my dog but I bathe in it / Sound rush, scent of the spring fields' – surely Gurney is racing against the wind in 'April Gale'? written about the Severn Meadows but reinforcing the same point (K, 2004, p.51). Or running alongside the streams: 'In October time – crystal air time and free words were talking / In my mind with light tunes and bright streams ran free, / When the earth smelt, leaves shone and air and cloud had glee.' ('When the Body Might Free', B, p.96; K, 2004, p.185) These are not detached pictures he is painting but a desire to pull us into the experiences. The poetry, like the man, is in a rush to gather these moments of being and the mobility is essential to the heightened perception and the feelings of well-being. The last verse of 'Old Times' reveals that Gurney was well aware of what was being taken away from him by his incarceration in the asylum. 'Old Times' spells out quite clearly that it was not just the Cotswold places but the ability to move swiftly in them that had been 'letting happiness in', feeding his music and poetry ('for a speed of thought') and making 'life worth knowing'. Now they are all gone.

One way of experiencing some of these sensations and moving a little closer to Gurney is to follow the walk **High on Cooper's**. Study the route outlined on the map on p.124 and read the commentary and poems on pp.126-127 – best of all, find the relevant OS map and go and walk it in person. You don't need to run it!

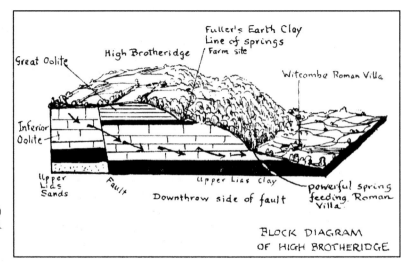

Fig. 7.1: Cooper's Hill and High Brotheridge; block Diagram. (W. Dreghorn, 1967) (*See* also the LIDAR image, colour illustration 15.)

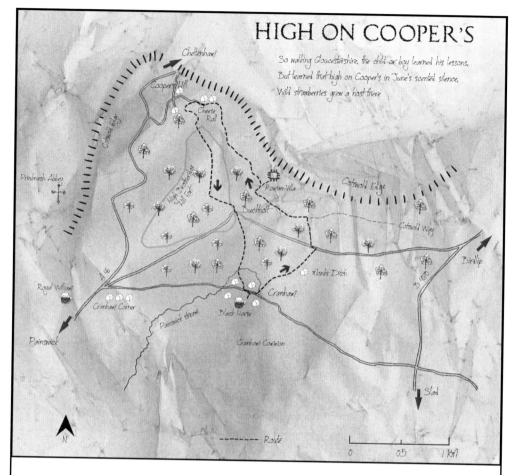

HIGH ON COOPER'S

So walking Gloucestershire, the child or boy learned his lessons.
But learned that high on Cooper's in June's scented silence,
Wild strawberries grew a host there

(See colour illustrations 13, 14 and 15)

Route Facts:

Distance/time
5.5km (3.5 miles)/2-2½ hours.

Map
OS Explorer 179 Gloucester, Cheltenham and Stroud.
OS Landranger 163 Cheltenham and Cirencester.

Start and Parking
The Black Horse Inn (897129) is the starting point for the walk. If you are taking refreshment at the pub, park in the large pub car park up the steep hill to the right as you face the pub. Or, drive on up to the Common and find a safe place on the side of the road.

Refreshment
The Black Horse Inn at Cranham. Normal opening hours.

So, walking Gloucestershire, the child or boy learned his lessons,
But learned that high on Cooper's in June's scented silence,
Wild strawberries grew a host there,

('Culpeper', GA, 1925)

Walking was an essential part of Gurney's life and the Cotswold Edge was a favourite area.
He loved the challenge of gaining height; the euphoria that accompanied the mix of hard
physical effort combined with the sense of wonder and achievement at reaching the summit;
the joy of wandering through sweet-scented beech woodland and recognising the flowers and
shrubs. The diverse landscapes of the Cotswold Edge, with its beech-woods, common lands,
high hilltops, small springs and hidden valleys, gave him all this and is exemplified in the walk
that follows. It starts at the 'village pub' on the edge of Cranham Common, crosses Cranham
stream, and climbs up into the stately beech-woods of Buckholt and Witcombe Woods.
The walk now skirts the edge of High Brotheridge Iron Age Camp, hidden beneath the trees.
After passing the remains of Witcombe Roman Villa, it reaches the hamlet of Cooper's Hill
and climbs to the open grassy summit of the famous Cheese-Roll. The return route takes
you across the ditches and banks of High Brotheridge Camp, before dropping back down the
steep wooded slopes of Buckhholt and back to Cranham.

High on Cooper's Hill, looking north along the Cotswold Edge in June.

WALK 3
HIGH ON COOPER'S

1. Start at the Black Horse Inn, which stands at the top of a steep hill in the middle of Cranham. When you look down at the village, the settlement seems to be completely enclosed by the Cotswold beech-woods. For Gurney, these woods seem to symbolise the beauty and stability of the Cotswold countryside, evoked in letters and poems alike: 'autumn Cranham with its boom of colour' ('That Centre of Old'); 'And Cranham, Cranham trees, And blaze of autumn hues' ('The Fire Kindled'); 'of tree or watercourse flowing by Cranham' ('Autumn').

2. Do not turn down the steep hill, but walk past the pub. At the junction with the main street, turn right and walk up as far as the village hall and the Sheepscombe turning, then turn left down a marked bridleway. If you want to see the spring that is the source of Painswick Stream and a wonderful example of Gurney's 'stream sources happened upon in unlikely places' ('Cotswold Ways'), then take a short diversion down the small grassy path between the last two houses on the left, and walk about 50m to a shady hidden grove. Here you will find a spring feeding a small pond; the latter was built specifically for the local pottery industry (Cranham Historical Society, 2010). One of the main reasons for Cranham's site was the existence of the spring line here, where the Oolitic limestone meets the Lias sands and clay and there are several springs dotted around the valley at this height, all feeding the stream that eventually runs through Painswick.

Back on the walk route, follow the bridleway across the edge of Cranham Common, a typical Cotswold common with rough grass, wild flowers like cowslips and orchids in profusion in the spring and summer, and blackberries in the autumn. The common only exists in this form because of continuous grazing by cattle, sheep and horses. The profusion of ash and elder saplings at the edge of the common shows the process by which the woodland would rapidly return if there was no grazing and management. Continue down the path into the woods and to the wooden bridge over the stream. You are now surrounded by mature beech, part of the Cotswold Commons and Beechwoods National Nature Reserve (www.naturalengland.org.uk).

3. Follow the track uphill as it becomes stonier and seems sunken into the hillside. This is the ancient trackway Monk's Ditch, and to the right you will see the gardens of Monk's Ditch House. Reaching the Birdlip–Cranham road, cross over before turning down a track next to a bungalow and eventually past a large new house. Once through the old gateway you are in Witcombe Woods, part of the Witcombe estate, owned for generations by the Hicks-Beach family. Join the Cotswold Way going westwards (to the left), running along near the bottom of the woods. You will begin to see glimpses of the pastures and the reservoir in Witcombe embayment below you to the right; in the summer, this can be a delightful experience, peeping out from the rich shady woodland into the brightly lit meadows with the blue gleam of the reservoir. Gurney's poem 'Possessions' (see p53) regrets the wartime demand for timber that led to many of the Witcombe trees being felled; particularly on the slopes to the east of where you are standing.

4. You now follow the Cotswold Way to Cooper's Hill. The track can be muddy and rutted in wet periods. In spring, the delicate colour of the new beech leaves gives a pale lemon glow to the woodland: 'Lemon-green the morning drips / Wet sunlight on the powder of my eye' as another Cotswold poet, Laurie Lee, described it ('April Rise'). Later in May and June, whole areas are awash with the blue haze of bluebells and wild garlic flourishes, providing the strong smell for which these woods are famous. In my childhood, we knew them as 'the garlic woods'. In spring and summer, the path is full of typical beech woodland flowers – such as wood anemone, wild geranium, celandine – and in the autumn it is rich with shades of red and brown leaves. Even in winter, the delicate tracery of beech twigs and branches presents a more stark splendour, often lit by low sunlight. After descending into a valley occupied by a stream, take the right-hand fork down to a field gate leading into a sheltered embayment, site of the Witcombe Roman Villa. Since Gurney's day, the site has been excavated and can be viewed at any time. Alternatively, you can just enjoy the deep calm and beauty of this valley. Gurney's poem refers to an autumn visit to one of the villas he knew – he may have been referring to Witcombe or to Dryhill. He speaks of the frustrations of trying to capture the 'fire and thrill' of his emotions and of paying due respect to the Romans.

ABOVE THE VILLA (extract)
The wind of autumn has touched there, the beech leaves have changed.

All the willowherb of all the world falling steep to the Villa

Where once the Romans ranged, is a wonder of light chanced

Upon ... O friend are you not drunken with the
sea of far lost mystic colour?

And I with the Roman unknowing in me then,
watched the fall
Of the high hill to pasture, and wondered if master
I might ever be of the thoughts in me did fire and
thrill
To have black on paper, golden in fame my dear
dreams and flooding faster.

(GA, 1925)

5. Return to the undulating main track, which is now
running below the main embankments of the High
Brotheridge Hill Fort (see colour illustration 15). Pass
an isolated cottage (Woodcot) on the right, before
leaving the woods and following the road into the
main village of Cooper's Hill. Note the views of
Brockworth and the Vale of Gloucester, dominated
now by factories and houses. At the parish notice-
board you will be at the foot of the Cheese Roll.
On the May Bank Holiday, large Double Gloucester
cheeses are rolled down this steep slope to be chased
by local people (see www.cheese-rolling.co.uk).

6. Follow the Cotswold Way signs through a gate
and up the gentle wooded slope to the side of the
Cheese Roll. Climb steeply through the woods then
leave the Cotswold Way to bear sharp left up a
grassy slope ('O up in height! O snatch up, O swiftly
going / Breathing was loving', 'Old Thought') and
come out on Cooper's Hill Summit by the flagpole,
from where the cheeses are launched. Here is one
of the best views in Gloucestershire, out across
the Vale of Gloucester, taking in the city itself with
cathedral glimpsed if the light is right, the Malvern
Hills to the north-east, the outlier of Chosen Hill
and the Cotswold Edge to the north. Behind you is
the remains of Cooper's Hill Common, much more
extensive when Gurney walked here (he refers to
it as Cooper's Heath in his poem, 'Dawn', see p.27).
Turn your back to the flagpole and go up the slope
and into the overgrown Common ahead (ignore
footpath going to right). Cross several bank and
ditch structures – you are now traversing one of
the inner earthworks of the High Brotheridge Iron
Age Camp (see colour illustration 15). Gurney often
mentions it in his writing. Alongside the path, you will
find many limestone-loving wildflowers, including the
bee orchid, hen and chickens and scabious. When I
was a child we called this area 'the wilderness' and
Gurney's poem 'Wilderness' evokes these memories
so well that I am placing it here, even though he may
be referring to Crickley Common.

WILDERNESS

The wildest place for brambles, the sweetest for
strawberries
With the great edge of Wales, and ridgy Malverns, ...
O Common of thousand flowers, and the great love
of June,
Which gave all things to the Hill – and later all
blackberries.
Higher the Roman Camp, [turning?] kept a stern
Reminder of what once History had shaped in
bringing
From Southern lands the true soldiers with strong
hands,
Whom now the harebell defeats in his delicate
swinging
(air stirred), and Briton all, on Rome passed and won
Yet praised by these hands living with love and warm
Mixed of both bloods and to each mastership with
love clinging.

(GA, 1925)

7. Soon you are back in the deep woodland of
High Brotheridge, with huge mature beech trees
and layers of dead leaves and leaf mould beneath
your feet. The path is not always clear, but head in
a southerly direction straight through the woods,
and following the line of an inner earthwork of High
Brotheridge camp. This path can be muddy in wet
months, but in May you will be rewarded by a sea
of bluebells and in autumn by a 'boom of colour'.
After about 1km, you meet the field edge of High
Brotheridge Farm, at which point you turn left and
drop down to Buckholt sawmill and the Birdlip road.
Here was once an impressive gateway to High
Brotheridge camp but little remains now, as gradual
erosion by walkers and recent redevelopment of
the old Buckholt house have reduced the gateway
mounds (Cranham Historical Society, 2010). Cross
over to find the footpath on the opposite side of
the road, a few metres in the Birdlip direction.

8. Take care walking down towards Cranham as the
path can be rough, muddy and occasionally awash
with water, due to the disruption of natural drainage
channels when the new houses were built. If it seems
unsuitable for use, then walk further along the road
towards Cranham Corner to find another footpath
leading back to the village. Both paths are, at times,
narrow. Near the bottom of the slope, it doesn't
matter if you turn left or right. One path (right) leads
past the Cranham Scout Hut and the other (left)
stays in the woods before crossing the stream and
emerging higher up the village street. You are now
back in Cranham and can walk back up to the Black
Horse.

Crickley Hill

> If only this fear would leave me I could dream of Crickley Hill
> And a hundred thousand thoughts of home would visit my heart in sleep;
>
> (*De Profundis*, WE, p.91)

Cooper's Hill was dear to Gurney but there is no doubt that Crickley Hill held a special place in his mind. He turned to Crickley when in need of spiritual revival and creative inspiration. After all, from Crickley he could see most of his Gloucestershire set out before him – the river glinting in the sunlight, the play of clouds over the edge, the cathedral spires and the city of his childhood, the outlying hills of Chosen Hill and Robinswood, and the sharp noble line of the Malverns.

Crickley Hill is distinctive to the people of Gloucestershire too. It is in their vision whenever they look up and, like a sentinel, it guards what is now the main route east-west across the

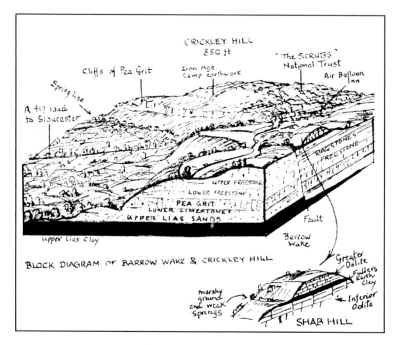

Fig. 7.2: Crickley Hill;
block diagram.
(W. Dreghorn, 1967)

Crickley Hill: 'Time's
wonder and crown.'
Picture taken from
Barrow Wake, 2010.

county. In fact, as we have seen in Chapter 2, its distinctiveness is closely related to the nature of its geology, landscape and history. Rising to 267m, Crickley is not the highest point but it is at an important turning point along the line of the edge. Whilst to the north, the headlands of Shurdington, Leckhampton, Cleeve, Nottingham, Oxenton and Langley Hills are 'closely riveted to the high plateau of the wolds' (Massingham, p.66) and present a relatively straight wall to the vale; further south, taking in Cooper's Hill, Cranham, Painswick, Haresfield, Stroud, Coaley and the hills round Dursley, is a region where the hills are 'flung out' to the west and separated by long winding combes and clefts. The distinction between north and south of Crickley is accentuated by the existence of a major fault line passing in a w-n-w/e-s-e line, closely related to the Witcombe embayment. We know too (Chapter 2) that the Crickley scarp marks a geological transition, and so also a landscape transition, west to east from the Liassic clays of the vale to the Inferior Oolite and Great Oolite limestones of the hills (Figure 7.1).

For Gurney, Crickley came to represent other more personal transitions, particularly in the post-war period – from a scholar at the Royal College of Music to a farm labourer; from the solitary creator to the lonely writer; and from someone showing signs of slight eccentricity to someone with mental problems severe enough to warrant commitment to an asylum.

Crickley appears as a named place in more poems than any other Gloucestershire place name. Using all collections of poetry and material published in Gurney's time or since, there are six poems with Crickley in the title or in the first line ('De Profundis', 'Crickley', 'Crickley Morning', 'Crickley Hill', 'To Crickley', 'Crickley Cliffs') and another twelve with the name of the hill mentioned within the poem. I have so far discovered in the archives three more unpublished poems with the name in the title or first line ('Crickley Heights', 'Heights of the Great Valley (Crickley)' and 'Rain Veil') and two more that mention the name in the poem ('Roman Cotswold', 'Quietitude'), but there are doubtless other references to find. Significantly too, Crickley's presence is felt on many other occasions once the reader gets to know Gurney's work and can apply a little local knowledge or read the landscape. For example, the fact that Gurney lived and worked at Dryhill Farm, just below Crickley, means that any mention of Dryhill usually refers to this area, as in 'Above Dryhill' and 'The Coin', which both talk about the Roman remains found under the Cotswold Edge at Crickley. Crickley is frequently referred to as the Roman Hill (e.g. in 'Quietitude') whilst 'Up on Cotswold' and 'Cotswold Slopes' are using Gurney's knowledge and experience of landscapes like Crickley to talk about the Cotswold Edge as a whole.

It is instructive to study these Crickley poems to see how the poet dealt with a 'special place'. What these poems, as a group, show is that Gurney envisaged Crickley not just in terms of a striking limestone scarp landscape with its assemblage of characteristic flora and fauna – though he did do that – but as a multi-layered presence rich in history, experience and personal meaning. As a poet and composer, he could 'read' Crickley, but only by opening himself up to the feelings, historic allusions and reflective thoughts emerging day by day and night by night as he walked, ran, sat quietly on the hill or, in some cases, remembered it from afar; 'Ages and ages dreaming there speak their heart to me' ('To Crickley') he explained.

'Crickley', eventually published in 2000 (RW, p.85), was one of the poems selected by Gurney in about 1924 to be part of his *Rewards of Wonder* collection, but there is evidence that it was written in the immediate post-war period, possibly in hospital (letter to MS, 28 September 1918) and revised later. It is a long poem, not easy to read with its many historical and classical references, but it does make reference to those themes that Crickley Hill inspired in Gurney. The poem paints a visual picture of the changing moods and landscapes of high hilltop throughout one day. The landscape is drawn in detail – the high common lands, the steep edge, the ploughed fields on the lower slopes, the grazing lands for sheep, and a range of plants, birds and animal life characteristic of the Crickley slopes. Gurney explains that 'Crickley gathers conies [the old Gloucestershire word for rabbits], starlings and lonely kites, Grass snakes and butterflies' and he refers to the assembly of trefoil, scabious, tansy, wild rose and bee orchid which characterise such limestone uplands. More importantly perhaps, we see how Crickley is associated in Gurney's mind with the early history of Gloucestershire, particularly with the early Britons and the Romans. He also saw Crickley as his ideal place for creating, and writing music and poetry (the

Left: Walking on Crickley Hill, the giant beeches in early March.

Right: Walking on Crickley Hill, cattle on rough pastures. (In 2010, belted Galloway were grazing.)

significance of finding the cottage in 1920 becomes apparent). He mentions walking, working, reading classic Greek texts, tea-time, wood smoke and the coming of evening, all offering the sense of peace and harmony necessary for creating: 'Making comes after that clarity / Of exact truth' ('Crickley'). All these themes reappear in later poems, and in his music.

The poem entitled 'Cotswold', for example, presents a visual image of Crickley Hill seen at dawn and dusk. 'But Cotswold wall stands up and has strength of its own, / Blue against dawn, Sunset's shield, and Time's wonder and crown.' ('Cotswold', RW, p.62) 'Cotswold Slopes' begins with a description that may not only refer to Crickley but surely has that place in mind. 'Wonderful falls makes Cotswold edge, it drops / From the roadway, or quarry or young beech copse / It gestures, and is below in a white flash of lucky places.' (RW, p.50) These are such striking images – walk along the path just below the summit of Crickley and you will see exactly how the edge seems to gesture downwards to guide your gaze to the white scar and the secret hollows hidden in long grass ('a white flash of lucky places'). Or stand on the edge at the Crickley summit as the sun is setting and be blinded by the brightness, then shocked by the vivid colours trailing across the western sky ('Time's wonder and crown'). Behind you the ground dips away, so that the Cotswold plateau is shielded (the high Crickley is 'Sunset's shield') from the brightest light, though still glories in the colourful sky display.

If you walk briskly or run along the Cotswold Way from the ancient Greenway Lane along the narrow bramble strewn path, across the rough sloping pastures and through the autumn beech woodlands to the summit of Crickley, you will find yourself taking in the earth-smell, 'turning brambles' and appreciating the 'White Cotswold [scars], wine scarlet woods and leaf wreckage wet' ('Old Thought') as you breathlessly climb the steep slopes. Find yourself on Crickley Hill in the rainy mist of a cool August evening and experience 'Crickley veiled by rain' ('Rain Veil') while the green of the fields below disappears ('green went out') and 'sheets of white rain' seem to slide past the steep earth and the road darkens beneath you. Walk on the footpaths above Dryhill Farm and you may pick up the theme of working on the land, the enjoyment of physical labour and the closeness to the land ('Felling a Tree', 'Above Dryhill').

As we have seen, Gurney was very interested in the historical evidence of earlier inhabitants of Gloucestershire. The Cotswold Edge was attractive to earlier settlers, partly for defensive reasons and partly because the lighter and thinner soils of the top were generally easier to plough than the thick clays of the vale. Crickley Hill shows signs of settlers living in hilltop enclosures since about 4000 BC, but the main hillfort was constructed in the Iron Age in the seventh century BC. In Gurney's day it was clear that the rounded mound and ditches and banks were evidence of earlier peoples, but at that time there seems to have been disagreement as to whether the Crickley Hill mounds were a burial site or a fort (*see* Murray for example, 1931, p.22). The archaeologist, Philip Dixon, excavated the site between 1969 and 1973, and we now know a lot more about this site (Dixon, 1979). Up on this exposed hilltop there was a complete fortified Iron Age town with an imposing double gateway and a main street lined with long houses. The walls were made of limestone rubble and timber. It was occupied for a considerable length of time, but Dixon thinks that some time in the third century BC it was abandoned and not subsequently reoccupied on a large scale again.

After AD 43, the Romans gradually spread out from south-east England, and by the start of the second century AD, the Celtic Dobunni kingdom had been taken over completely by the Romans. There are signs of some small-scale Roman activity at the site, possibly a village behind the Iron Age ramparts and also a second settlement in the west of the site where there was a guard house and living areas. Gurney seems convinced that Roman soldiers were stationed here, frequently mentioning their presence on the Crickley hilltop. Whether or not there was a Roman camp of any size, the Crickley area is rich in Roman associations. On either side of Ermin Street, as it makes a bend to climb up Birdlip Hill, lie Roman villas at Witcombe and Dryhill. Gurney knew both of these as features of the landscape – 'the bare line of the hill / Shows Roman and / A sense of Rome hangs still over the land', as he described it in 'The Bare Line of the Hill' (K, 2004, p.73). He was also curious to know about the lives of the people who lived there. Working at Dryhill Farm in the 1919–21 period had an extra attraction, since he was surrounded by evidence of Roman settlement and recalled it later in many poems, such as 'Up There' (*see* p.135), 'Red Tiling' and 'The Coin'.

The walk, **On the Roman Hill**, allows you to discover Gurney's Cold Slad cottage and to relive his experience of roaming along this hilltop – although one would need to walk at night and in all weathers to gain anything like the full experience! Study the map (p.132) and the accompanying commentary (pp.134-135), which together provide you with all the details. Best of all, find the relevant OS map and walk the route in person.

Looking at the Crickley poems, it is possible to trace some of Gurney's personal transitions in an emerging sequence in his way of seeing this place (although the poems were not written in this sequence). 'Crickley Morning' presents the joy and sensitive appreciation of the experience of morning breaking on Crickley Hill – he is reliving a real place and a real experience. 'Quietitude' hints at the creative relationship that is developing between poet and place ('in my pocket a sketchbook to write of all the beauty that I could') and this is explored further in 'Crickley Cliffs' ('to have a mind of music, a body of delight') and in 'Rain Veil', where Gurney begs the Roman ghosts to help him speak ('give me music and great speech to say of you what is to say').

'De Profundis', written about the traumas of being a soldier, represents a different process whereby Crickley Hill stands for something else – the peace and happiness of the life left behind. In 'Crickley Hill', this idea is developed further. When talking to another soldier in France, Gurney is transported back to Gloucestershire by the mention of the name: 'When on a sudden 'Crickley' he said'; 'we shared memories / And the old raptures from each other learned.' The name has now come to represent 'home', 'nation' and 'identity'. To continue this sequence, we need to place the poem 'The High Hills' next (though written 1920–22). In his depression and anguish, he realises how essential these hills are to his creativity and well-being; they have become a part of him. Hence they (and he) know only bitterness when apart and his mind is confused, 'walking into clarity is gone'. The final poem, 'To Crickley', is a cry for help from someone who is deeply disturbed and mentally ill: 'my soul goes there crying when it is hurt by God far' – even the memories of Crickley Hill and what it stood for cannot save him.

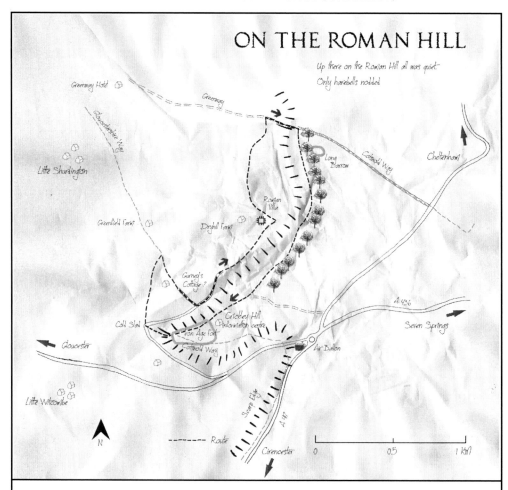

ON THE ROMAN HILL

Up there on the Roman Hill all was quiet.
Only harebells nodded

(See colour illustrations 16 and 17)

Route Facts:

Distance/time
4.75km (3 miles)/1½-2 hours.

Map
OS Explorer 179 1:25,000 Gloucester, Cheltenham and Stroud.
OS Landranger 163 1:50,000, Cheltenham and Cirencester.
Also useful are the walk maps provided by the Crickley Park Country Park,
available at the information centre.

Start and Parking
The walk starts at the information centre at Crickley Hill Country Park (929164).
There is ample parking in upper and lower car parks.

Refreshment
The Air Balloon Inn at the road junction (A417/A436).

Up there on the Roman Hill all was quiet.
Only harebells nodded,
And the pieces of limestone scattered in the spaces white,
Wondered not what I did.

('Quietitude', GA, 1925)

This walk is focused on Crickley Hill, Gurney's high playground and place of retreat, usually on his own and always creating poetry and music in his mind. It is one of the places featuring most frequently in the poems, often as 'the Roman Hill', where Gurney sensed the ghost of Roman soldiers and farmers. The walk is a short one but what it lacks in length, it makes up for in the diversity of scenery and the richness of allusions and memories of Gurney. What is more, the views from the edge display the rest of Gurney's Gloucestershire set out below. The route begins on Crickley Hill, amidst the remains of an important Iron Age settlement, standing high above the vale and the Roman Ermin Street. It descends the 'nose' of Crickley, passing a cottage that might have been the one Gurney briefly lived in, crosses the fields under the steep slopes of the edge and pauses at Dryhill Farm, where Gurney worked as a farm labourer. Climbing back up the scarp slope via the ancient drover's road, the Greenway, the walk follows the Cotswold Way along the high edge, passing through the magnificent mature beech woods, now being protected in Crickley Hill Country Park.

Wind-blasted trees in March on the scarp edge below Crickley Hill.

WALK 4
ON THE ROMAN HILL (CRICKLEY)

1. From the Crickley Hill Information Centre, walk down the road a short way to join the 'orange' and 'brown' marked walks. A viewing point display explains the amazing 180° panorama of the vale and distant hills. The eye travels from Cooper's Hill on the far left, to Bredon Hill on the far right, taking in the Forest of Dean, the Welsh hills of Sugar Loaf and Blorenge, the outliers of Robinswood Hill and Chosen Hill, and the striking silhouette of the Malverns. Carry on along the path, passing the remains of the Iron Age fort and town, and then veer to the right down an open grassy slope. This is classic limestone common land, with its assemblage of rough grass, wildflowers (e.g. harebell, cowslip, scabious) and occasional hawthorn and elder bushes. It owes its characteristics to the underlying rock and the continual grazing by sheep and cattle, nowadays maintained by the National Trust.

QUIETITUDE

Up there on the Roman Hill all was quiet.
Only harebells nodded,
And the pieces of limestone scattered in the spaces white,
Wondered not what I did.

It was early Spring, below hedges breaking in green
The coppice clothing with light,
Where soon the children should gather yellow marigolds in,
And the willow sprouts show bright.

In my pocket my sketch book to write of all
Beauty that I could –
But after the long climbing – the place majestical
Made lazy my mood.

So trying to guess what village I had never yet known
Lay under a mile forward…
I mused, hoping at night to work well from the longing
Now, keeping no vow or word.

And thought of all the mailed sentries that had kept
In past times watch here – now…
When only through their vigilance danger slept,
Or went uncaring the plough.

(GA, 1925)

2. Head straight down the 'nose' of Crickley, signposted as the Gloucestershire Way, and pass the large flat rock known as the Devils Table (colour illustration 17). Descend the steep, rocky path to reach Cold Slad Lane ('A'). Here, follow the Gloucestershire Way across the road and through three fields, until you reach the place where the Way crosses what looks like a rough ditch hidden in shrubs but is in fact an old trackway. The Gloucestershire Way continues onward and turns right downhill, but follow the old rough track uphill. It eventually passes a house on the right and the surface improves before it runs alongside what I believe may be Gurney's cottage. It meets his description of 'an old Cotswold stone house', under the shadow of the great rise of Crickley' and the track and cottage are marked on the 1896 and 1919 OS maps. The cottage is on the left, hiding amidst shrubs and with its own small overgrown garden; it is now disused but not completely derelict. It has a gateway onto the track and from here, until a recent footpath re-routing, a path led across the fields direct to Dryhill Farm, where Gurney worked as a farm labourer. It is easy to imagine Gurney out in the early morning on the high top of Crickley, his head full of Romans and the dawn light-show, returning to reflect and write in the tiny cottage. (If you prefer to miss out this Gloucestershire Way loop and the rough section of ditch, at 'A' you can walk along the Cold Slad Lane to meet the top of the track and walk down it to find the cottage.)

CRICKLEY MORNING

Morning struck the first steel of cloud light,
And steel and armour changed to flooding oceans
Of light, and with infinite slow cautions and motions;
Full power awaiting and signals of full delight.
Faded away strength to sea-shells of fashion exquisite;
Delicate; to tiny sea-shell trinkets of waves
Touched with unmatched separate pallors of light;
Rose-coloured, ocean matching; the last spirit to delight of music.

But there was coffee to my body's need,
And fire to be made – and of music a screed.
There was Dryhill meadow to calm the thought to birth,
And there were books of familiar and heart precious earth.
So put aside the matchless glories, for those who were more
Worthy, or loved not earth or writing as I did – to the door
Of the small cottage going in – to work out thoughts of musing
By the Camp – or the pine wood – or the marsh;
pen and ink to find the mood.

(RW, p.82)

3. From the cottage, walk to the top of the track and, at a path junction, follow the continuation of the lane. After about 100m, the lane bends left but you should go ahead through a gateway onto the path that runs through the pastures under the scarp edge. At the next gateway, do not go through it but turn left onto a signposted bridleway. Stop and look back to see Gurney's cottage peeping out of the trees with the Crickley slopes above. Follow the bridleway; for the next 1/2km, you are on fields that once belonged to Dryhill Farm, contouring round the slope above the farm and catching sight of its rooftop and chimneys. The farm is now a private house, and the footpath which led immediately to it has been discontinued, so this is the best view you will get. These are the fields on which Gurney would have raked hay, gathered root crops or herded livestock and wondered about the Romans whose villa was located next to the farmhouse and whose pottery and coins he occasionally found.

Up There

On Cotswold edge there is a field and that
Grows thick with corn and speedwell and the mat
of thistles, of the tall kind; Rome lived there,
Some hurt centurion got his grant or tenure,
Built farm with fowl and pigsties and wood-piles,
Waited for service custom between whiles.
The farmer ploughs up coins in the wet-earth-time,
He sees them on the topple of crests' gleam,
Or run down furrows; and halts and does let them lie
Like a small black island in brown immensity,
Till his wonder is ceased, and his great hand picks up the penny.
Red pottery easy discovered, no searching needed,
One wonders what farms were like, no searching needed,
As now the single kite hovering still
By the coppice there, level with the flat of the hill.

(K, 2004, p.188)

Where the field path meets the field corner, do not go through the gate uphill into the woods but turn down alongside the field edge, imagining the Roman villa to your left and passing a spring that trickles into a stone trough. Perhaps it is one of those 'old troughs' that Gurney had in mind when writing 'Cotswold Ways'. This spring fed the Roman villa. The path down the field eventually crosses the Dryhill Farm House driveway and reaches a gate into a lower field.

4. Once in the field, walk a few metres straight ahead, but after that turn uphill to the right, making for a blackberry bush, the field corner and another

gate. Looking back you get another view of Dryhill Farm and can appreciate its sheltered foot of scarp and springline location. Go through the gate and follow a footpath which occasionally bends downhill, but generally stays close to the upper edge of two fields. Note the view of Gurney's favoured outlier, Chosen Hill, from the second field. Eventually you reach Greenway Lane, formerly a drovers' road, now only used as a road in its upper section, while the lower part is a deeply sunken and shady track. Gurney wrote about such unsurfaced country roads, 'Daylight colours gray them, they are stained blue by the April / Skies on their pools and summer makes carpet of dust / Fit for the royal; Autumn smothers all with colour / Blown clean way by the withering winter's gust' ('Roads', Blunden, p.85).

5. Walk up Greenway Lane until you turn right for the Cotswold Way, reached by a short flight of steps up from the road. The return route is easy – just follow the Cotswold Way all along the high edge. The first section is a narrow path right on the edge, with relatively young beech-wood to the left. Notice some coniferous trees amongst the beeches. Gurney mentions the firs above Dryhill Farm and remembers the poet Robert Bridges, whose work he had clearly been reading:

Cedar Mountain (extract)

Under the firs I thought of Robert Bridges,
Who set these memories sighing far away from the sand
Of piny branches growing on Cotswold ridges
And looked up to the enormous, the Roman mound
(where I had also helped plough earth ages fruitful now).

(GA, 1925)

6. After a pathway goes off to the right (linking with the Dryhill route), the scarp edge path climbs again and enters more mature beech-wood. You may find you are diverted from the edge itself as the National Trust is protecting the giant beech trees for which this area is famous. At times the trees on the scarp edge at Crickley seemed to Gurney to assume a more threatening manner, particularly when he was in a low mood. Some of the most arresting imagery of Gurney's later poems conjure up the gloom and menace of wind-shaken trees. 'There is a coppice on Cotswold's edge the winds love; / It blasts so, and from below there one sees move / Tree branches like water darkling.' ('The Coppice', K, p.277) The path emerges through a gate into the upper Crickley Hill car park.

Walking on Crickley Hill,
May Blossom.

It would be unthinkable, at this point, not to at least mention Gurney's music and, in particular, the 'Gloucestershire Rhapsody'. This orchestral piece, written in 1921 when Gurney was at the height of his Crickley explorations, represents his desire to produce a significant piece of music rooted in the Gloucestershire landscape. Performed for the first time at the Three Choirs Festival in 2010, the 'Rhapsody' has a first section which seems like an evocation of sunrise on the Cotswold Edge. After three poignant notes on the horn which, like the dawn appearing on the eastern horizon, introduce the Edge, the music then swells and builds 'as if following the contours of a great hill' (Ian Venables, 2011). In the remaining four sections of the Gloucestershire Rhapsody, themes from Gloucestershire's history unfold – early Britons, Romans, Elizabethans, soldiers marching (Roman and / or First World War). After reading the poetry of Crickley, I am in no doubt that this is the great hill to which music alludes, for example:

> There dawn rounding the north strikes dimness through
> A wind stirs tremulous about the leaves, and shows
> Curves like any carved thing
>
> ('Crickley', RW, p.85)

and

> Crickley cliffs blared a trumpet ever, ever golden,
> A flourish of trumpets against the late afternoon light.
> Rome spoke out intangibly yet matchlessly,
> And defied land and high air with boy soldiers' might.
> Such huge tramplings of brass sound about
> Cliffs of white stone…
>
> ('Crickley Cliffs', GA, 1925)

Just as Gloucestershire's history unfolds against the backdrop of Crickley, so did Gurney envisage the events of his life, as Gloucestershire boy, musician, poet and soldier, playing out against this vision of Crickley. 'All love from all memory called out', as he explained it in the poem 'A bit from my "Gloucestershire Rhapsody"'. The hill has become a metaphor for the dynamics of place and the march of time. In this sense, his music and his poetry are not two different interpretations but one unified creative expression of the place.

8

THE SOUL HOPELESS GONE

THE HIGH HILLS
The high hills have a bitterness
Now they are not known,
And memory is poor enough consolation
For the soul hopeless gone.
Up in the air there beech tangles wildly in the wind –
That I can imagine.
But the speed, the swiftness, walking into clarity,
Like last year's briony are gone.

(B, p.54, also in K, 2004, p.181)

The Poet of Gloucestershire

Gurney's Gloucestershire was real. He is a poet of Gloucestershire; he lived in the county and wrote from direct experience about the places all around him. When he wrote 'To my county where I was born, and the earth / entered into my making and into my blood', this was not just rhetoric. His poems reveal a direct engagement with these real places and this can be seen in many of the poems presented in this book (e.g. 'Gloucester' and 'The Old City' in Chapter 5; 'By Severn' and 'First Framilode' in Chapter 6; 'Cotswold Slopes' and 'Crickley Morning' in Chapter 7) in which place names, geographical features and first-hand observations are essential elements of the image. Whether he is referring to the changing landscapes experienced while traversing the Cotswold Edge or the varied riverscapes along the different stretches of the River Severn, the faithful and intimate descriptions are such as only one who has been there could provide.

Geographers also recognise what has been called a 'sense of place', or the essential character of the place resulting from the interplay over time of its physical features (geology, landscape, weather) and its human features (settlement, community, land uses). Again Gurney's poetry seems to evoke 'sense of place' easily and naturally, as if the very fact of expressing his own connection with the landscapes and places enables him to draw out their essence. Seamus Heaney, writing about Thomas Hardy and Dorset (2002, p.232), suggests that the spirit of the place was 'already immanent in the place from which Hardy sprang … Hardy's country, in other words, pre-dated Hardy. It awaited its expression.' This not only seems to fit Gurney's relationship with Gloucestershire very well, but it was recognised as such by Gurney himself. 'O Cranham, Minsterworth, Framilode, Maisemore,' he wrote in a letter to Marion Scott (September 1915), 'It is you that have poured into my as yet defective mould that fluid of beauty which shall one day take form in me and make others aware of your graces and sweet looks.' For Gurney, music and poetry were ways of capturing the true essence of these landscapes and places, and he felt that it was his responsibility, as someone blessed with creative energies, to interpret and express

A sense of place – Severn Meadows in flood, February 2009.

them. Although he is describing specific locations, he seems to sum up the essential atmosphere and feeling of all Severn Meadows and all places on the Cotswold Edge in this part of Gloucestershire. Other examples abound. Writing about the Cotswold scarp (for example in 'Old Thought', 'Crickley Hill', 'That Centre of Old', 'The Bramble Patch') he conjures up the airy breathlessness of the high Cotswold Edge, the startling views, the easy relationship of farmer and land, and the rich sensuousness of the beech-woods running along or below the summits. The many poems about the Severn Meadows appearing in *80 Poems or So* (e.g. 'Sedges', 'Dull Afternoon', 'April Mist', 'First Spring') evoke a landscape of riverside pastures, elm trees, sedge, and the knowing presence of fishermen and boatmen. If the role of the regional geographer is to identify and describe regions with distinctive characteristics and a sense of place, then Gurney was a very good regional geographer.

Gurney's Gloucestershire, as defined by the places he mentions, is quite a small area and is focused on the twin points of Crickley Hill and Minsterworth (one on the Cotswold Edge and one in the Severn Vale). In fact, Gurney has provided his own definition of his Gloucestershire in the last four lines of the poem 'While I Write' (K, 2004, p.262). It seems to have been his war experience that helped crystallise this revelation:

> War told me truth, I have Severn's right of maker,
> As of Cotswold: war told me: I was elect, I was born fit
> To praise the three hundred feet depth of every acre
> Between Tewkesbury and Stroudway, Side★ and Wales Gate★★

★ Side is usually written as Syde on recent maps; ★★ by Wales Gate, Gurney means the point at which the Forest of Dean hills rise and the road to Wales (current A40) breaks away from the plain. This is around the village of Huntley.

The map, colour illustration 12, is an attempt to represent Ivor Gurney's Gloucestershire, drawing on Gurney's poetry and writings, with the help of an artist and map-maker, Roger Ellis. Surrounding the twin-centred core of Crickley and Minsterworth is a wider area covering about 16km of the Severn Vale upstream and downstream of Gloucester, the Cotswold Edge between Langley Hill and Coaley Peak, and the high Cotswold uplands stretching inland for about 10km from the Edge. This varied area contains Stroud, Brimscombe, Bisley, Painswick, Syde, Cranham, Cooper's Hill, Leckhampton and Cleeve on the Cotswolds, and Arlingham, Framilode, Minsterworth, Maisemore, Ashleworth, Staunton and Tewkesbury in the Severn Vale. It was the direct source of Gurney's creative inspiration throughout his life, both in his poetry and his music. Although there are occasional poems about Gloucestershire places outside this area (e.g. Northleach, the Windrush Valley, Chipping Norton) these are more detached observations, rather than expressions of intimacy.

Writing about the work of Patrick Kavanagh, Seamus Heaney (2002, p.135) spoke about the kind of poetry which reveals a direct attachment to the place that is its source. He stated:

> It is supplied with a strong physical presence and is full of the recognitions which existed between the poet and his place; it is symbolic of affections rooted in a community life and has behind it an imagination which is not yet weaned from its origin, an attached rather than a detached faculty.

I think that we can say the same, certainly about those poems between 1913 and 1922, written when Gurney was still either living in direct touch with the Gloucestershire countryside or able to return to renew his intimacy with it. Gurney himself elaborated on this deep-seated connection in his essay 'On Earth' (2009, p.158). He also wrote a poem in 1925 entitled 'The Local Poet'. In this, he explained his need, as a local poet, to be in direct contact with ('attached to') Framilode, the October woods and the Cranham watercress stream; in the trenches he became 'lethargy sodden; dumb'.

> THE LOCAL POET
> As I lay in the dugout
> My heart would adventure
> Out to the bare woods
> On green of my own shore
>
> Of Framilode – or high
> Octobers woods of night;
> Days of unrestricted colours
> Clouds shadowing all delight.
>
> Immortal delight; on by
> The Cranham watercress
> To drink tea, or muse of high
> Music, or Roman marches
>
> Or talk, O happy boy
> With all a boy's freedom …
> We limp in dugouts now –
> Lethargy sodden; dumb.
>
> (GA, 1925)

Place, Time and Identity

Gurney is also much more than a local poet with the possible narrowness of vision that this might imply. Gurney uses his poetry not only to produce images of specific Gloucestershire places but also to illuminate more general qualities of place, time and identity. In 'Yesterday Lost' (p.119), for example, he moves from describing the morning light on the Cotswold Edge –'the changed light, the curve changed mistily' – to recognising that beauty is such a fleeting experience, and that being human means we live in a constant state of loss – 'a sense of mornings once seen, forever gone'. Of course, in this poem, he also hints at his special relationship with the place, such that he can keep it (the moment of beauty and ecstasy) alive in his imagination – 'my possession'. In 'There Was Such Beauty' (p.85), Gurney is moved almost to tears by the harmonious setting of 'town, tower, trees, river' in the valley and the 'gathered loveliness of all the years'. We do not need to know exactly which valley, or to be in Gloucestershire to understand the point he is making about the effect of such 'natural' beauty and harmony on the human emotions. The interesting point is, however, that as the preceding chapters have shown, Gurney does need to be in Gloucestershire to present these feelings to us. Taplin (1989) agrees with this: 'the 'local habitation' is essential to the kind of truth-seeking, exact poet that Gurney was. The universal had to spring from the particular (p.153).

Gurney's sense of history was acutely developed. As shown in Chapter 5, growing up in Gloucester ensured that he was surrounded by the past, the ghostly presence of Romans, Saxons, Danes, Normans and Elizabethans forever hovering on the edge of his vision. He seemed to accept, as normal, the way in which time and place interweave, and so his poetry rambles through historic periods just as much as it ranges through space. In the Gloucester poems like 'The Old City', this characteristic is, perhaps, not surprising; before modern redevelopment, walking Gloucester, to use Gurney's words, must have 'seemed a living thing' for all its inhabitants. But historical continuity is also a strong feature of the poetry of the High Hills and the Severn Meadows. The Romans of Crickley, Abbot Serlo's monks fetching Cooper's Hill stone for the abbey, the centuries of boatmen on the Severn – these are not just detached references in Gurney's poems, they are intricately interwoven to remind us just how much the past is still a part of the present.

Jeremy Hooker (1982), referring to 'Cotswold Ways', explains that Gurney 'has a gift for at once naming things and conveying their shapes and textures, which renders place as the presence of historical time, but without conflating widely separated periods or smoothing out their differences.' (p.124) The poem 'By Severn' (Chapter 6) reveals that literary allusion could be used to the same effect. The weaving of Shakespeare and Elizabethan theatre into the description of Wainlode Cliff does not read like an unnatural device but as a natural and masterly way of conveying a sense of the long traditions of English cultural life alongside the importance of the English landscape. This is about English identity.

Although born in a town, Gurney was a countryman at heart and he had a countryman's understanding of the close relationship between the people and the place. In Gloucestershire he saw the rural landscape being shaped and cared for by the ordinary men and women – the Cotswold and Severnside farmers, the hedgers, the fishermen and, like his friend Harris, the lock-keepers. His poetry frequently reminds us of this intimate human-place relationship and of the necessity and dignity of such tasks. In fact, for Gurney, this was what characterised England – a deep-seated recognition of the dignity of work and the everyday contributions of the 'common man' to England's landscapes. In 'The Hedger', 'Felling a Tree', 'The Mangel-Bury' and, perhaps most clearly, in 'The Lock-Keeper', Gurney celebrates the physical labours of such people but also their practical wisdom and their intimate understanding of the natural world around them. However, this is not done in a patronising way. When Gurney refers to his 'net of craft of eye, heart, kenning and hand. / Thousand-threaded tentaculous intellect' (K, 2004, p.84), he isn't looking back to an over-idealised or romanticised vision of the past; he is bringing our attention to the knowledge, hard-won skills and experience needed to understand and protect the natural world on which we depend. The modern term for this might be stewardship.

In a different way, the poem entitled 'Changes' talks about the villas built to house the new urban workers, 'set up where the sheepfolds were', and in which 'plate glass impudent stares at the sun'. Gurney is sad that the old ways are swept away, 'threshing for ever is done', and that 'new things are there, shining new-fangled gear'. He is concerned about the thoughtlessness –'the mixtured hotch-potch' of new and old.

In all these poems of Gloucestershire (particularly in the 1918–22 period, *see* Chapter 3), Gurney seems to be putting forward the idea of a satisfying and productive society in which people labour hard but with dignity, and in which the beauty and wholeness of the countryside is recognised. This was what he hoped would be the basis of the England to which the soldiers returned. In 'A Wish', he imagined 'villages on the land' and good housing with plots of land 'Where one might play and dig, and use spade or the hand / In managing or shaping the earth in such forms / As please the sunny mind or keep out of harms.' (K, 2004, p.200) In this, he, like many other soldiers, was disappointed. They came back to find housing shortages, no proper work and no real recognition, as they saw it, for the sacrifices and hardships they had made. Some of Gurney's most bitter poems are cries of frustration because of his own desire for recognition and for work. But it is not just his own difficulties that he is bemoaning in poems like 'Strange Hells' (K, 2004, p.141), nor is it an escapist looking back to a past golden age. It is the sense of loss for the place that England might have become; an ideal of English identity that his poems had nurtured.

Morning light on a frost-covered Crickley Hill, 2009.

Being in-Place

There is another approach to Gurney's poetry which offers a fruitful way to understand his poetry, his place and the person he was. A phenomenological approach focuses attention on the experience of 'being in-place'. Whereas the established Western tradition of art, as seen in painting and literature, is based on the idea of detachment from the landscape or place, on standing back and observing what is assumed to be an objective and separate reality, phenomenology is opposed to this. It suggests that the fundamental quality of being human is 'being in-place', an idea derived from the work of Martin Heidegger, the geographer and philosopher. He used the term 'dasein' – being here (Heidegger 1962). It is also taken forward by other thinkers such as Merleau-Ponty (1969), who developed it in relation to landscape. Phenomenologists argue that we cannot have a detached view of the place we are in, because we are a part of it. Being, belonging and perceiving are happening at the same time. This implies not a series of detached viewings or experiences of the place/landscape but a constant process of dialogue between the person and the place.

> As I contemplate the blue of the sky I am not set over against it as an acosmic subject; I do not possess it in thought, or spread out toward it some idea of blue … I abandon myself to it and plunge into this mystery, it thinks itself in me.
>
> (Merleau-Ponty, 1969, p.214)

Interestingly, a new generation of cultural geographers is revisiting the phenomenological approach to landscape and place, providing a new emphasis on how our being-in-the-world takes shape – for instance through walking, photography, painting, playing sport, exploration, and literature and poetry (Wylie, 2007; Rawling, 2011). Using this approach, we can see that the 'mystery' of Gloucestershire places might be seen as thinking through Ivor Gurney. As he himself explained in a letter to Marion Scott, 6 October 1915: '…Minsterworth orchards, Cranham, Crickley and Framilode reach. They do not merely mean intensely to me; they are me…'

In 'The Cloud', the setting is a hot May day, in which the heat is such as to dazzle and blind the walker, but Gurney is mesmerised by the wholeness of skyscape and landscape. Rather than merely describe a bright blue sky with a large cloud moving over the landscape, he directs our senses into the scene so that we feel the darkness of the overhead cloud moving over the azure blue of the sky, are tantalised by the contrasting light and dark, and feel with Gurney an almost mystical union of earth and sky. It is difficult to know where the onlooker ends and the sky begins.

THE CLOUD

One could not see or think, the heat overcame one,
With a dazzle of square road to challenge and blind one,
No water was there, cowparsley the only flower
Of all May's garland this torrid before-summer hour,
And but one ploughman to break ten miles of solitariness.
No water, water to drink, to stare at, the lovely clean-grained one.

Where like a falcon on prey, shadow flung downward
Solid as gun-metal, the eyes sprang sunward
To salute the silver radiance of an Atlantic high
Prince of vapour required of the retinue
Continual changing of the outer-sea's flooding sun.
Cloud Royal, born called and ordered to domination,
Spring called him out of his tent in the azure of pleasure
He girt his nobleness – and in slow pace went onward
A true monarch of air chosen to service and station;
And directed on duties of patrolling the considered blue.
But what his course required being fulfilled, what fancy
Of beyond-imagination did his power escape to
With raiment of blown silver …

(B, p.78; K, 2004, p.119)

What is amazing about this poem is that we have, all in one piece, the movement and experience of the poet and walker ('with a dazzle of square road to challenge and blind one'), the strong involvement of the writer in the scene ('the eyes sprang sunward to salute the silver radiance') and yet the sheer accuracy of image (the meteorological details of an Atlantic high, cloud as water vapour, the unusually hot May). This is a countryman's understanding of weather conditions bound up with a poet's sense of being in-place. Gurney was acutely aware of weather, geology, light and dark, daily patterns and rhythms in the environment and seasonal changes, but these were not cool detached observations; they were immediate sensual experiences.

In 'The Cloud', movement is essential to the experience, as was discovered with other poems written about the Cotswold Edge (Chapter 7). In fact, there is a long tradition of linking walking and poetry. Roger Gilbert's book *Walks in the World* (1991) points out that even Theocritus and Horace, Dante and Petrarch, Spencer and Milton represented themselves as walkers in a landscape. More recently, we think of the Romantic poets, particularly Wordsworth and Coleridge, as walking poets. Indeed Wordsworth was well known by the local inhabitants of Grasmere for his peculiar habit of composing lines out loud as he walked the footpaths, apparently finding the rhythms of walking in harmony with the rhythms of poetry. Gilbert suggests, however, that the Romantics were not so much walk poets as poets who walked, because they used the outer landscape as a prompt for reflection and meditation. 'Tintern Abbey' is a good example where the descriptions of the landscape are separated out from the thoughts being promoted. Gurney's dependence on walking was, as we have seen, all to do with his way of 'being-in-place', making him a more genuine 'walk poet' in Gilbert's definition. For Gurney, the poem was not about the landscape as a detached subject, it wasn't even about the experience of walking in the place or landscape, the poem *was* the experience. As a result, currents of thought become inextricably interwoven with the sensual experiences of walking in a place, exactly what we find in 'Old Thought', 'Early Spring Dawn', 'The Cloud' and other poems written from direct experience. For Gurney, it is worth noting too that he was fascinated by all forms of moving through the landscape, not just walking and, as I think, running, but also cycling and sailing. The words he uses in relevant poems suggest that his creativity was stimulated by these as well. For example: 'swift as a running horse', 'to find music at last, my dear thought flowing in my mind quick' in 'Dawn', the cycle ride poem (p.27); and 'my boat moves and I with her delighting', 'asking fulfilment of the heart's true and golden passion (long dimmed) now gets hold of truth and an action' in 'March', one of the sailing poems (p.112). In each case, the movement, the joy and the spurt of thought are virtually instantaneous.

Gurney has provided us with a description of his in-place creative process in another poem entitled 'When from the Curve of the Wood's Edge' (K, 2004, p.44); he helpfully summarises the three stages in the last two lines of the poem:

'When from the Curve of the Wood's Edge.' Blackstable
Woods, Sheepscombe, from the Sheepscombe–Cranham road.

The fire, the flood, the soaring, these the three
That merged are power of Song and prophecy.

First is 'the fire' which is the first spark of inspiration,
imagination and love invoked by experiencing
a place or landscape at first hand (as we have seen,
usually by moving through it). So, in this poem, it is
not just the sight of a woodland edge but the whole
experience of being where, as Gurney describes it,
'tree meets plough' and the 'power' of the place
'spreads to envelop me'. He is filled with delight and
joy and feels 'tiny song stir tremblingly'. Then comes
the 'flood' of emotion – 'the kindling, the beating at
heaven gate' before the feelings overpower him and 'the flood of tide … bears strongly home'.
Finally there is the spiritual ecstasy ('soaring') which moves him 'to purify' his thoughts and so
to prepare himself to set them down on a page ('fit my heart for inhabiting the high House of
Song'). There is more than a hint of Hopkins in this poem, although whereas for Hopkins the
intrinsic power of the place arose from God, in Gurney there is a more pantheistic Wordsworthian
feel about the place in its own right. According to the notes in Kavanagh (2004), Gurney would
not let Marion Scott submit this poem for publication in the Royal College of Music magazine
(1919/20) because 'it was too intimate'. It is interesting to find how many of Gurney's poems
confirm this need for the inspiration to come direct from an experience in-place. The 'sight of
earth and rooks made passion rise' ('February Dawn', p.104); 'Who walked in dawn to find the
fitting word' ('The Golden Age', p.218); 'Give me out of truths / Of wide sight of valley / Fore
Severn, far Severn / Spinney or water sally' ('Prelude', p.260); 'Out of the blackthorn edges I
caught a tune' ('Love Song', p.218). (All K, 2004)

We also know from his letters and poems that another essential stage in the creative process was
to retreat to a quiet and secure place indoors, preferably with a cup of tea, a warm fire and maybe
a cigarette, in order to reflect on the experience and write down the words of the poem or the
notes of the music. As he explains in 'Prelude': 'Let me but have a room / Of golden night quiet –
/ Peace in a lonely gloom / Mixed of mixed rich light / And dark; and remember some / Height
of Cotswold, plough of valley.' He had hoped to find this creative bolthole in his cottage at Cold
Slad (see 'Midnight', p.66); he certainly found it, but briefly, at his aunt Marie's house in Longford
1920–22 ('Going Out at Dawn', K, p.105). Finding the final right words and shape of his poem
was not an easy task. Gurney saw this as a craft skill, needing his full attention and numerous
trials. As we have seen (Chapter 5, p.91) he used the term 'squaring' to describe this final part
of the process, explaining in 'Compensations' that although 'the poet's true place is in that high
wood', nevertheless 'virtue lies in square making – / The making pleasure' (K, 2004, p.99). It may
be that, in some cases, the desire to improve his poems in this way resulted in a less free-flowing
place experience. The revisions made to 'Old Thought' (GA) provide a good example – Gurney
had changed the last line from 'White Cotswold, wine scarlet woods and leaf wreckage wet' to
'White Cotswold with the breathing earth, and leaves hurting, bloodwet', so changing the mood
from that of joyful exuberance to something darker and more considered. Both Lancaster (2007)
and Thornton (2007) suggest that Gurney was always torn between the looseness of free writing
and the attempt to achieve squareness – 'he aspired to squareness but is inclined towards free
inclination', as Lancaster (p.58) describes it.

Did Gurney, the musician, draw on the same sources for his musical composition? And did
he follow the same creative process? Those who have written about his music (Venables, 2002
and 2010; Lancaster, 2007; Banfield, 2007; Frederick, 2007) seem quite clear that the places of

Gloucestershire were one of the most important sources of his inspiration. In his essay 'Springs of Music' (1922), Gurney tells us the same thing: 'the springs of music are identical with those of the springs of all beauty remembered by the heart.' Later in the same essay, he seems to be saying that music is the more significant art: 'the chief use of Poetry seeming to one, perhaps mistaken, musician to stir his spirit to the height of music.' However, I do not take this to mean that one is more important than the other but that they are two parts of the same creative urge. 'The fire, the flood, the soaring' of sublime thought, as described above, result in the artist capturing the words which flow from the landscape, and these can then be written down in a poem, or transformed into music. Lancaster (2007, p.48) confirms this idea of music being 'another language into which literary thought can be directly translated'. Gurney composed a comparatively small number of song settings for his own poems (fifteen, of which 'Severn Meadows' is the best known) as if his own poetry needed no further transformation by him (Lancaster, p.48). Venables (2002) suggests that when setting other people's poems to music, Gurney the song-writer was drawn to poems with a natural rhythm: 'the hidden music behind the words.' (p.9) However, looking at Gurney's poem 'Crickley Cliffs', and Gurney's orchestral piece 'Gloucestershire Rhapsody', it is possible to see that Crickley Hill is not only the inspiration for both but, as described on p.136, that words and music seem to be part of one unified image of this special place, drawing on his own walking experience and the marching Roman soldiers.

Being Out-of-Place

This way of looking at Gurney's poetry begins to tell us not just about his poetry but also more about the man and his dependence on being in his Gloucestershire places. If 'being in-place' was so important, then 'being out-of-place' must be significant too, and suddenly we can see the huge significance of Gurney's incarceration in an asylum, away from Gloucestershire. Some of his most bitter poetry is expressing this place absence:

> There is a coppice on Cotswold's edge the winds love;
> It blasts so, and from below there one sees move
> Tree branches like water darkling – and I write thus
> At the year's end, in nine Hell-depths, with such memories;
>
> ('The Coppice', K, 2004, p.277)

As Gurney himself seems to have predicted in 'The High Hills', without access to the direct experience of being in Gloucestershire, his 'soul is hopeless gone'. It would be tempting to see this as a simple story and to look for evidence to back this up. When he was in Gloucestershire and could walk the countryside, he was generally contented and, apart from some spells of mental instability, he was settled and his creative juices flowed. When he was away from these places and his illness became more severe, he was unsettled, depressed and could not create good music and poetry any more. This is how the story should go, but we know, of course that it is not as simple as that. Some of his most creative periods of writing poetry and music were when he was absent from Gloucestershire, especially in the 1915–17 period when he was in the army, and again in 1922–26 during the early years of Dartford Asylum. There are many works of high quality throughout this time. In addition, the reference to Gloucestershire places did not fade or cease when he could not be there; indeed, the mentions of Gloucestershire places are greater not fewer during the Dartford years. However, none of this invalidates the 'being in-place' idea. Gurney just had to find different ways of being there, and that was mainly through his memory and imagination. My contention is that we can trace a process of change in the way that Gurney's close identification with his Gloucestershire places is expressed, and that this can be traced in the content, language and style of his poetry.

In Gloucestershire from 1890–1911, as a child and young man, Gurney was directly in contact with these places, and his identity and creativity were fashioned in this joyful learning relationship (Chapter 2). From 1911 to 1917 (Chapter 3), although the absences, first in London and then in France, were painful, they were temporary and he found ways to renew the contact (e.g. recovering from depression in Framilode, 1913; using his leave in 1916 to cycle to Ryton). In France he drew on his Gloucestershire experience in his mind by writing poems about absence from Gloucestershire ('After-Glow', 'The Fire Kindled', 'De Profundis') or more usually comparing and relating places and events to Gloucestershire examples ('Trees', 'Ypres-Minsterworth', 'Half Dead'). Poems of this period appear in the two published books (*Severn & Somme* and *War's Embers*), but there are other poems not written until 1917–22 that also hark back to this period (e.g. 'Crickley Hill', 'That Centre of Old'). Overall they show a direct identification with the places concerned, and recognition of their uniqueness as far as the writer is concerned.

After the war, he was able to return to Gloucestershire (1918) but his deteriorating mental state meant that this was not easy. The experiment of living at Dryhill revealed that it wasn't just a case of living back in his old haunts, and the desire to re-launch his professional career as musician meant that London called him as well (Chapter 4). In this period, Gurney's poems alternate between pleasure and pain. The pleasure is more apparent, particularly in *80 Poems or So*, and is due to him renewing his acquaintance with the Gloucestershire countryside (e.g. 'Lovely Playthings', 'First Spring', 'Coming Dusk', 'Above Dryhill'), the city ('There Was Such Beauty', 'The Old City – Gloucester', 'Above Maisemore'), in rediscovering the joys of walking ('The Walking Song', 'Old Thought') and of creative inspiration ('When from the Curve'). The pain was a result of anxiety and a sense of loss brought on by his spells of depression ('What Evil Coil', 'The Bronze Sounding', 'Moments', 'The Not-Returning'). There are also hints of bitterness at the feeling that England and Gloucestershire were not the ideal places of return that he had imagined in France ('Time to Come', 'Swift and Slow', 'North Woolwich', 'Changes', 'Strange Hells'). What is interesting about the poetry of this period is the beginning of a sense of loss, even though Gurney is actually back in Gloucestershire. His mental illness and depression are beginning to take him 'out-of-place' and so away from the sources of his creativity – hence in 'The Bronze Sounding', he talks of the vivid autumn beauty of the woods between Cranham and Birdlip ('a gong of colour') but fears that his illness means 'the body now no longer takes in distance as slow thought' i.e. he won't be able to walk and be inspired by the place. The same sentiments appear in 'The Not-Returning' – 'never comes now the through and through clear / tiredness of body on crisp straw down laid' – pointing out that without his physical involvement in the countryside he will not be able to create –'Poetry, friends, music, the old earthly rewards. / No more they come. No more. / Only the restless searching, the bitter labour, / The going out to watch stars, stumbling blind through the difficult door.' (B, p.46; K, 2004, p.168) Gurney had hoped to return to his place, to find himself 'in-place' again. But it wasn't that easy. The idea of return or retreat is a common theme in pastoral writing, but usually a joyful return to an ideal place – Gurney's return is often turned to pain by his illness.

In the asylum years after 1922, Gloucestershire really was lost to him. After admission to Dartford Mental Hospital in December 1922, Gurney

A coppice on the Cotswold Edge.

never returned to Gloucestershire again – until he was buried there in 1937. Gloucestershire became a place of memory and imagination only, and it is apparent that the poetry changes as the man, locked away in the asylum, changes. And, of course, the increasing debilitation and anguish of his untreated bi-polar condition must be factored into this as well (Blevins, 2007). At first, there was an outpouring of bitterness and outrage over his fate, as in 'There is a Man' and 'To God' – the latter with its haunting first lines: 'Why have you made my life so intolerable / And set me between four walls.' (K, 2004, p. 197) Then, as he began to write more, Gurney was able to draw heavily on his memories of Gloucestershire; after all, as he had explained in 'The High Hills', he could still remember and imagine. The title of *Rewards of Wonder*, the collection that came out of the 1922–24 period, may be significant in this respect – does Gurney see his memory and the ability to write these poems as his reward for being in Gloucestershire all those years? I pointed out in Chapter 4 that some of his best 'place poetry' appears in this selection, although there are occasional hints ('Memory', 'October', 'Poem for the End') that this may be the last time he can rely so heavily on his memory. Many of the later poems (1924 onwards) are very different. Increasingly, the fact that they are remembered and not experienced becomes apparent. The North American poems are a good example of this, with their strange (to us) device of using a Civil War battle site or a place name as the prompt for memories of childhood, Gloucestershire and the war. So too are the many poems about Elizabethan poets and musicians, and the long autobiographical poems. Gurney's atlas map of the Civil War (bought for him by Marion Scott), his reading and his desire to put the record straight about his life are all more real now than his Gloucestershire places. Instead of the place speaking through Gurney, we begin to see Gurney's fears and anxieties of all kinds speaking through the place memories. Gurney recognised what was happening to him: 'They have left me little indeed, how shall I best keep / Memory from sliding content down to drugged sleep' ('Memory', K, 2004, p. 264); 'It is Winter, the soon dark annoys me – / Who cannot remember Severn / Her warm dark lights ('It is Winter', K, 2004, p. 265); 'Here no dreams touch me to colour / Sodden state of all dolour' ('The Depths', K, 2004, p. 285). To refer again to 'The High Hills', it is not a detached beauty that he is missing – after all, he can imagine the beech trees tangling in the wind. What he cannot do if he is not present is experience 'the speed, the swiftness, walking into clarity' – that is the upsurge of joy and creativity that comes with direct involvement in this place.

Seamus Heaney compared being 'in-place' and being 'out-of-place' in terms of what he calls attachment and detachment. Commenting on the detached nature of the poetry of Patrick Kavanagh's later period, he remarks:

> We might say now that the world is more pervious to his vision than he is pervious to the world. When he writes about places now, they are luminous spaces within his mind. They have been evacuated of their status as background documentary geography, and exist instead as transfigured images, sites where the mind projects its own force. In this later poetry, place is included within the horizon of Kavanagh's mind rather than the other way round. The country he visits is inside himself.
>
> (Heaney, p. 136)

For me, this precisely sums up what was happening to Ivor Gurney. His Gloucestershire places were included within the horizons of his mind and not the other way round. The country he visited now was himself. He was 'out-of-place'. Heaney explains how this is recognisable in the poetry of Kavanagh. 'At the edge of consciousness [in a late poem] we encounter the white light of meditation; at the edge of consciousness in the early poems the familiar world stretches reliably away.' Applying this to Gurney, we could take 'Old Thought' or 'East Wind' as the earlier poems where the familiar world of the Cotswold Hills stretches reliably away into the distance – the reader can feel the landscape directly; whereas in a later poem, such as 'The Coppice' or 'Hell's Prayer', written in Dartford, Gurney can refer to the memory of wind rising on the Cotswold ledges, but behind and beyond him are the asylum walls and himself, 'In Hell, I buried a score depth, writing verse pages.' ('Hell's Prayer')

The Last of the Book

> There is nothing for me, Poetry, who was the child of joy,
> But to work out in verses crazes of my untold pain;
>
> ('The Last of the Book' extract, K, 2004, p.231)

The illustrated map in the middle of the book is the actual Gloucestershire of Ivor Gurney, and is reproduced as Figure 8.1 overleaf. Figure 8.2 is a model or map to compare with it. It suggests that we can best understand Gurney's life, his creativity and his poetry by starting from his direct relationship with Gloucestershire; it can be laid, figuratively speaking, over the other map and it reveals what Gloucestershire meant to Gurney and how Gloucestershire has been shaped by Gurney's images. The previous, more conventional, map, Figure 8.1, was focused on the place as if it were an objective and separate thing from Gurney himself. But Figure 8.2 is different in that it is not concerned with Gloucestershire *per se* but with Gurney's sense of being in- or out- of place (i.e. with the person-place relationship).

Looking at these two maps and the accompanying notes, we can see that the relationship between Gurney and Gloucestershire is a crucial factor in explaining the development of his creativity, the character of his music and poetry, and the over-arching shape of his life. In a very real sense, place was Ivor Gurney's making; it was also his unmaking.

> THE SONGS I HAD
> The Songs I had are withered
> Or vanished clean
> Yet there are bright tracks
> Where I have been,
>
> And there grow flowers
> For others' delight.
> Think well, O singer
> Soon comes night.
>
> (B, p.21)

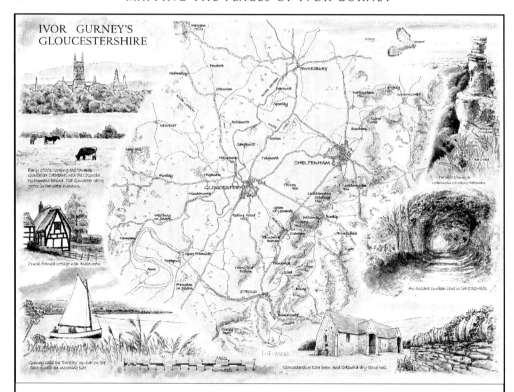

Fig. 8.1: Ivor Gurney's Gloucestershire.

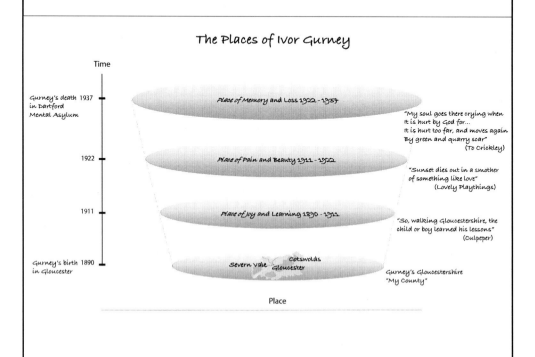

Fig. 8.2: The Places of Ivor Gurney.

Place of Joy and Learning, 1890–1911 (in-place)

- The awakening of joy; the experiences of the child and boy in a historic town and diverse countryside
- Exploring Gloucester and the Severn Meadows with family and friends
- School and local friendships and mentors (Cheesman, the Hunt sisters)
- Learning music, composing and working in the cathedral
- The golden days with Harvey and Howells; walking, sailing and beginning to explore the hills
- Laying the foundations for his creativity and place dependency

Place of Pain and Beauty, 1911–22 (in- and out-of-place)

- Disruption to old place connections and making new ones
- London, the Royal College of Music, new friendships (including Marion Scott) and new influences
- First signs of mental illness (1913) and realising the importance of place to his well-being (the pain as well as the beauty)
- France, the army and the war – companionship, trauma, poetry writing and letters
- *Severn and Somme* (1917) and *War's Embers* (1919) published
- Drawing on memory, but memory which could be rekindled, revived by actual return to e.g. Framilode, Crickley
- Returning to Gloucestershire and deepening his intimacy with the place. Outpouring of music and poetry, 1917–22
- *80 Poems or So* prepared but rejected for publication
- Crickley Hill and Dryhill Farm, the experiment in living and working at Cold Slad
- Mental breakdown, 1922

Place of Memory and Loss, 1922–37 (out-of-place)

- Direct connection with Gloucestershire places lost after entry to Dartford Asylum in 1922; Gloucestershire becomes a place of memory and imagination.
- Memory of recent experience underlies *Rewards of Wonder* collection, and music and poetry still flow in the mid-1920s
- Eventually, Gloucestershire places are reconstructed or re-framed to take unresolved worries and anxieties about himself, Gloucestershire, the war, and England in general – e.g. 'The Mangel-Bury', 'The Bridge', autobiographical poems like 'Chance to Work', 'The Wish', and the North American poems
- Maps, atlases and reading assume a big part of his life. Helen Thomas' OS map takes him back to Gloucestershire
- Loss expressed in many poems – both personal ('The Depths', 'The Coppice') and more general concern about Gloucestershire's beauty being unexpressed ('Musers Afar will Say', 'Soft Rain') and ideals of England being abandoned ('I Would not Rest', 'What Was Dear to Pan').

BIBLIOGRAPHY

Banfield, S., 'Gurney the Musician', *The Ivor Gurney Society Journal*, no. 13, pp. 85-112 (2007)

Barnes, A.F. ed., *The Story of the 2/5th Battalion Gloucestershire Regiment 1914–1918* (Gloucester, Crypt House Press, 1930)

Bingham, J., *The Cotswolds; A Cultural History* (Oxford, Signal Books, 2009)

Blevins, P., 'Ivor Gurney's Illness; The Tide of Darkness', *The Ivor Gurney Society Journal*, no. 13, pp. 159-74 (2007)

Blevins, P., *Ivor Gurney and Marion Scott* (Woodbridge, Suffolk, Boydell Press, 2008)

Boden, A., *Stars in a Dark Night* (Gloucester, Alan Sutton Publishing, 2nd Edition, 2004)

Boden, A., *F.W. Harvey; Soldier, Poet* (Gloucester, Alan Sutton Publishing, 1988)

Boden, A., 'Gerald and Joy Finzi: Striving for Ivor Gurney', *The Ivor Gurney Society Journal*, no. 15, pp. 9-42 (2009)

Clarke, J., *The Architectural History of Gloucester from the Earliest Period to the Close of the Eighteenth Century* (Gloucester, T.R. Davies, 1850)

Coppin, J. ed., *Between the Severn and the Wye: Poems of the Border Counties of England and Wales* (Moreton in Marsh, Windrush Press, 1993)

Cranham Local History Society, *Cranham; the History of a Cotswold Village* (Bodmin, King's Lynn, The MPG Books Group, 2005)

Dreghorn, W., *Geology Explained in the Severn Vale and Cotswolds* (Newton Abbot, David & Charles, 1967; also reprinted by Fineleaf Editions, 2005)

Finberg, H.P.R., *Gloucestershire (Making of the English Landscape)* (London, Eyre Methuen Ltd, 1975)

Fortey, R., *The Hidden Landscape; A Journey into the Geological Past* (London, Bodley Head, 2010)

Frederick, A., 'The Craft of Beauty; an Interdisciplinary Model of Criticism for the Songs', *The Ivor Gurney Society Journal*, no. 13, pp. 61-72 (2007)

Gilbert, R., *Walks in the World; Representation and Experience in Modern American Poetry* (Princeton, NJ, Princeton University Press, 1991)

Grigson, G., *Faber Book of Poems and Places* (London, Faber & Faber, 1980)

Gross, P., *The Water Table* (Northumberland, Bloodaxe Books, 2009)

Gurney, I., 'The Springs of Music', *Musical Quarterly*, Vol. 8, no. 3, pp. 319-22 (1922)

Gurney, I., 'By Ashleworth', *The Ivor Gurney Society Journal*, no. 15, pp. 43-4 (2009)

Gurney, I., 'On Earth', *The Ivor Gurney Society Journal*, no. 15, 158-60 (2009)

Gurney I., 'On Sailing', *Archipelago* 3 (Oxfordshire, Clutag Press, 2009)

Harvey, D., *Justice, Nature & the Geography of Difference* (Oxford, Blackwell, 1996)

Harvey, F.W., *Collected Poems* (Coleford, D. McLean, The Forest Bookshop, 1983)

Heaney, S., 'The Place of Writing', *Finders Keepers; Selected Prose 1971–2001*, pp. 232-45 (Faber & Faber, 2002)

Heaney, S., 'The Placeless Heaven: Another Look at Kavanagh', *Finders Keepers; Selected Prose 1971–2001*, pp. 134-44 (Faber & Faber, 2002)

Heidegger, M., *Being and Time* (Oxford, Basil Blackwell, 1962)

Hibberd, D. and Onions, J., *Poetry of the Great War: An Anthology* (London, Macmillan, 1986)

Hill, G., 'Gurney's Hobby', *Collected Critical Writings*, K. Haynes ed. (Oxford, Oxford University Press, 2008)

Hill, S., *The Spirit of the Cotswolds* (London, Michael Joseph, 1988)

Hipp, D.W., *The Poetry of Shell Shock: Wartime Trauma and Healing in W. Owen, I. Gurney and S. Sassoon* (Jefferson, NC, McFarland & Co., 2005)

Hooker, J., 'Honouring Ivor Gurney', *Poetry of Place: Essays and Reviews, 1970–81*, pp. 120-29 (Manchester, Carcanet, 1982)

Hoskins, W.G. (first published 1955), *The Making of the English Landscape* (London, Penguin, 1985)

Howells, H., 'Ivor Gurney: The Man', *Music and Letters*, Vol. 19, no.1, p.14 (1938)

Hurd, M., *The Ordeal of Ivor Gurney 1890–1937* (Oxford, Oxford University Press, 1978)

Hyett, F., *Gloucester in National History* (Gloucester, Kegan Paul, Trench, Trubner & Co. Ltd of London, 1906)

Kirby, D., *The Story of Gloucester* (Stroud, Sutton Publishing Ltd, 2007)

Lancaster, P., 'Gurney's Duality: Well-Spring, Correlations and Conflicts', *The Ivor Gurney Society Journal*, no.13, pp.45-60 (2007)

Lancaster P., 'Reconstructing Gurney in the Archives', *The Ivor Gurney Society Journal*, no.16, pp.109-118 (2010)

Lucas, J., 'Edward Thomas, Ivor Gurney and English Socialism', *The Ivor Gurney Society Journal*, no.4, pp.19-34 (1998)

Lucas, J., *Ivor Gurney (Writers and Their Work)* (Tavistock, Devon, Northcote House Publishers, 2001)

Massingham, H., *Cotswold Country, The Face of Britain* (London, Batsford, 1937)

Mead, R., *Walking the Cathedral Cities of England*, Globetrotter Walking Guides (London, New Holland Publishers, 2003)

Merleau-Ponty, M., 'What is Phenomenology?' in *The Essential Writings of Merleau-Ponty* (New York, Harcourt, Brace & World, 1969)

Murray, A., *The Cotswolds*, Crypt House Pocket Series (Gloucester, Crypt House Press, 1930)

Natural England, National Landscape Character Areas of England, accessed via http://www.naturalengland. org.uk/ourwork/landscape/englands/character/areas/soputhwest.aspx, September 30 2010

Oswald, A., *A Sleepwalk on the Severn* (London, Faber & Faber, 2009)

Palmer, Christopher, *Herbert Howells: A Centenary Celebration*, pp.352-53 (London, Thames Publishing, 1992)

Parsons, I.M., *Men Who March Away: Poems of the First World War* (London, Chatto & Windus, 1965)

Pilbeam, A., *The Landscapes of Gloucestershire* (Stroud, Tempus Publishing Ltd, 2006)

Plunkett Greene, H. and Scott, M., 'Ivor Gurney: The Man', *Music and Letters*, Vol. 19, no.1, pp.2-7 (1938)

Rattenbury. A., 'How the Sanity of Poets can be Edited Away', *The London Review of Books*, Vol. 21, no.20, 14 October 1999, pp.15-19 (1999)

Rawling, E., 'Putting Gurney in his Place, a Geographical Perspective', *The Ivor Gurney Society Journal*, no.16, pp.7-30 (2010)

Rawling, E., 'Reading and Writing Place; A Role for Geography Education in the Twenty First Century?' *Geography, Education and the Future* (London, Continuum, 2011)

Scott, B., 'The Obverse of the Canonical: Ivor Gurney and the American Civil War', *The Ivor Gurney Society Journal*, no.4, pp.43-58 (1998)

Scott, B. and Walter, G., 'Glory Crying for Poetry: Ivor Gurney's American Poems', *The Ivor Gurney Society Journal*, no.4, pp.59-79 (1998)

Stallworthy, J., *Anthem for Doomed Youth* (London, Constable & Robinson Ltd in association with the Imperial War Museum, 2002)

Taplin, K., 'The Poet's True Place: Ivor Gurney', *Tongues in Trees; Studies in Literature and Ecology*, pp.146-56 (Green Books, 1989)

Thomas, M. ed., 'Ivor Gurney' in *Time and Again; Memoirs and Letters*, pp.110-12 (Manchester, Carcanet, 1978)

Thornton, R.K.R. ed., *Ivor Gurney; Collected Letters* (Manchester, MidNAG & Carcanet, 1991)

Thornton, R.K.R., 'What Did They Expect?', *The Ivor Gurney Society Journal*, no.13, pp.1-18 (2007)

Thornton, R.K.R., 'Having a Particular Home; Ivor Gurney, Edward Thomas and Walking', *Dymock Poets and Friends*, no.8, pp.56-67 (2009)

Venables, I., 'The Music of Poetry', *The Ivor Gurney Society Journal*, no.8, pp.7-16 (2002)

Venables, I., 'To Make Musical History for England and Out of Gloster Stuff – The Orchestral Music of Ivor Gurney', *The Ivor Gurney Society Journal*, no.16, pp.91-100 (2010)

Walter and Thornton, Introduction in *Ivor Gurney: 80 Poems or So*, pp.1-16 (Northumberland, MidNAG & Carcanet Press, 1997)

Whitman, W., *Leaves of Grass* (The World's Classics Paperback Edition, Oxford, Oxford University Press, 1990)

Wylie, J., *Landscape* (Abingdon, Routledge, 2007)

APPENDIX

SOURCES OF GURNEY'S POETRY

Note About Sources for Gurney's Poetry

I have drawn on all available sources for the poems used in this book, both published and unpublished, and the main items will be listed presently. In the book, an abbreviation has been used to indicate the source of the poem. Where a published poem has been quoted significantly or in full, the source, date and page number are given; where it is merely a mention of the poem title, only the source is quoted. Note that the *Severn & Somme* 1917, *War's Embers* 1919, and Blunden 1954 versions of many poems have been used, but the modern reader can find many of these, with usually only slight differences in wording, in Kavanagh's *Collected Poems* 2004. This book contains many poems published for the first time, thanks to permission from the Ivor Gurney Trust. These poems are marked in the text with the abbreviation GA (Gurney Archives, in the Gloucestershire Archives) and they remain the copyright of the Ivor Gurney Trust. For those wanting the full reference, these are listed below:

Severn & Somme, London, Sidgwick & Jackson, 1917 (S&S)
War's Embers, London, Sidgwick & Jackson, 1919 (WE)
Poems by Ivor Gurney: principally selected from unpublished manuscripts, with a memoir by Edmund Blunden, E. Blunden ed., London, Hutchinson, 1954 (B)
Poems of Ivor Gurney, 1890–1937, with an introduction by Edmund Blunden and a bibliographic note by Leonard Clark, London, Chatto & Windus, 1973 (C)
Collected Poems of Ivor Gurney, chosen, edited and with an introduction by P.J. Kavanagh, Oxford, Oxford University Press (K, 1982)
Ivor Gurney: *Severn & Somme and War's Embers* 1987, Critical Edition, R.K.R. Thornton ed., Ashington: MidNAG; Manchester: Carcanet (S&S/WE)
Ivor Gurney: *Selected Poems*, selected and introduced by P.J. Kavanagh, Oxford, Oxford University Press (K, 1990)
Ivor Gurney: *Best Poems and The Book of Five Makings*, R.K.R. Thornton and George Walter ed., Ashington:MidNAG; Manchester: Carcanet, 1997 (BP)
Ivor Gurney: *80 Poems or So*, George Walter and R.K.R. Thornton ed., Ashington: MidNAG; Manchester: Carcanet, 1997 (80P)
Ivor Gurney: *Rewards of Wonder*, George Walter, Ashington: MidNAG; Manchester: Carcanet, 2000 (RW)
Ivor Gurney: *Collected Poems*, P.J. Kavanagh ed., Manchester: Carcanet, 2004 (K, 2004)

The Ivor Gurney Archives in Gloucestershire – formerly unpublished poems, as listed:

Culpeper 4 lines	Archives Box 1925 Chronology 1 Orange Exercise Book, Poems of Gloucesters, Gloucester and Virginia 52.2 p.61
The Salt Box (all)	Archives Box 1925 Chronology 1 G44.27
Petersburg (all)	Archives Box 1925 Chronology 1 Orange Exercise Book, Poems of Gloucesters, Gloucester and Virginia 52.2 p.61
Fort Yukon 8 lines	Archives Box 1925 Chronology 1 Gurney 15. 248
Dawn (all)	Archives Pictures and Memories 1925 Maroon Exercise Book p.176
The Man (a few lines)	Memories of Honour Archives 21A p.79/80
LLanthony (all)	Archives Pictures and Memories 1925 Maroon Exercise Book p.136
The Little Way (all)	Archives Box Chronology 2 'Eight Poems' G44.18
Ship Over Meadows (few lines)	Archives Pink marbled notebook 1922
Twyver Begins (all)	Archives Pictures and memories 1925 Maroon Exercise Book p.126
Harper's Ferry (all)	Archives Box 1925 Chronology 1 Orange Exercise Book, Poems of Gloucesters, Gloucester and Virginia 52.2 p.69
First Framilode (all)	Archives Pictures and memories 1925 Maroon Exercise Book p.22 (also pub. in Archipelago 3 Spring 2009)
Arlingham (all)	Archives Pictures and memories 1925 Maroon Exercise Book p.90
Above the Villa (all)	Archives Box 1925 TS Poetry Collection, Threepenny Exercise Book G21.20
Wilderness 11 lines	Archives Box 1925 Chronology 1 Orange Exercise Book, Poems of Gloucesters, Gloucester and Virginia 52.2 p.68
Crickley Cliffs (few lines)	Archives Pictures and Memories 1925 Maroon Exercise Book p.152
Quietitude	Archives Box 1925 Chronology 1 Orange Exercise Book, Poems of Gloucesters, Gloucester and Virginia 52.2 p.3
Cedar Mountain (5 lines)	Archives Box 1925 Chronology 1 Orange Exercise Book, Poems of Gloucesters, Gloucester and Virginia 52.2 p.66
The Local Poet (first 16 lines)	Archives Box 1925 Chronology 1 G15.8

INDEX

Visit our website and discover thousands of other

History Press books.

www.thehistorypress.co.uk